C000228101

PANDAMONIUM!

PANDAMONIUM!

PANDAMONIUM!

How Not to Run a Record Label

SIMON WILLIAMS

NINE
EIGHT
BOOKS

NINE
EIGHT
BOOKS

NEB 008

First published in the UK in 2022 by Nine Eight Books
An imprint of Bonnier Books UK
4th Floor, Victoria House, Bloomsbury Square, London, WC1B 4DA
Owned by Bonnier Books, Sveavägen 56, Stockholm, Sweden

@nineeightbooks

@nineeightbooks

Hardback ISBN: 978-1-7887-0728-2
eBook ISBN: 978-1-7887-0729-9
Audio ISBN: 978-1-7887-0730-5

A CIP catalogue record for this book is available from the British Library.

Publishing director: Pete Selby
Senior editor: Melissa Bond

Cover design by Paul Palmer-Edwards
Typeset by IDSUK (Data Connection) Ltd
Printed and bound in Great Britain by Clays Ltd, Elcograf S.p.A

1 3 5 7 9 10 8 6 4 2

Nine Eight Books is an imprint of Bonnier Books UK
www.bonnierbooks.co.uk

Now I see the sadness in the world,
I'm sorry I didn't see it before.

– 'Mother I've Taken LSD'
by the Flaming Lips

CONTENTS

★

IN SPITE OF THESE TIMES

I am beyond delighted to say that I had a massive role in the creation of one of the least-read *NME*s of all time – one that was to mark my farewell to life as a full-time music journalist. And all without lifting a finger.

The cover date tells us it is from 31 March 1999, a year of years. In big red and orange letters across the middle the headline screams: HERE'S PANDA! SULTANS OF NING BEARS ALL. In the top left-hand corner sits a frothy pint of Carling with a tagline of 'Darling Premier! New release on Vivid Beermat.' To the top right, a live picture of a frothing Rat from Ned's Atomic Dustbin accompanies a shout of 'NEDS HEAVEN: Big shorts, Steve Lamacq and why fraggle rocks.'

The main front image is a black and white picture of some doofus with his face (very badly) painted like a panda. He's lying flat on his back on the ground with his tongue poking out. In his right paw is something that is definitely not a cigarette. The picture was taken backstage at Glastonbury Festival circa 1995. This much we know because we is he and he is we – it's a picture of your author in his natural habitat, happily pissed and rolling around in the grass with a roll-up.

There are more words on the bottom half of the cover. Those words read as follows:

* FARMER'S BOYS * GOTHS *JOHN HARRIS *
NEW WAVE OF NEW WAVE *
* SUPER FURRY ANIMALS * RADIOHEAD * THE
BLUETONES * ASH * EMBRACE *
* KEBABS * STEVE PERRYMAN * CHARLIE
WRIGHTS * SAINSBURY'S
WALTHAMSTOW * 'I ONLY SNOGGED HER' *
'IT'S EASY FOR YOU TO SAY'
* MARK SUTHERLAND * 'STICK IT ON THE OLD
BUNGOUS' * LIGHTNING
NEVER STRIKES – KAPOW! * SKUNK ROCK *
BLUE POSTS * . . . AND NO CHEESE *

Tucked right underneath the *NME* logo, in the tiniest of type-faces, it says: 'We'll miss you when you're gone', a poignant response to my frequent office shout out of, 'You'll miss me when I'm gone!'

At the risk of spoiling the rest of this here book, that is a pretty mesmeric summary of my life up until that point. Some bands, some flatmates, some bars, some music scenes, some catch-phrases . . . and no cheese. This is hardly surprising as this had been carefully put together by writers and sub-editors and general roustabouts who I'd been working with and gigging with and drinking with across eleven years of lobe-flapping, globe-trotting, strobe-boggling rock 'n' roll writing palavers. Because this *NME* front cover was one of a kind, a kindly leaving gift. One copy only. Worst. Sales. Ever.

PANDAMONIUM!

At another risk of spoiling the fun it is no exaggeration to say this story contains a million more gear changes than a gazillion laps of the Monaco Grand Prix. This tale is a mutant hybrid of neon-lit highs and near-death lows.

If you have this book in your hands, you may well have read some of those words of wisdom in the *NME* between 1988 and 1999. Or there is slightly less of a chance you may have bought a *Jump Away* . . . fanzine from me in the mid-'80s, or listened to my Dalston tones on Xfm in the mid-'90s, or been entertained, or indeed sickened, at one of our Club Smashed! or Club Spangle or Club Panda or Club Fandango live shows at any point over the past thirty-odd years.

We may have shared gig space at the Lyceum in 1982. We may have shared dancefloor space at Pigeons in 1987. We may have shared bar space at the Powerhaus in 1992. We could well have shared drinking space at the Water Rats in 1996, or the Dublin Castle in 2002, or the Bull & Gate in 2007, or the Shacklewell Arms in 2014, or the Victoria in 2021, or . . . oh, you know. Yet, despite all of the above, in spite of all those times, the chances are you haven't got a clue who I am. Sometimes I'm not quite sure either.

What we are certain about is that what has dominated proceedings for half of my so-called life is Fierce Panda Records. You may have heard of this label with the big heart and the small purse; the skinnyfit company with the fat furry face; the indie tiger with the golden ears glinting in the dark recesses of the gloriously fetid toilet circuit. But what is a record company? Who is a record company? Why is a record company?

First true fact: you don't have to be a lunatic to run a record company but – oh, hang on – you *do*. You also need to be a bit nerdy, a bit dweeby, a bit needy. Are you the kind of person who

3

buys a new notepad to start a fresh to-do list and carefully writes down: '1) start a new to-do list' so you have something to instantly cross off? Were you the kind of pop kid who sat staring down at the gramophone as the vinyl record went round and round and the logo kept spinning and spinning until you got a bit dizzy . . . Jet Jet Jet Jet . . . EMI EMI EMI EMI . . . WXYZ WXYZ WXYZ WXYZ . . .? Were you the kind of person who accidentally spent their school dinner money on that absolutely vital new Food single? Did you ever go to Better Badges in Covent Garden to make your own badges of bands too new to have their own badges on sale or, in some extreme cases, make badges for bands who would never exist? Did you used to give your own personal records your own catalogue numbers? Did you cut lyrics out of *Smash Hits* magazine and put them in the appropriate 7-inch sleeve (where they still lie)? Crucially, are you moderately happy in your own slightly offbeat body, the kind of person who goes to gigs to see completely unknown bands in the hope that you'll accidentally find the new Coldplay, if not, at the very least, the very latest hot combo?

If you have nodded along to all of the above and muttered, 'Uh-huh', or 'He knows me so well', or 'Yikes, yeah!' under your breath then stop reading right now and throw this book into the fire, or perhaps the nearest second-hand literary receptacle, possibly at your local recycling centre, because you are either already a record-company owner or you are in significant danger of becoming one.

Second true fact: I certainly never intended to run a record company. Nobody does. Like any other slightly grubby latchkey kid growing up in the 1970s, I wanted to be a footballer or a racing driver or an astronaut – Tottenham Hotspur warhorse Steve Perryman strapped into a John Player Special Lotus 72 wheel-spinning on the Milky Way, perhaps. The usual. Even up until my late twenties my so-called career prospects still revolved around music journalism, radio presenting or gig promoting; truth be told, even after Fierce Panda started for the first couple of years it was little more than a hobby, a curio, a gentle distraction from the day-to-late-night-to-day procession of gig bookings and gig reviews and just general gig-out giggings.

Oh sure, it all started with fun and lager. In 1994, Fierce Panda was launched on a wing and a prayer by three music hacks very much lurking in the pre-Britpop indie undergrowth. There were some chirpy six-track compilation EPs with cheeky bands like Ash and Green Day and Supergrass. Then we went a bit punk rock, with a small 'p' and a wee 'unk'. Then we got a little bit fixated with Suzi Quatro living in Chelmsford. As you do. Then, in 1995, we almost sullied the nation's top-forty furnishings with the sweariest fucking single release since 'Killing in the Name', thanks to a couple of chaps called Noel and Liam. And then, in 1996, everything started to go very, very mad. By which point it was too late. Way too late.

Third true fact: because the tragic truth is you don't choose to run a record company, the record company chooses *you*. It sizes you up, checks you out, susses the cut of your indie jib. Then, like some immense parasitic wasp that you only seem to ever hear about on the more gruesome sections of the *QI* televisual programme, it invades your very being. I'll spare you the grisly details, apart from these: 'When the baby wasp is born, it eats the cockroach alive from the inside, in a special order, to keep it alive for as long as possible, because the meat goes off very quickly.'

At first all is serene. You are in control. You name the label, nurture it, cuddle it when it looks a bit sad, inject it with new music when it looks a bit forlorn. You take it to gigs, buy it beers and introduce it to friends. And then the label begins to gain confidence. It starts helping out, making cups of Yorkshire tea (other brands are available, but they're not quite as good), nipping down to the shop for snacks, carrying you home from the pub. And then one day you wake up and you realise, to your absolute hungover horror, that the label is in control.

From a cheeky little in-joke with a daft name releasing one record as a tribute to a batshit scene you suddenly have a catalogue of over 500 singles and 130 albums. You have a label roster heaving with twelve and a half acts. You have nine tracks, three albums and one T-shirt coming out before Easter Monday, and it's now 24 February. You have a release schedule that is longer than Peter Crouch's long chaise longue – it's essentially never-ending. Not only that, but the label is running you ragged with its insatiable appetite. It wants more bands. It wants more songs. It wants your soul. Feed me. Heed Me. Bleed me dry.

You are helpless, hapless, hopeless. That lovely little label you used to run is now running you.

Running you right into the fucking ground.

30 DECEMBER 2019, 9.48 A.M.

Have you ever said goodbye to your loved ones? Like, really, really said goodbye to them? Like, knowing that you know and knowing they don't know that you will never see them again? Like, choking back the silent tears as you lean over to kiss the girls goodbye in their beds, murmuring farewell platitudes in the midst of their mid-morning slumbers? They sink back into sleep as you slink down the stairs, a stranger in your own house, quietly turning the backdoor key. He's leaving home. Bye-bye.

The usual 23-minute walk to Stowmarket station for one last train to London, just heading out, out, out. A final look at the Orwell Bridge, curving over the Ipswich skyline like a brutalist concrete rainbow. A farewell wave to the waterscapes of Manningtree, with the cranes of Felixstowe docks towering in the distance at the far end of the Stour Estuary. The only way now is through Essex, clattering through Colchester and Chelmsford and then hitting the billowing outskirts of London as we sprint past Romford dog track.

From Liverpool Street I walk to Moorgate and get the bus to the art shop in Islington to pick up a scalpel, paid by cash to cover my furry furtive tracks. I think London is deserted, but I might be making that up. I go to the top-secret Fierce Panda HQ (Unit 2.0, Leroy House, 436 Essex Road, London N1 3QP), smack bang on the corner of Balls Pond Road and Essex Road.

I'm not scared.

1

UNDER LONDON SKIES

When I was five years old, my father threw himself off a bridge and into the River Thames: 6 July 1971. Splash rang out in an empty sky. His body was found, washed up and washed out, on the foreshore at Putney. I remember my mother reading about his death in the newspaper. Open verdict, said the coroner. I can't remember the funeral. I don't know where he is buried, if he is indeed buried. In fact, I can't remember much about my dad at all.

Judging by the few black-and-white pictures I have of him, he was not a Beatles-loving bohemian. He is wearing a suit and tie, a trilby, black-rimmed spectacles, a serious-faced cross between comic Peter Sellers and a vacuum cleaner salesman. He was much older than my mother. He knew this because he was a maths teacher. She didn't know this until they signed the marriage certificate. Uncle Jimmy and Auntie Norma always said he was a very nice man. Everyone liked my dad. Apart from my dad.

My release date was 26 September 1965 in Clapton, in the Salvation Army Mothers' Hospital, the week the Walker Brothers hit number one in the hit parade with 'Make It Easy on Yourself'. When I was one year old, the Williamses made the move from Stoke Newington to Walthamstow, fully five decades before the hipster migration across the Valley reservoirs. An upgrade from a tower block flat with panoramic views to a semi-detached on Forest View Road – three bedrooms, a garage, a marriage, a little blond baby boy and a grown-up job at Chapel End High School. From an inner-city high rise to the suburban high life, in so many ways.

But not enough for the father who always wanted to go a little bit further: he wants a new car, a better job, a bigger house, another baby – maybe a little blonde girl this time. But there's nothing left in the tank, or the bank. Mortgaged to the hilt and beyond with a job for life and a lovely young wife and a little blond baby boy, my suit-wearing, trilby-tilting dad is trapped in straitlaced suburbia while the super soaraway '60s happen to everyone else. Trips to Wood Street station, not tripping at Woodstock Festival. Nowhere to run, baby, nowhere to hide.

One day things had become so bad in my sad dad's head that my mother moved myself and her out of 98 Forest View Road and into a bedsit in Palmers Green. Both of us sleeping in the one room, with two grapefruits in the kitchen and three rabbits in the back garden hutch. One other day my dad kidnapped me from infant school, took me back home to Walthamstow. He took me up to Epping Forest for a picnic, eating giant yellow lemon curd sandwiches overlooking the giant yellow Tonka toys tearing down trees, gouging through the foliage, laying down lanes and lanes of tarmac for something called the M11. He tried to look after me, tried to love me.

He handed me back to my mother a week later, unable to handle his little blond boy. He couldn't be a proper big dad for me. I don't remember why. Maybe I couldn't ever be a proper little son for him. I never saw him again.

Not everything is lost for ever: I do remember being sick in a yellow Ford Anglia, being driven by Dad's friend Daphne. Possibly caused by eating something called 'pizza' in a Golden Egg restaurant on the long way home from seeing Dad's Welsh side of the family in Pontyberem (between Camarthen and Llanelli, turn lleft at Llannon). This I know because I still have a battered Paddington Bear suitcase with half of a faded address scrawled on the lid. A Polaroid crammed with me and a cluster of Welsh cousins, three lovely girls, all of us going to Welsh Sunday school; everyone turning to look at the little blond Williams boy from London Town, four years old, sitting there in blissful, bashful silence, not understanding a single Welsh word being spoken about him.

I remember a visit to a van hire place at Bell Corner in downtown Walthamstow, on the junction of Forest Road and Hoe Street, right near Lloyd Park; opposite the tatty cinema with the mysterious XXXs on the front over there and the Bell pub over there. We are going on holiday. But we can't afford much. My parents take a look at a lovely big Ford Transit camper van. Giant steps up the back, comfy furnishings, cosy kitchenette. That's my bed, on the corner sofa. I love it. Compared to home this is a crystalline palace on wheels.

We eventually drive off in a bruise-coloured Bedford van. No windows at the back. No comfy kitchenette. No furnishings, lovely or otherwise. A Bedford with no bed. How ironic. It takes us the long way to the Costa del Cornwall. I'm sick. Frequently. Mattresses are thrown down in the windowless back. I'm sleeping near the petrol tank, the kid of gasoline, fumes filling up my pillow. Every trip to top up at Combs Ford Esso centuries later still takes me straight back to that last family holiday. Lovely Polperro dazzling by the sea, shining by night; sleeping near the gas tank, parked up in a public car park. That petrol emotion.

We go on an evening fishing trip on a small trawler: the compact family Williams packed together like sardines, on a pilgrimage for pilchards. Or are we? The boat pulls away from the dock. My mother looks around for my dad. He is still standing on the harbourside, trilby titled back, the father slowly getting smaller and smaller as we chug further and further out to sea. He's off to the pub, sparkling black-rimmed eyes shining in the harbour lights, Polperro dazzling by night. Clever dad. He's waving goodbye. In a very real sense, my father was always waving goodbye to me.

30 DECEMBER 2019, 4.47 P.M.

I need to write a list of final funeral demands – the musical choices are very important. I need to update the release schedule so label manager Chris Disorder, aka Chrisorder, knows what will be going on in the months ahead. I need to leave a list of important contacts – manufacturers, lawyers, accountants, investors, bankers – who will need to be told what I've done. And I need to write one last letter explaining what I'm going to be doing and why I'm going to be doing it.

Essentially, I am sick and tired of being sick and tired. This is not going to be a cry for help; this is going to be a howl of total defeat. I have to do these things in the office so I can type them and then print them all out. I want them to be as clear as possible. No scrawled last-minute notes. No bloodied dribbling scribblings. No agonising, everlasting ambiguity. Stop your sobbings.

I head around the corner to the Alma pub around 5 p.m. for a drink and to edit my witterings with a battered biro – old **NME** *habits die hard. At one especially curious point I calculate that I am running approximately fifty-five minutes late. For what? Can you actually be late for your own death?? I head back to the top-secret Leroy House to make the last tweaks and to print out the final words. Close up the empty HQ for the last time. Empty the bins in a way I can't empty my head. Silently turning the office door key. Sloping along the long, deserted corridor, down the two flights of stairs. Past the Christmas tree in the foyer, lights shivering in the winter breeze as I make my final exit through the entrance. He's leaving Leroy House. Bye-bye.*

2

MOTHER OF GOD

Forest View Road sits on the north-eastern tip of Walthamstow, hemmed in by the Chingford to Liverpool Street train line rattling along behind the back garden, and the North Circular Road sweeping through from Woodford to Edmonton at the end of the dead-end street for the dead-end kids. To the north, beyond humpy Wadham Bridge sits the heights of Highams Park. To the south, the rest of Walthamstow, sprawling, crawling, seemingly endless E17 with its two Tube stations and three train stations and its Hoe Street and High Street and hi-de-hi side roads and glowering pubs.

Some houses still took deliveries of coal from the grim-faced coalman in his grimy cap and eggs from the delicate eggman (woooh) and Corona pop and silver tops rattling in their crate from the ever-whistling out-of-tune Unigate milkman. The scrap metal merchant crawled by once a week in a Ford Transit pick-up, ringing his bell to encourage us to bring out our dead fridges and mangled mangles. At night you could hear the roar of the crowd from

Walthamstow Stadium dog track. E17 was quite the place. Apart from the greyhounds on *Sportsnight*, you also had wrestling from Walthamstow Assembly Hall on *World of Sport* with Big Daddy, Giant Haystacks and tiny screaming grannies. Throw in Green Pond Road, home of Walthamstow Avenue FC, the Olympic-sized swimming pool near the George Monoux school, and the scrub of grass at the back of Thorpe Hall primary, our notional home soccer-balling pitch, and you could surely have held some kind of global sporting event in E17 in '77.

What could be a better place for a latchkey kid to live in the 1970s? This was the era of all-day FA Cup finals you can still remember ('Pearson, put through by Greenhoff, Jones is after him, Pearson shoots . . . goal!'), games of football that lasted eight hours with the other dead-end kids, with jumpers for goalposts, lamp posts for goalposts, small brothers for goalposts. Out here in the commuter belt before computer games, smartphones and girlfriends, we had to make our own daft entertainment, fuelled by frozen Jubblys throughout the long hot summers, bombing through Epping Forest on Chopper bikes while the ERF lorries chuntered down below on that thing called the M11.

I clearly remember all the other kids had brothers and sisters and both parents in full effect. No dead sad dead dads there. Neil and Steven Corchoran's old man had a Jensen Interceptor and an eight-track cartridge machine pumping out 'Band on the Run' by Wings. They went on holiday to somewhere outlandishly exotic called the Isle of Wight. They went on that holiday in a big Ford Transit camper van. It looked very, very comfortable, crystalline even. Then there were the Andrews Brothers, Mark, Paul, Stephen and little Kevin, always loud and fun and exuberant and living their best chaotic lives. Buying Jasper Carrott albums for something called Father's Day and then playing them before wrapping them up, crying with laughter. These were houses of fun, and not just because oldest brother Mark was so smitten with Madness he eventually went out and bought a saxophone.

Following the nights spent in the bed-free Bedford van, the best holiday I had as a child was actually pretty local, like a primitive early staycation. It was up the road in Whipps Cross Hospital in the spring of 1974, where I ended up with a broken arm and a broken leg, up in traction after being knocked down by an orange Ford Capri. This was the '70s, after all. Gliding beneath sickly yellow hospital lights, I can remember the hullabaloo when they lifted me from the stretcher to the bed, but I can't remember any pain. Years later, David Beckham would be born here, as would Harry Kane, as would Chrisorder's son Indy. My mother would virtually die here in 2012. I can't remember any pain then either.

Me? As an eight-year-old I had a terrific time. I was there for about six weeks, but I could have happily stayed there for ever. The nurses were lovely and caring, my friends brought gifts and sweets, and magazines and books and Spurs paraphernalia – programmes, photos, 'get well soon' cards from the Saint Martins (Peters and Chivers). The ward was a riot of colour and life and laughter, a playground for damaged goods. I didn't have to tiptoe around anyone anywhere here – not that I could do much tiptoeing with my plastered leg hanging from the ceiling, but you get my point. Maybe all the other patients were dead-end kids who preferred hospital to home.

The other damaged kids told me amazing stories about how there was a big colour TV in the TV room at the end of the ward, but I couldn't get into it with my ol' dirty plastered leg in traction. But this was okay, because the one thing the hospital ward had was the radio, which was tuned to Radio 1 and was on all the time. To this day, specific songs I hear on Capital Gold or Radio 2 can take me straight back to that bed on that ward in that hospital in March 1974. 'Billy, Don't Be a Hero' by Paper Lace, 'Rebel Rebel' by David Bowie, 'The Air That I Breathe' by the Hollies, 'Tiger Feet' by Mud, the Wombles' 'Wombling Song'. Cozy Powell was dancing with the devil while Suzi Quatro was going down to the devil gate, down to the devil gate, down to the devil gate drive – what Godless magick was this? Oh, and there was 'Seasons in the Sun' by Terry Jacks. *Always* 'Seasons in the Sun'.

A glut of glam, a rustle of the softest rock known to denim-kind, some guys dressed as Bungo and Tomsk. Throw in afternoon tea and biscuits with Diddy David Hamilton and it cemented a love affair with radio that remains fruity and concentrated nearly fifty years later.

Ours was not such a house of fun. I'm not sure if my mother ever recovered from the death of what would be her one and only husband. She was never lacking in company – there were a few boyfriends in the years that followed, and she actually had a good eye for a decent bloke who could put up with her urchin son. To add to the general all-round oddness, after my dad died, I stopped going to local schools in Walthamstow and shifted to Houndsfield juniors in Edmonton, where she taught art in the senior school next door, which was a properly bullish '70s comprehensive – more Biffa than Francis Bacon, at the very least.

Fittingly, at home there was love, but it was definitely a tough love. An I'm-only-doing-this-for-the-best-for-you love. The old this-is-hurting-me-more-than-it's-hurting-you love. There was a perpetual parental dichotomy. Maybe she was struggling to play both roles of mother and father at the same time. It was certainly a life of cigarettes and alcohol. More specifically, it was a life rife with softpacks of Peter Stuyvesant and draught sherry. You heard right. I'd be sent off to the off-licence on MacDonald Road, just next to the surgery, where I'd hand over an empty bottle, which they would take out to the back (presumably not to the surgery) and fill with some ghastly, glutinous fluid that I would carry back home at arm's length, like a rabid and possibly radioactive raccoon. Any spillages would be sticking around for weeks on end, melting through the furniture and carpets. This was a dark, dark drink for dark, dark days.

On top sober form, she was a bohemian intellectual. As a teacher in the '70s she was Labour with a capital L. As a self-made woman of books and reading and psychology she had broken free of the family constraints of growing up as a teenager in the north-east. She painted in oils, played squash, went sailing and played flute for a mosh of Morris Dancers, although rarely all at the same time. Fittingly, she bought a Morris Mini Minor that was older than me. It was royal blue. She painted it black. The black doors fell off. The back doors would've fallen off as well if there had been any. Insert your own metaphor here.

There were trips to London on this marvellous modern beast called the Underground, which appeared out of the underground at some Space Age landing point called Walthamstow Central. It had been opened in 1967, giving us a world of silver machines thundering through endlessly dark tunnels. Rattling along in the smoking carriage I would marvel at the way in which my mother's discarded butts would collect oh-so-perfectly in the grooves of the wooden floor, like they were designed for life, destined for each other.

Inevitably, my friends adored her. Her stories, her cigarettes, her alcohol, her intellectualness, her very bohemianism. She was everything their sensible parents could never be – matey, sweary, boozy, *fun*. I craved the nuclear family. They craved the atomic option. But they were only there for the good times, not the hungover times, when the sound of silence would settle on number ninety-eight like a clammy draught sherry shroud.

It took me slightly too long to realise that she liked children, but she *really* liked children who drank booze and smoked tabs and could talk like adults. Grown-up children, in fact. I suppose you could say her method worked – the lack of maternal mollycoddling made me independent. But not as exasperatingly, enthrallingly independent as I would eventually become.

30 DECEMBER 2019, 6.54 P.M.

A 73 Routemaster bus ride to the Tavistock Hotel in Fitzrovia. Time to check in before checking out. Bloody love Routemasters. Bloody love Fitzrovia. Bloody love the Tavistock Hotel. Its prices never change, unlike the likes of Premier Inn, who charge a Premier Beyoncé booty tax and ramp up the prices in Euston and King's Cross whenever she plays in town. We discovered the Tavistock when Death Cab for Cutie played around the corner at ULU and stayed here after the show. All those years of trying to find a decent student-free pub pre-gig and it turns out there was a bloody great big hotel bar within crawling distance of the venue.

Apparently hotels are quite the place for suicides. It's neutral territory. Family won't discover the body. Someone else has to clear up the bloody mess. Like a bird with a broken wing you ultimately drag yourself to a strange, dark corner to die. Truly, the Tavistock's Woolf & Whistle Bar – we are in Bloomsbury Square after all – is where nobody knows your name.

I embark on a fabulously low-key farewell tour of the West End: a sombre you-hoo to ULU at the end of Malet Street; a sober wave to UCH, birthplace of daughter Scout; skulking past Habitat and over Tottenham Court Road, left on to New Cavendish Street, crossing Charlotte Street, ex-home to Xfm, and on to the Ship.

It's closed.

Bollocks.

This is not part of the plan.

Better try the Stag's Head up the road. It's open, open wide. I have my last Amstels. I bump into a friendly Radio 2 producer and, it is fair to say, Stag's Head regular. We talk about the olden days, the golden days. She gets a taxi home to continue her life. I make my last walk back to the Tavistock to polish off mine, down through the deserted West End streets, back past UCH and ULU and into the W&W bar.

One last drink. Stuff to do.

Some final emails back in my room. No clues. No tears. No doubt. I build a shrine – the farewell note, the release schedule, the list of contacts, Nelson the Panda sitting proud.

At 2 a.m., I take three handfuls of painkillers and go to sleep, endless sleep.

3

LOVELY LITTLE SWAN

When I was twelve years old, I wanted to go to a pop concert, my first ever, but my mother wouldn't let me. The year is 1978. A million lives away, the cities are being rocked by the fall-out from punk rock, not to mention new bands who sound a bit like a new band called the Fall. In reality, by this point the Sex Pistols are a busted flush, the seminal Roxy venue has been dead for a year, the true punk originators are already scattering to the wind. In our reality meanwhile, in Edmonton in north London, us first-year Latymer grammar school boys are going ever-so-gently out of our minds to the cosmic orchestral sounds of *Out of the Blue* by the Electric Light Orchestra. 'Mr Blue Sky', 'Wild West Hero', 'Sweet Talkin' Woman' . . . this melodically overloaded double album dominates our lives on the radio and in the record racks as much as 'Turn to Stone' turns relentlessly on our Stone Age gramophones.

Starting on 2 June 1978, they would go on to play eight shows at the massive Wembley Empire, where tickets ranged from an alarming £2.75 right up to a frankly mindboggling £4.25. My best schoolfriend Stephen Langford was going along with some other excitable students. A good crew out for some serious AOR fun. And yet for some bizarre reason my mother would not let her blushing boy go with them on the London Underground to Wembley. I say 'for some bizarre reason' because we lived in a house full of music, from Simon & Garfunkel to Gilbert & Sullivan via Mozart and Dylan and the Wombles. She'd bought me my first radio. She bought me my first record player. She even bought me *Out of the Blue* by the Electric Light Orchestra to play relentlessly on that first record player.

Perhaps she didn't want me gallivanting out and about on what was – quite literally – a school night. Perhaps she didn't want me causing chaos with first-year scallywags on the year zero '70s streets of west London. Perhaps she thought the £2.75 charge for the cheap seats was a scandalous cost too far. Perhaps she just didn't want to unleash my inner gigging demons and thereby condemn her son to a life of dodgy bars, darkened back rooms and drooling along to bands with names like Dead Kids and Death Cab for Cutie and Desperate Journalist. Well, that bloody well worked, didn't it?

In fact, you could say it was almost as much of a shock as starting school in the first place. I'd been comfortably the fourth smartest in the playground in Houndsfield juniors. Actually, all four of us smartarse kids ended up going to Latymer. But while the other three revelled in the new environs I cowered in the classroom. With a lower sixth and an upper sixth, the age range was from eleven at one end of the school to eighteen at the other – some of these people had proper beards. Latymer was a bit posh, although it wasn't private and it was very mixed, but it took me about four years to get up to speed with the demands of the entire educational process – it didn't help that I was the smallest in a class full of toweringly advanced Amazonian girls who must have been all of 5 foot 2 – by which point I was sixteen years old, so I could send myself off to gigs and the educational process started to diminish in importance.

It wasn't all bad. I was a dependably enthusiastic, if mildly incompetent, member of the school cross country and football teams, and as the kit was a white shirt with blue shorts and blue socks the local vibe was very, very Tottenham, what with White Hart Lane being just up the road and the glorious Hotspurs being freshly relegated to Division Two. And, in lieu of any connection with the complexities of French language or physics, I bloody loved lunchtime football in the playground.

But I never felt as though I fitted in. Most of the kids were from the sweet suburbs where north London rolled its Metro-landing way into Middlesex: Southgate, Enfield, Winchmore Hill (cue the classic Piccadilly line joke: 'Excuse me, is this Cockfosters?' 'No, it's mine, madam.'). Big houses, big families, big hopes, big aspirations. I was from the wrong side of the tracks, the loutsider from E17, the creased kid from the east, the runt of the litter. (Actually, my classmate Jane Ogden lived nearby to me in Highams Park, but as a girl she was always an adult in a teenager's body and lived in a big house with big hopes and aspirations. Ergo, not runty.)

The school run was on the top deck of the 144 bus along the North Circular Road, which picked me up on Wadham Bridge, opposite the Sun Inn Chinese takeaway. Down to Wadham Lodge sports ground, over the Crooked Billet roundabout (to your right, Walthamstow Dog Stadium), past the Unigate milk depot, the Polygram Records plant, the Thorn EMI HQ – proper factories for proper workers – on past Pickett's Lock sports centre, through the Angel (Edmonton, not Islington), turn right at the North Middlesex Hospital. It was quite the journey.

It wasn't all sitting on the 144, kicking around tennis balls and chewing through the tuck shop Burton's beefy potato puffs though: when I was a wee nipper there was an older cool dude who swaggered around with peroxide blond hair and a guitar case. One day I saw his picture in *Sounds*; turned out he was in a mod band called Back to Zero, and he is at the front of quite the Latymer celebrity queue. Debbie Smith, guitarist from Curve and Echobelly, went there. Phil Barker from agit-punks Lack of Knowledge was in my year, as were Simon Armstrong and Richard Blackborow from indie dreamboats BOB. Previously, Bruce Forsyth had been a student. Later on, *NME* writers Mark Beaumont and Leonie Cooper went through the same educational system. In even later years, James Blake would glide his electronical way along those same shiny corridors. Ipso facto, I am barely in the top ten of the coolest showbiz people at my own school, and that's before we get to the people who've gone on to write books on psychology and politics and economics and all that intellectual malarkey, like one Professor Jane Ogden in fact.

Economics, politics and psychology were none of my specialist subjects. In fact, I wasn't quite sure what my specialist subjects were by the time I bopped into my mid-teens. This reared its pretty ugly head when I had a chat with a so-called careers advice officer in some shabby office in Edmonton Green shopping centre. They asked me what I liked at school. Basing my answer on the utter joys of colouring in maps of long-since perished African countries a decade earlier as an eight-year-old, I said geography. 'In that case,' said the tired, shabby man in his tired, shabby office, 'perhaps you should consider becoming a long-distance lorry driver.'

The benefits of a grammar school education, eh? I did not end up driving meat products across the highways and pie-ways of Europe to the hungry people of Hungary. My first ever Saturday job was in a bakery positioned very neatly at the Baker's Arms in Leyton. I can't for the life of me recall the name of the shop, but it definitely wasn't Greggs or Percy Ingle and the slogan on our work T-shirts was 'Mister Dusty Makes Fresh Bread Crusty'. I'd start work before the first bus had even rolled down the hill from Highams Park, so I'd have to walk all the way across a deserted Walthamstow listening to the dawn chorus and watching the streetlights dim.

Glenn was the main baker, a proper cheeky geezer and a West Ham fan. I learned how to bake perfectly fresh crusty loaves of bread and overcook rolls just enough they couldn't be sold, they had to be taken home for free. We talked about the Jam and he taught me how the jam makes it right into the middle of dough-nuts. I loved it there. Sometimes I could finish up and be back home in time for *Football Focus*. Other times I'd walk up Hoe Street and go record shopping in a place called Small Wonder.

If the name rings a doomy bell, that might be because you are a goth, or in total gothic denial, because the Small Wonder label released 'Killing an Arab' by the Cure and 'Bela Lugosi's Dead' by Bauhaus amid snotty singles by Patrik Fitzgerald, Cockney Rejects and Angelic Upstarts. Unsurprisingly then, the Small Wonder Records record shop was punk – not the slightly silly early '80s punk of the Exploited or the Anti-Nowhere League, but proper anarchic underground punk, with the Crass commune a crow's flight away in Epping Forest.

It was a pretty angry place. In my teenie mind's eye, the counter was about 20-foot tall and the music was played at a thunderous volume, but I still scurried in to buy my indie schmindie records.

I once squeakingly asked if they had 'Revolutionary Spirit' by the Wild Swans on 7-inch vinyl. Over the thunderous sound of 'Yes Sir, I Will', Pete Stennett the owner told me in various uncertain terms that it was only available on 12-inch, the cost of which my meagre earnings from the bakery at the Baker's Arms couldn't justify. Basically, the baker's boy didn't have enough dough. Such sweet, jammy irony.

31 DECEMBER 2019, 7 A.M.

I awake, feeling heartily refreshed. Morning is bloody well broken.

Bollocks.

This is most decidedly not part of the plan.

Another two fistfuls of painkillers, until I can't swallow any more without gagging. A hot bath. A cold scalpel. No pain, just numb cutting, cutting, cutting. Up the arm, not across the wrist. Crimson clouds spill out into the dull dawn water, submerged under a blood-red tide. All surface, no feeling. Dozy now, desperately hoping to just fade away in the bath. Slipping down, choking on my own bloodied water, diluted like so much gory squash.

I am sure there is an exact science to this, but I'm buggered if I can work it out.

Back on the bed, bleeding. Another doze. Bloodstained fingers crossed this time. Awake again, this time to the sound of housekeeping rampaging efficiently through rooms along the corridor. They mustn't find me. Because then they'll try to save me. I hurriedly, fuzzily, get dressed, dismantle the shrine, pack a bag I thought would never be packed again, skulk out head down through reception and out under the glum grey skies crushing Tavistock Square. And you will know me by the trail of bloodied hotel towels.

Slouching outside the British Library with the eager tourists staring up at Harry Potterland next door. It's a kind of magic. Back on a 73 bus. Past the Orchard HQ in the Lighthouse, that funny pie-shaped building in the middle of the King's Cross traffic flow. Right past the Scala, up the hill and turn left just past the Lexington. Bloody love Routemasters. I am now making it up as I go along. My plans are in tatters. Lucky it's winter – the oversized overcoat covers the bloodsoaked toilet roll haphazardly wrapped around my wrists. I suspect I am not looking too good.

4

LET THE DAYS DRIFT AWAY

Lacking an older sibling to steal records from, or any friends especially interested in this music malarkey, apart from making tentative semi-terrified forays into Small Wonder on Hoe Street I had to make my own journey into sound. I'd missed the Danny Baker generation where it seemed billion-selling chart singles were for sale at the back of every haberdashery, ironmongers and car showroom, but as the '70s sneaked into the '80s the world was not lacking in other oddball outlets for records.

There were the wobbly freebies on the front of magazines and cereal boxes – I still have the flexi disc of 'Pop Art Poem' by the Jam from *Flexipop!* filed next to the flexi of 'Dead Man's Curve' by Nash the Slash from *Smash Hits*, filed next to the Elton John and Kiki Dee flexi that came frreeee with Frosties.

Then there were off-the-wall marketing deals, like the Clearasil spot face wash offer: you collected three labels from the top of the boxed packaging and sent them off to a mysterious address and they would send back the 7-inch version of your chosen top

PANDAMONIUM!

ten smash hit of the moment. Or should that be smash zit? A little bit limiting in scope, to be honest, but that offer begat me free copies of 'Leaving Me Now' by Level 42, 'West End Girls' by Pet Shop Boys, and 'Kayleigh' by Marillion, which was handy because Keely from the west end of Enfield had indeed just left me. I wasn't even especially spotty. Leastways, I wasn't after piling through gallons of Clearasil.

Woolworths was obviously a brilliant high street staple. I bought my first single, 'Jilted John' by Jilted John, from the Walthamstow High Street branch (full price 89 pence and counting), but soon appreciated that the Woolies' bargain bin was always a great source of failed glory. On Wood Street was a record shop that had stacks of ex-chart singles, ex-jukebox too judging by the big holes in the labels – I pretty much had my fill of Soft Cell, OMD and Gary Numan's synthpop glories from their tattered racks. And even your run-of-the-mill newsagents would often have a wee box of dog-eared 7-inches on the counter, the Chrysalis logo on the Blondie label fighting for attention with the crisp packets.

But what this cruising and perusing really uncovered were a litany of unloved nuggets. Tracks you heard once or twice on the radio (perhaps because they were only ever played once or twice) and, pre-internet and Spotify, then had to head outside to search for in local haberdasheries or chart return shops. Sometimes they were cheap because a major label was trying to hoick them into the charts. Sometimes they were cheap because the same major had given up with the hoicking and the hyping.

The junk shop loitering wasn't without its credibility hazards: you could buy Tears for Fears' 'Mad World' when it was number sixty-five in the charts and breezily assume it was destined to crash and burn, and then a month later it would be in the top bloody three. Similarly, 'Take On Me' by A-ha was seemingly re-released to fail every three months for ever, until the famed love story video rocketed it to success and you were left looking as leftfield as a Phil Collins B-side.

In essence, however, this tactic usually meant I ended up with a tremendous amount of terrific records by bands few people have ever heard of, would-be headline acts who never made it past the opening slot of life: the morosely pop-tastic 'This Is the Shirt' by Two People; the shimmeringly epic 'Glasshouse' by the Promise; the billowingly graceful 'Time' by Music for Pleasure; 'Barriers' by Tony Martin, a splendidly enticing DIY New Order-lite nugget; 'Happy Together' by Sophie and Peter Johnston, a synthpop pebble that surprisingly caused many a ripple in Peelie's pond.

None of these were in any way 'indie' or 'alternative'. A large number of these acts I never even saw play live – the Promise did support Frankie Goes to Hollywood at Hammersmith Odeon, and history tells me that Music for Pleasure played with Talk Talk at the Dominion, mind you. But for the most part I considered these records to be little miracles lurking on the margins. And these are songs I still play to this day because, rather conveniently, some lunatics have put them all on YouTube. More often than not there is no promo video, just a static image of the original dog-eared artwork and the music, often preceded by the crackle of needle settling on vinyl. Sometimes I suspect those uploading lunatics are the actual artists themselves.

Even as a young pop pup ignorant of the machinations of whatever the music industry was, these records made me realise that not everyone can be as big as U2, not even the relentless slew of supposed new U2s like Cactus World News and the Chameleons and the Alarm. It made me realise that some bands are destined to leave one, maybe two, great singles and fade away. It made me realise that there was another level beyond the 'normal' entry point for new bands. And it made me *really* realise how to value the role of the underdog. After all, if it's hard to live life as a one-hit wonder, what must it be like to exist as a none-hit blunder? Absolutely wonderful, I hope.

Another way of looking at it is that some of the best songs in the world never got into the top forty. Annie Nightingale once ran a competition on the pre-*Evening Session* evening session to find the ten best ever non-hit singles. I can't remember who I voted for – what am I, some kind of indie nerd?? – but I'd bet my very last bottom dollar my top ten featured 'Marliese' by Fischer Z, 'Felicity' by Orange Juice, 'I Ran' by A Flock of Seagulls and 'Whatever Is He Like?' by the Farmer's Boys. And perhaps 'A Letter from Afar' by B-Movie and 'Streets of London' by the Anti-Nowhere League. Oh, and maybe 'Revolutionary Spirit' by the Wild Swans and 'Love My Way' by the Psychedelic Furs.

Apart from that, I can't remember a thing, but I do know four of my choices coincided with those of my fellow nerdling listeners, and for my pleasure and pain I got sent a much-cherished Annie Nightingale Radio 1 pen. I also got the heart-swelling sense that your record peaking at number forty-one was an indie badge of honour. Only twenty years later would I learn how that so-called honourable badge could pierce a broken indie heart with its cold pointy metal pointlessness.

★

In 1989, as UCAS legend has it, Manchester University was overwhelmed with applications from spotty tykes mesmerised by seeing the Stone Roses and Happy Mondays on *Top of the Pops* and wanting a bit of that flarey Flowered Up life hanging at the Hacienda. I was years ahead of them. In 1984, I wanted to go to the University of East Anglia, purely because of night-time Radio 1. More pertinently, it was because of the push the music scene in Norwich was getting from John Peel and Kid Jensen.

My first gig was at the Lyceum, at the end of the Strand by Waterloo Bridge. It's home to a never-ending run of *The Lion King* now, but before Simba we did the samba to feverishly up-and-coming acts. In essence, the Lyceum was the Astoria of the day, a lovely velveteen old ballroom. My second gig was there as well, on 5 December, when U2 were poised to burst into the mainstream with their *War* album. Zerra 1 opened and the Alarm were middle on and blew everyone else off stage with their '68 Guns', and I bought a U2 War tour sweatshirt for a tenner, which equates to roughly £300,000 in today's merchandising money.

Anyhooo, back to 10 October 1982, when I made my gigging debut at an indie-funk face-off between Norwich and Bristol. There were seven bands playing: Maximum Joy, Animal Magic, Dislocation Dance, and Design for Living formed the West Country contingent; the Higsons, the Farmer's Boys and Popular Voice came from the east. I thought all gigs were like this, and I thought I especially loved the three bands from Norwich. I was very wrong on one count, but I was very much right on the other.

In the many years ahead, Norwich Arts Centre would become my favourite venue outside of the grizzly puddles of north London, and only partly because it was a semi-reconstructed church. There was no stopping me as I started to fixate on the local scene lurking beyond the sacred confines of St Benedict's Street and bought records by the Higsons, Serious Drinking, Popular Voice, Testcard F, Gee Mr Tracy and the Farmer's Boys. Especially the Farmer's Boys, or if we want to be pedantic, the fARmeR's bOys. (Note to self: I wish I'd called us fiERce pANdA.) I don't think indiepop had been invented then, but if it had they would have personified the musical tag. Simple, swooning songs about drinking and dressing up played by four glamour-free blokes. No drummer on drums, just Mark on bass, Stan on guitar, Frog on keyboards and singer Baz standing behind an ironing board with a portable Casio keyboard in the middle and a pint where the iron normally stands.

Everyone thought they looked daft, but they were beyond caring. Squint hard enough and they were kinda like one of the first post-Postcard bands. They were more about wearing nerdy spectacles than providing any gigging spectacular, but they were certainly my band. I bought their singles from Small Wonder: 'I Think I Need Help' on Waap!, 'Whatever Is He Like?' on Backs, all three versions of the 7-inch of 'More Than a Dream', i.e. one on Backs, one on Backs (distributed by Sony) and the EMI reissue when they sold their souls to the corporate devil and I had to go to a chart return shop to buy it.

I knew the chart return record shops very well. They were the ones who put the *Music Week* chart on the front door and who got all the freebie promo merch from the major label reps. I gorged on Farmer's Boys' paraphernalia filched from uncaring shopkeepers: posters for 'For You', weird dangly plastic things for 'Apparently'. I bought 'Muck It Out' on 7-inch, 12-inch and pig-shaped picture disc. I bought 'For You' on 7-inch, 12-inch and double 7-inch gatefold package. I just thank the sweet lord that they split before multi-multi-formatting days of the late '80s, when you'd have to remortgage your lovely home to buy everything by the House of Love, or the ghastly onset of CD1 and CD2 releases in the '90s.

I was, quite frankly, infatuated. I wrote them letters and posted them to the address on the back of their record sleeves; they sent back badges, notes, stickers and a fanzine (farmzine?) called *Griff.*

I carefully collated cuttings, cuttings, cuttings of their live and record reviews, their interviews, even their adverts from the music press. I taped their sessions off the John Peel and Kid Jensen shows. I bought their bootleg cassettes from Camden Market stalls, mostly featuring session tracks I'd already ripped off the radio and live shows I'd already seen. I even delved into the curious realm of the test pressing.

I travelled across London for teenage gig-shaped experiences – out to the Mean Fiddler in Harlesden, in to the Electric Ballroom in Camden Town, up to North Middlesex Polytechnic in Trent Park. I went to see them on my own at the Venue in Victoria playing with the Chameleons and was accompanied by a company of wolfish school friends at a brilliantly sold-out Hammersmith Palais on 13 December '83 with the Higsons, Serious Drinking and Popular Voice and absolutely no funk bands from Bristol, and I tore down a gigantic gig poster from outside the Tube station on the way home.

Like some indiepopping Paddington Bear, I once scurried determinedly to their record company EMI's HQ, in Manchester Square in London Town (the one where John, Paul, George and Whoever are leaning over the balcony on the *Red* and *Blue* album sleeves). In reception, I asked to see 'someone who had something to do with the Farmer's Boys'. I think everyone was so surprised I wasn't asking for a chance to kiss Sir Cliff's bottom they let me upstairs with my marmalade sandwiches to a Very Big Office where the major label marketing department must have been, although I had no idea at that time what a majorly labelled departmental market was, and I left with a suitcase full of records and promo gear.

As an even weirder aside, when we were in the sixth form at Latymer we would get professionals from various industries to come along to our Lecture Theatre (outside of which during an icy mid-winter game of lunchtime playground football I had once slipped and, hands safely stashed in pockets, crashed forward onto the concrete. Luckily, I landed safely on my face and only broke my nose for ever. I was whisked up the road to North Middlesex Hospital where, under gloomy yellow lights, I sat for four hours until I looked like a fat panda, and a doctor came along and gave my fat panda face a poke and said, 'Yes, that's broken. But it's far too swollen now for us to do anything to fix it.' Phew wow indeed) and give talks about their vocations.

One day a man from EMI came along and talked about his job working at the major label. Truth be told, him talking about working at a major label didn't sound very exciting until one of the students asked him about new bands and he said it certainly wasn't all about kissing the bottoms of Sir Cliff and Queen all day long. 'In fact,' he said, 'we've just signed this new band called the Farmer's Boys.' At which point – and I shite thee not, rogue reader – my fellow students in the auditorium cheered and turned to look at the bashful indie boy with the bent nose blushing at the back.

I never went to study at the University of East Anglia – the lure of the London underground scene was too strong, and more pertinently my useless A-level grades weren't strong enough. But I'm still convinced that had the Farmer's Boys had another 126,865 fans as devoted as me they would have stood a chance. As it was, they ended up releasing a cover version of Sir Clifford's 'In the Country', which I actually heard on Radio 2 in an ice cream emporium in Mousehole. On the week of release, I went to Sounds Right to buy the 7-inch, the 12-inch and the weird flower-shaped picture disc. The next week I went back and studied the *Music Week* chart in the window with great, possibly alarming, intensity. 'In the Country' wasn't on there, primarily because it had missed the top seventy-five by seven places.

No disaster, as we've seen from the creeping likes of Tears for Fears. Sure enough, the following week it was there in the window, up from eighty-two to number fifty. Up it went again the following week, 5 August, this time to forty-four. Sadly, the Pointer Sisters, Dio and Miami Sound Machine's 'Doc-Doc-Doctor Doctor Beat' had gone straight in at forty-three, forty-two and forty-one respectively. To add insult to injury, A Flock of Seagulls had hopped up from forty-three to forty with 'The More You Live, The More You Love', a song even I can't recall today, and I actually have a soft spot for the band.

They were scarcely on their own in the cool runnings: that week alone in the top forty the Kane Gang, the Bluebells, the Mighty Wah! and Echo & the Bunnymen (not to mention Billy Idol's secretly terrific 'Eyes Without a Face') scowled among the Kershaws, Moyets and Frankies. However, the Farmer's Boys, aka the fARmeR's bOys, would never get near the chart again. Actually, the next single, 'Phew Wow!', did peak at fifty-nine, but apart from that neo-near-hit the fARmeR's bOys, aka the Farmer's Boys, would never, ever get near the charts again.

Mark and Baz reformed as the Avons and released an excellent EP and an album of world-weary janglepop, delivering Americana from the Norfolk Broads bijou. We went up to Norwich to interview them for the fanzine when they played a hometown show at UEA. We did a smashing interview and I vommed up my afternoon Kronenburgs on the sculpted lawns outside – the nearest I would ever get to behaving like a student on the UEA campus, and therefore a special moment. They talked freely about the Farmer's Boys years, memorably describing a possibly apocryphal hi-falutin meeting at Manchester Square where one A&R man told A&Nother that he'd been tremendously busy getting Belouis Some a new haircut. Imagination indeed.

A couple of years later, we went to see Julian Cope at Tufnell Park Dome, circa 'World Shut Your Mouth'. Deliciously dark days. Checked shirts and Levi's begone – this was a night for the leather box jacket and PVC trousers, in the middle of an overcrowded crowd of tearful Teardrop Explodes fans in leather jackets and PVC trousers. In the middle of a heatwave. An experience in gigging meltdown in north London years before the Meltdown gigging experience became de rigueur on the South Bank. Cope had his mad angular mic stand and the last of his few remaining pop sensibilities. Also, on keyboards, he had Frog from the Farmer's Boys. If you were at that show and you can recall a slightly drunk, very sweaty and immensely mournful cry of 'FROOOOOOOOOOOG!!' ringing out from the middle of the crowd, much like a foghorn – or, if you will, a froghorn – blowing across the Tufnell Park Sound, then you have a very good memory.

A thrillion lifetimes later we did them (well, Baz, Mark and Stan) as the Great Outdoors on Fierce Panda. They say never meet your heroes. They are wrong. We released two singles by them when we were in Walthamstow and they supported some bunch of chancers called Coldplay at the Bull & Gate. This was quirky for several reasons: first, it was fifteen years since the Farmer's Boys had split, so the Great Outdoors looked very much like the elder statesmen of the evening, especially next to the fresh-faced students headlining. Second, the room was totally packed with A&R people boasting about the excellent new haircuts they'd just got their primetime artists, none of whom could leave the room because they knew they wouldn't get back in again, so they had to endure the Great Outdoors' lovely indie flappings, which, if memory serves me correctly, involved a semi-ironic Take That cover. In a way, it was a passing of the baton, from one Panda pop legend to another. Leastways, Coldplay were themselves about to sign to EMI.

My love affair with Norwich would pay off eventually when, in 1992, I was sent to review the first ever Sound City, which saw the opening of the local Waterfront venue. I'd had a big hand in the writing of a special *NME* pull-out preview of the event, in the sense that I'd written the entire thing, with an overview of the history of the Norwich music scene, in which a phone interview with John Peel was a special highlight. A month or so later, editor Danny Kelly said perhaps I should have got some sort of writing credit for writing the entire thing. He had an excellent point.

One inaugural Sound City night, Nick Cave and the Bad Seeds played the main Waterfront, with the Catherine Wheel in the other room. While we were sitting in the foyer of the Nelson Hotel – quite literally my favourite place in the world apart from a beach in the Cyclades or a tatty venue in a Camden side street – getting prepped for the show, a tall, dark stranger strolled over, waving an impossibly thin cigarette at the end of an implausibly skinny arm.

'You got a lighter, mate?'

'No, sorry I haven't.'

'Hmmph.'

So our tall, dark stranger loped off, searching for a light to guide his way back to the holy bar. And I became best buddies for ever with Mister Nicholas Cave.

Bloody loved the Catherine Wheel. They were on a Norwich label called Wilde Club. Great local set-up, putting on live shows at the Arts Centre, releasing carefully handpicked records, thinking deeply about things. After a few such carefully thought-out releases, they put out a compilation album called *I Might Walk Home Alone*. Every indie label should release a compilation album called *I Might Walk Home Alone*.

The Farmer's Boys' place in the pantheon of indie greatness, meanwhile, is not entirely assured. Beyond the wilds (or indeed, Wildes) of East Anglia their name scarcely resonates. Orange Juice were cooler and funkier, the Housemartins more tuneful and ruthlessly commercial, and the Smiths ultimately stole their great Oxfam-overcoated student thunder. But they were still mine. And I still learned so much in those three years of fandom: be nice to your lunatic fans; be loyal to your favourite bands; be nice to people; grow a floppy fringe.

And they opened doors I didn't know existed on emotional, sartorial and musical levels. When they weren't playing with bands from Norwich or Bristol they gigged with Orange Juice, with Aztec Camera, with the Daintees, with Strawberry Switch-blade. It was my introduction to the universe of scruffed-up charity-shop chic, a world of the checked shirts, the rolled-up Levi's, the DM boots, the Greek fisherman's cap, those dead men's overcoats. And it was my entrance to those regional pock-ets of underground passion around the nation – beyond doing the Norwich knowledge, Postcard in Edinburgh, Factory in Manchester and Zoo in Liverpool were the main names in the label frame, and it led me to rummaging around Kitchenware Records in Newcastle with the likes of Prefab Sprout, the Kane Gang and Hurrah!, excellent local bands for handsome local people – agog on the Tyne, indeed.

Ultimately, the Farmer's Boys were done for by the middle of the decade, but they led me to some kind of indie tipping point, which was the Miners' Benefit in 1985, on 21 January, the one at Brixton

Academy where Aztec Camera, Orange Juice, the Woodentops and Everything but the Girl pooled their alternative resources and pulled together for the striking underground workers, i.e. the miners rather than Tube-drivers. Roughly 120 per cent of the audience were decked out in checked shirts, charity-shop overcoats and rolled-up Levi's, the indie ranks united by the racks of Oxfam as much as the bands were by the right to fight against Thatcher's mentally bullish coal-mining philosophies.

Except that when it came to the drawing of straws backstage to work out the running order, some unnamed people drew the shortest of the straws and got sniffy about having to go on first, and so an irked Edwyn Collins legendarily stormed *on* stage, bewildering the late stragglers still coming into the venue, who'd expected his Orange Juice band to at least be in with a chance of headlining, what with 'Rip It Up' ripping up the charts not so much earlier, and who split the band up during their set.

I didn't see this in the flesh (of my flesh) because for once in my life I was one of those stragglers, dear reader. But that was okay, in a way, because in my wee weird musical world indie was about to get a whole lot indier.

31 DECEMBER 2019, 11.21 A.M.

Back to the top-secret office I thought I'd never see again. Fingerprint ID entrance, just like 007. No time to die. Yet. Stumbling back up two flights of stairs. Back along the long corridor, past the deserted offices – domestic violence charities, gay violence charities, African violence charities, architect violence charities. Slumped on the Fierce Panda sofa, pondering the next move. Can't stop now.

Another fistful of painkillers. Can't take any more. Think, man, think.

When you frequent certain places, you notice weird little things. For example, in the toilet opposite our office door there are old pipes running up above head height, just beneath the ceiling, plumbing relics from a previous building usage. I've often sat below idly wondering if they could sustain the weight of a human body. I am now about to find out.

I'm standing on the toilet seat, strapping a leather belt around the middle pipe, choosing the right hole to make sure it fits snugly around my neck. Wish me luck.

I jump off the toilet, hurtling into infinity and beyond.

The pipe holds. But the belt snaps. I crash to the floor, cursing loudly. Lying by the blasé basin I try to see the funny side. For once in my infuriatingly ongoing life, there isn't one.

I end up back on the brilliant orange office sofa, slumped and lumpy. I have now been trying to kill myself for fourteen hours. Jesus, this death thing is hard. On a brighter note, nobody knows where I am. It's New Year's Eve. No one will be coming into the office for days, probably a week at least.

I need to sleep. Why don't you let me?

5

I KISS THE FLOWER IN BLOOM

In 1986, indie was a little bit of a niche concern for the *NME*. In fact, you could say they put the 'indie' into 'sideline', in spite of that year's release of the *C86* cassette, which captured twenty-two shiny, sometimes shouty new alternative acts. Even the Smiths, the band most associated with the paper and the most coveted by the readership since the Jam split up, only made number nine in the *NME* writer's end-of-year album run-down, lagging behind Prince, Anita Baker, Janet Jackson, Sonic Youth, Cameo, Paul Simon, the Fall and Run DMC. And that was with *The Queen Is Dead*, which even a Morrissey non-sympathiser like me can recognise as an excellent record. In the writers' top-fifty singles, meanwhile, only three of the *C86* acts made it in – Shop Assistants' 'Safety Net' at thirty-one, The Wedding Present's 'Once More' scraping in at forty-nine, and Age of Chance hitting the top ten with their version of 'Kiss' by Prince, who himself took top spot with the original version, the fruity little sexbomber.

So even by the niche standards of the *NME*, *C86* was a left-field release. But consider that out of those twenty-two bands a grand total of sixteen of them released their first records in 1986 and you can see why the *C86* release really was a bolt out of the blue, which is precisely why it resonated with elusive pop kids like myself when the Mighty Lemon Drops appeared, seemingly out of nowhere, on the cover in the spring, singer Paul Marsh as skinny as a starving stray dog. Contrary to cynical opinion it's not all jangly and twee – that would make it unbearable, even for a twee jangly spangler like me. There's actually a decent sonic balance struck with the thunderous indignation of Big Flame and A Witness (five of the bands were from the impressively unstable Ron Johnson Records stable), the wobblesome stomp of Stump, the Delph-righteous comic chewings of Half Man Half Biscuit.

But overall it set out the classic, definitive indie stall in spades, a core of bands unwittingly united by a certain tetchy intelligence allied to a thoroughly enervating naivete, a dizzying DIY ethos. Looking at the tracklisting, modern consumers might think that The Wedding Present were cast adrift at the end of Side Two. In cassette-flipping reality this meant that once you finished their 'This Boy Can Wait (A Bit Longer)' track, the tape was ready to roll back at the beginning of Side One. Curiously, some of my very favourite tracks were by bands who I'd never like again, like 'Velocity Girl' by Primal Scream, although to be fair many a wise person has suggested that without 'Velocity Girl' there would have been no 'Made of Stone' by the Stone Roses.

Conversely, some of my least favourite *C86* tracks were by bands who I subsequently went on to love and cherish across various album releases, notably McCarthy and Close Lobsters, whose tunes – 'Celestial City' and 'Firestation Towers', respectively – didn't really stand out among the rowdy cassette crowd.

Certainly, if future indie delights 'Red Sleeping Beauty' by the former and 'Never Seen Before' by the latter had been on there, it would have been love at first bite. Then again, I've subsequently read that some bands were so dubious about the validity of what was ostensibly a mail-order tape project that they deliberately chose to put inferior tracks on there, somewhat undermining, if not quite entirely defeating, the project. Other bands went even further and turned down the chance to participate at all.

For the passing indie nerd, there were some lovely little links to the past and the future as well: Dan Treacy, a true DIY originator as the driving force in TV Personalities, had his Dreamworld label represented by the Mighty Lemon Drops. The similarly playfully troublesome Robert Lloyd, ex-Prefects, was present and correct via his Vindaloo label, which contributed the hysterical We've Got a Fuzzbox and We're Gonna Use It. In truth, for the average excitable dweeb the labels resonated as much as the artists: Creation, Subway, Glass, Probe Plus, 53rd & 3rd, Reception, Pink. Then there were the inner indie workings – Head Records was run by Jeff Barrett, later boss of Heavenly; Ian Broudie, future Lightning Seed, produced the Bodines; on a slightly more geographical bent, for us Walthamstow locals there was a frisson of joy upon hearing that McCarthy and the Wolfhounds were from the near east, i.e. Barking and Stratford respectively. Small wonder I'd walk myself around the darkened streets of E17 with *C86* playing so loudly and proudly on my Sony Walkman WM-4.

Looking back, the tape bonded me with the *NME* for the very first time. Up until that point, I'd bounced around between *Record Mirror*, *Sounds*, *Melody Maker* and the never-less-than-exuberant *Smash Hits*, usually depending on who'd written about the Farmer's Boys that week. The haughtily intellectual '80s *NME* of Paul

Morley was more than my very little brain could comprehend, but *C86* somehow brought everything down to my level. It was a genuine generational thing. A bona fide underground thing. An independent thing. An indie thing. *My* indie thing. And it changed my life, simply because there was a whole week of *C86* shows at the ICA, so I had to leave the slightly chilly comfort of my post in the freezer department on Sainsbury's nightshift. My time had come. My supermarket sweepings were at an end.

But we needed a shop where we could buy the new releases by these fresh fruitcats, some kind of retail hub that could act as a meeting point for like-minded indie dweebs hiding behind their fringes. Luckily, this being Walthamstow, we had one. Enter Ugly Child Records, which had arrived on Hoe Street in 1984 when Small Wonder exited stage left. Same shop, same stock, same state of shock, now run by a couple of passive/aggressive/passive/slightly more aggressive stoner dreamers called Nigel and Jeremy. Vinyl was their rock in trade, racks and racks of dub and hardcore and rap and goth and reggae and positive punk, which made it some kind of raging anti-Woolworths.

It was less scary than Small Wonder – or perhaps I'd grown a bit since the Baker's Arms baker boy days – but it was still edgy, still snotty, still not averse to suggesting to the accidental record-buying tourist that they fuck off up the high street if they wanted to buy that new Michael Jackson album. Crucially, it was nicely stocked with releases from the ever-expanding *C86* generation and beyond, like Microdisney and Furniture and Hurrah! and One Thousand Violins. Even more crucially, that elusive 12-inch version of 'Revolutionary Spirit' by the Wild Swans had been passed down the retail chain by Small Wonder and was now marked up at a whopping £15, which is about 16,000 streams in today's curious musical currency.

And what we needed now was a nightclub, somewhere to hear the alternative sounds of the day. Walthamstow didn't have one but Stratford did, a place called Pigeons where every Friday they played indiegoth crossover classics to a gently crazed crowd. What we also needed now was a venue, some kind of live arena where we could see these new bands in full effect. Luckily, this being Walthamstow, we had one and bloody lovely it was, too. The Assembly Hall sits at right angles to the Town Hall and still stands as one of my favourite buildings in London, with a reeling-around-the-fountain water feature out front and wooden panelling inside, where drinks are served through a booze hatch to 1,000 thirsty lost souls. There was a new guy in town, down from Scotland, some big shot from the top estate. He was called Dave McLean. He took over bookings at the venue and there was a paradigm shift.

Rebranded as WAH 17 (Walthamstow Assembly Hall + E17 – geddit?), and prompted by Dave's trips to chat to the knowledgeable stoners at Ugly Child, the venue that had previously played host to 'Peter Pan' pantos, *World of Sport* wrestling ('Big Daddy's behind you!') and a gig by New Order on 25 September 1981, suddenly tapped into popular alternative culture: Pop Will Eat Itself, The Wedding Present, Half Man Half Biscuit, the Bolshoi, Doctor and the Medics, Zodiac Mindwarp and the Fall all came to the party, accompanied by various cool support acts and excellently leftfield vibes.

And, if WAH 17 was ever found wanting, you could toddle along to the Royal Standard to see Nigel Ugly Child and his good mate Ian Ballard putting on the Wonder Stuff and the Darling Buds, or not putting on the Stone Roses as the case may be, because the band insisted on headlining. (As a rather fraught side note, toddling to the Wonder Stuff show was definitely the

PANDAMONIUM!

most convenient mode of travel – the night before they played, the King's Cross fire happened, smack bang in the middle of the Victoria line.) Crucially, I thought *all* towns were like Walthamstow. It took me a very long time to realise this was not the case.

Nothing lasts for ever. Dave McLean moved on to start Riverman promotions – we'll meet him again in a few chapters' time. Unfortunately for both myself and a fairly large chunk of what we can loosely describe as Ugly Child's customer base, it wasn't just the Wild Swans who were flying ever further out of fiscal reach. I remember having to choose which Creation single to buy each week as frequently I couldn't afford all the releases I desired. Nigel from Ugly Child now remembers a lovely warm communal alt-rock spirit from the local music-loving waifs and strays, which, if lovely warm spirit alone could pay the heating bills and the rent, could have kept the shop going for ever. But by the end of the '80s they'd sold their last Close Lobsters single before being forced to close.

One final Christmas Eve, Nigel Ugly Child handed me a 12-inch record in a brown Ugly Child paper bag. He had gifted me all £15 worth of 'Revolutionary Spirit' by the Wild Swans. 'It's not like anyone is mad enough to pay that price for it,' he sniffed gruffly. He had a point.

31 DECEMBER 2019, 5 P.M.

The sun is setting, a frozen fireball sinking over the chimney tops and trumpeting tower blocks of Canonbury. I'll just lie here awhile. Give me the beat boys, and free my soul. I want to get lost in your rock 'n' roll and drift away. No more hassle. No more worries. No more tears. Enough is enough.

The dusky silence is suddenly shattered by the intercom phone. Someone is pressing the panda button on the front door. I can't reach the receiver on the wall. Too far, too far gone. But who is it? Think man, think. It is now 5 p.m. on New Year's Eve. That can't be a delivery man. It won't be a band member. It won't be Chris or Alice or Roger or Andy or Lloyd or anyone else from the pandango posse. It won't even be bailiffs.

It could be a mistake. It might be someone trying to get into another office. It may well be sensationally optimistic burglars. Or maybe Liann is panicking back home in Suffolk. She hasn't heard from me since yesterday morning, primarily because I didn't think anyone would be hearing from me again after last night. Maybe she's called our friends Russell and Sarah and asked them to check on me. They only live five minutes away.

Problem is our office is at the far end of the Leroy House, the very furthest point from the main entrance. The entrance itself is unmanned at this time, and even if someone did let them into reception, they would be confronted by a set of fire doors that need a key fob to get through.

This is a sliding security doors moment, for sure.

6

WORD ON POWER

So we needed a fanzine.

Before *C86* sauntered onto the horizon, I'd moved out of the family home and headed straight to the heart of bedsitland: 386 Forest Road. A terraced house on the main drag from the North Circular slicing through to Tottenham Hale. Standard Sheriff Fatman-style landlordery behaviour over four stories of wonky floors and never-finished decorating with rooms divvied up by plasterboard to make even more rooms, like some endless bedsit recurrence. There were already artists in residence: Pete the road sweeper, Brian the builder, Ken the bus driver, Robert from the Marigold gloves factory on the North Circular Road (actually a rubbery corporate cover for the Durex products being made inside) and John the American cello player who was marginally fixated on Hawkwind. In one way it was like hanging out with a really shit Village People tribute act. In another, they were like the father figures I'd never had, not even in my maddest dreams.

When they weren't getting up at the crack of dawn to go clean-
ing the streets of Westminster or construct houses in Notting Hill
these people absolutely loved to live to drink and take drugs,
ideally both at the same time. It was a battered bedsitland full of
tattered men, divorcees or bachelors, the workers lurking in the
shadows, lost to a system they actually helped to keep functioning. But their lives were stupendously uncluttered, a working-for-
the weekend routine of bookies and boozers and later-than-late
nights getting merrily wrecked in the communal kitchen listening to cassettes of Pink Floyd, Led Zeppelin and very especially
the Beatles' *Sgt Pepper* on the in-house ghetto blaster.

Brian the builder was my favourite. He was a fighting ban-
tamweight, tough as old East End boots. He had a wife and two
kids on the other side of E17 and he absolutely loved skinning
up and talking about music and listening to the records pumping on my stereo, lovely flowing melodic flowerings by the Red
Guitars and the Railway Children and other bands beginning
with 'arrr'. It was a brilliant education, not least because I pretty
quickly worked out that taking speed rather than getting stoned
at midday was a much more efficient way of writing a fanzine. I
also quickly worked out that if the fanzine was going to be paid
for, work would be involved.

So my further education continued at the Polytechnic of
Sainsbury's on Walthamstow High Street. As modern as can be
in 1984. Multi-story car park upstairs. Woolies just up the road,
where I'd bought 'Jilted John' by Jilted John for 89 pence. It
started as a summer job and then, as the A-level grades ground
me down, became a full-time course. And I loved my time at
Sainsbury's. Got a tidy job on the delicatessen counter slicing
ham, slicing spam, slicing ham and egg gala pie and cutting, cutting, cutting really thin slices of mortadella . . . and no cheese.

PANDAMONIUM!

I moved onto the shop floor, couldn't stay still. Worked the fridges, marching out the platoons of Mr Men yoghurts. Clambered up to the exalted heights of the position of Head of Bread before hitting the night shift on detergents – I still get that bold smell of Bold every time I go shopping – before landing on my cold feet in the freezer department. I even tried to be professional and applied for a Sainsbury's management course but got turned down at the first step – a recurring theme.

We were working old school hours, pre-Sunday trading explosion and the relaxing of the licensing laws. There was overtime on the Sabbath, double your money working Sunday morning shifts restocking the decimated shelves of desiccated coconut followed by free roast potatoes and pints of XXXX with the lunchtime strippers in the Royal Standard. Right next to the deli counter was the bakery. Another recurring theme. There was a girl working there called Marie, who loved her music as well. We'd buy our records from Ugly Child, go to gigs up in town. Some young couples start a family. We started a fanzine together.

The world, it is safe to say, was not waiting for us to start that new fanzine together. My first taste of this indie publishing subculture was watching 'The Legend!' standing at the bar with his farmer's wife shopping basket selling his fanzine at a Housemartins show at Hammersmith Clarendon. The clamour from the customers! The glamour of the endeavour! There was also *Blah Blah Blah*, there was *Trout Fishing in Leytonstone* and in one issue of *Are You Scared to Get Happy?* – itself named after a Hurrah! song – there was a two-page spread on the Farmer's Boys written and designed in the style of classic E. H. Shepard-style Winnie the Pooh. It was the most exciting thing I'd ever read.

Our fanzine was called *Jump Away . . . Carlos Fandango*. The
'Jump Away' bit allegedly came from Irish Robert from the
Durex factory, who one day said, 'It was just a hop and a skip
and a jump away.' Carlos Fandango was a showroom dummy
we borrowed from somewhere, the name nicked from the
Hamlet cigar advert when the bloke got his souped-up Ford
Anglian wide wheels stuck in a farmyard gate. If this sounds like
some kind of meta-in-joke, then just wait until you get past the
cover. Mine and Marie's first interview was with the Icicle Works
at the Electric Ballroom at the end of 1985. Totally unaware of
PR protocol, the two of us mooched to the stage door at the end of
the gig, asked if we could speak to the band, and got let backstage.
I would never have had the gumption or the courage to do it by
myself. We ended up with the band back at some place called the
Columbia Hotel. Good grief! Are all interviews like this??

Doing the fanzine was brilliant. The writing, the re-writing, the
photocopying, the re-photocopying. It was a world of typewriters,
Pritt stick and a scalpel cutting, cutting, cutting out tabloid headlines and music paper photos and setting out Letraset. The second issue was called *Jump Away . . . Nelson Pandela* and it starred
my very own childhood panda, the third was *Jump Away . . . Mr
Wang*, who was another mannequin we found in the Walthamstow
Arcade, and the fourth was *Jump Away . . . Madam Whiplash*, which
was edited by a doll clothed in a bin liner – a toy doll, if that makes
it any better. By the time of the fifth issue, I'd completely lost the
plot and gone fake Norwegian and called the fanzine *Jomp Avak . . .
Gerkhin Fawshawt*, with Barry Manilow on the front cover with a
free unwrapped condom stapled to his face. It was all hilarious at
the time. In fact, it's still quite amusing, to be honest.

The idea of editing ourselves was mad nonsense. I had no
idea what a 'word count' was. If that Mega City 4 feature was

four pages too long, you'd just go down the newsagent's, down by the Bell pub, and photocopy it down until it fit. It might take a few trips to the newsagent's but that's okay, it's a nice day. And 'deadlines'? What are they now? You just wrote and wrote and wrote until you'd written enough and it came out when it was printed. But even I could see that the levels of self-discipline required were incredible, as was the sense of achievement when boxes of the magazine were delivered.

If a fanzine was supposed to represent a feral alternative – a feralternative, if you will – to the mainstream music press we were perhaps a little bit of a let-down to begin with. We heartily aped the weekly tropes – judging by the number of times I ripped it off, I spent a lot of time reading *Melody Maker* – but by the end we were starting to make our own way, doing features on new bands like the Ogdens and the Ryecatchers at the Bull & Gate, interviewing an up-and-coming Harry Enfield before he performed on a comedy night at the Royal Standard. In hindsight, it was brilliant journalistic training – by studiously ripping off the weeklies, and indeed other fanzines, we were accidentally understanding our craft.

Alongside the standard live reviews and interviews with the likes of the Darling Buds and Hurrah! and the Wolfhounds there were cartoons and tabloid spoofs and photo love stories – this was the peak era of *Viz*, after all. The contents careered from the meta in-jokes about pandas and mannequins to Very Serious Pieces on Apartheid and the State of Independents, as well as the imminent folding of Walthamstow Avenue FC into West Essex United (which, by a series of tortuous backflips and non-league grindings, resulted in Walthamstow Avenue and nearby Leytonstone & Ilford both being squashed into the behemoth known as Dagenham & Redbridge), which meant that *Jump Away* . . . was essentially a blend of furious seriousness and laidback flippancy, but not without a degree of pride in its presentation and publication and its brash indiepopness.

Whether or not it was essential reading is another conversation entirely – I fear that fanzines are merely for fun, not for life – but looking back at the State of Independents feature rather than just the standard whinge about bands selling out to the Major Label Man, man, it's actually a very neatly pieced together and balanced piece of work, which is a weird thing to appreciate all these years later. It's even weirder looking back and trying to gauge where that brazen chutzpah came from. Most bands were welcoming, enthusiastic even. Maybe they appreciated our honesty, or our intensity, or our stupidity. Maybe they just liked being liked. Perhaps my steady diet of nothing but cheap amphetamines, deep dish pies and gallons of cooking lager helped.

If there wasn't enough madness inherent in spending your waking hours, weeks and eventually months writing, designing and finally creating an entire fanzine from scratch, you then had to go and sell it. One thousand copies. Good luck. And sell it we did, on mail order, in Rough Trade, in Ugly Child, and at gigs – especially gigs. Back then the music weeklies would do the odd fanzine round-up, which helped postal sales no end, and I have excellent memories of Mick Mercer giving us some nice words in *Melody Maker* back when I was working in an indestructible envelopes factory in downtown Woodford. My job was to build the cardboard boxes they used to pack the finished indestructible envelopes in. I was indeed 'Living in a Box' at the start of the production line. I wore a boiler suit. I was the lowest of the low. I soon started hanging with the cool kids who liked music and drugs and dated a girl on the indestructible envelope production line called Sarah, who had an uncanny ability to look like Tracy Tracy from the Primitives. But even those cool kids would boggle at the idea of going out to a gig in the West End on a Wednesday night.

Eventually I got tired of waking up too late to catch the dawn-breaking 123 by Lloyd Park to make the morning shift in Woodford and started looking for another Crap Job to pay for the gigging fanzine fun. This was fine as the world was full of Crap Jobs back then. You'd just go to the Crap Job Centre on Hoe Street, pick a card from the display panels, take it up to a Crap Job Centre jobber and get yourself a Crap Job. One day one card said: 'Local Record Company seeks staff.' Thrilling!! Took it up to the Crap Job Centre jobber and got the Crap Job! At the Local Record Company! Fuck you, Living in a Box, I'm on the glory road to the heart of the music industry!

Turned out the 'so-called' 'record company' was actually a 'record distribution centre' in a warehouse over from Blackhorse Road station, whose main clients were those paragons of underground musical virtues Boots and Asda and whose most popular products were gatefold sleeved albums by Alexander O'Neal and Daniel O'Donnell and O'MD (I thang yew). I'd graduated from making cardboard boxes for indestructible envelopes to packing cardboard boxes full of songs by an indefatigable Irishman. And, of course, it was a brilliant place to work. I found the cool kids who liked music and took drugs. If you looked hard enough, i.e. at the racking on the end of aisle three, you could also find the 'indie' section, which quite literally consisted of 7-inch versions of 'Crash' by the Primitives and 'April Skies' by the Jesus and Mary Chain. At the end of the shifts, we'd go and drink Castlemaine and get royally XXXXed in the Royal Standard around the corner.

By now, Marie had done the sensible thing and moved on, exiting stage left to move to Exeter. A million lifetimes later we put her supremely talented teenage daughter, Maz Totterdell, on at Pub Fandango at the Bull & Gate with another young up-and-comer called Nadine Shah. A good gig. Wheels within wheels. I carried on regardless. Come 1987, peak sales were to be had at Panic Station at Camden's Dingwalls. An indie club, every Monday night, free entry with a plastic Panic Station card and a liberal booking policy that saw a procession of potentially terrific new talent tread the boards. There was Primal Scream, the Blue Aeroplanes, the Stone Roses, the Chesterfields, the La's being blown offstage by One Thousand Violins. These were very Happy Mondays indeed, and the crowd was knowledgeable and enthusiastic and very fanzine-friendly.

There was a weird quirk though: one week sales would be great – you'd turn up penniless with a carrier bag of fanzines, sell quite a few copies, enough for some drinks to sustain you through the three or four bands, maybe leave you with some spare change for a kebab on the way home. Class. The next week the sales would be rubbish, and you'd struggle to get enough money for a second pint. Seemed like the punters had already bought a fanzine, another fanzine. Seemed like some-one was getting there before me. But who could it be? Turns out the other 'zine was called *A Pack of Lies*. It was intense and tetchy, not without flashes of humour and the ubiquitous cartoon cut-outs, but much tougher than *Jump Away*. Much spikier and gnarlier – *punker*. No pandas or mannequins or meta in-jokes here. It seemed to be entirely written by some angry bloke in Essex called Steve L. Our paths would cross again.

Luckily there were other hotbeds of 'zine sales: the Bull & Gate in Kentish Town was especially great, not least because it was the first venue where I could embrace the absolute madness of compère Jon Fat Beast and the ever-whirring luminosity of

Timebox and the Pop Club and Hype and a never-ending procession of mental indie performers alongside a seemingly ever-
changing live-room decor. And, in a way, just as important as
the bands were the punters: a thousand years later I said that at
its very best the Bull & Gate was a meeting point for the fraggle
rockers, the indie shysters, the gothic dreamers, the popstarship
troopers; it gave the loners a home and the hopeless a cause,
because these people were part of Generation Vexed. It was
also, inevitably, a breeding ground for music journalists, A&R
people, promoters and, in the case of Bull & Gate workers the
Popinjays, and Gem, who was in the Contenders and who would
later join Oasis, future pop stars. One night there a young Voice
of the Beehive actually asked *me* if *they* could be in *my* fanzine.

Elsewhere, London was awash with creative student unions
that put on ace bands and sold cheap beer to captive indie kids,
who therefore had spare money to invest in a passing fanzine.
The Queen Mary University union, aka QMU, on Mile End
Road, was a great night out, but the University of London Union,
aka ULU, on Malet Street in Fitzrovia, was even better. Kinda
800 capacity, cheap studey beer, loads of captive indie kids.

So I'm on the fanzine prowl at a Pop Will Eat Itself show at
ULU, 15 January 1988, a lonely carrier bag man on full sales
alert. Amble up to a couple of girls chatting by the main door into
the live hall. Roll out the standard sensational indie salesman pat-
ter: 'Hello. Would you like to buy a fanzine?'

The one with the long auburn hair glances at the front cover,
then looks up questioningly.

'Are you Simon? I've been looking for you!'

Turns out one of these girls, the one with the long auburn hair,
is called Helen Mead. And she's the Live editor at the *NME*.

Couldn't make it up. So I haven't.

31 DECEMBER 2019, 5.46 P.M.

I am now sick and tired of being sick and tired of being sick and tired. In short, I think I have lost the will to die. I reach for the mobile for the first time that entire day and slowly scroll through the messages: Liann politely asking where I am. Liann again, slightly panicking. Where am I? And again, this time slightly tempting: we've bought you New Year's Eve pies. Then there's one from Russell, all cool, but knowing that Liann is panicking. It was him at the door, pressing the intercom.

I slowly text Russell back. One message. Five words that change everything.

'Hello. I'm in the office.'

He responds swiftly.

'Hello Simon. I think you'd better give Liann a call. She's very worried.'

'Could I pop round? I'm afraid I've done something a little bit silly.'

'Of course! I look forward to hearing all about it!'

An anxious, slightly embarrassed moment of text silence.

'I think I might need to go to hospital.'

Another longer moment of text silence.

'Ah. Well, better get round here then.'

It sounds a touch facile, but if you read our text conversation in the style of Biggles indulging in some stiffly upper-lipped banter with Ginger it makes a lot more sense.

7

GOT APPREHENSION

The world, it has to be said, was not in dire need of any more coy
boy writers clutching their fanzines to their wee palpitating indie
hearts in 1988. *Sounds*, *Melody Maker* and *NME* were all running
at full steam and fully for sale in the nation's newsagents. The
Legend!, Bob Stanley, Push, Mick Mercer, John Robb, Andy
Ross, Andy Winters . . . all of these and many more were loitering around the Bull & Gate and the Fulham Greyhound and
the Night & Day and wherever else fruity new bands lurked.
The eloquent likes of John Tague and Stuart Maconie were both
freshly blown into the *NME* on the northern winds. And that
Steve L who I'd shared fanzine perils with? He turned out to be
some sub-editing indie kid called Steve Lamacq who was courting the Live editor, Helen, hence her curious and indeed surprising enthusiasm for my fanzine selling skills at ULU.

For any coy, shy indie boy writer the early months at the *NME*
were a bit of an eye-opener, mind you. C86 Forest Road had
no landline telephone so, in this pre-mobile universe I would

commandeer the phone box on Greenleaf Road for my business dealings. After several highly entertaining conversations with the Live desk answering machine, I worked out that to get any work it was easier just to get the Tube to the office, which was originally in Commonwealth House in Holborn before moving to the twenty-fifth floor of King's Reach Tower, aka IPC headquarters, aka Satan's Cock Tower according to David Quantick, on the South Bank overlooking the Thames by Blackfriars Bridge. On a clear day I swear you could see Hackney.

My first words were for Helen's Live section, and those words were about the live performances by Eat and the James Dean Driving Experience at my indie-home-from-home, Panic Station in Camden. When I did manage to get more live reviews commissioned, written, typed and handed in on A4 paper I was most alarmed to discover that any excess copy was just cut out and not carefully reduced to point six on the photocopier in the newsagent's down the road. In actual fact, they didn't even need to go to the newsagent's as they had their own industrial-sized copying machine down by the art department, but still they just cut the review to fit it on the page, regardless of context or contemptuously excellent kiss-off lines.

Worse still, loads of my early commissioned gig reviews were spiked – i.e. dumped and left unused, unread, unloved – due to lack of space in the final Live pages (where all last-minute adverts were dropped in, squeezing our valuable wordage space). This simply didn't happen in the fanzine world, where every word was precious, every paragraph thoroughly precocious. In fact, in a weird way, going from the fanzine world to the *NME* was like making that massive leap from junior to senior school, except with fewer beards as the modern hipster look looked far from cool in the late '80s.

But still it was brilliant. If you've got the drive and the self-discipline, not to mention the requisite 30 degrees of lunacy, to sit on your bed and build an entire fanzine from a few flexi discs, a mini-envelope of cheap speed and several flashes of creative vivaciousness, then a 250-word live review from the Bull & Gate is no problem whatsoever, even if it gets cut by a third. And you get paid! (You even get paid half for the spiked reviews!) And your name is on things called Guest Lists! And you get sent free records and free T-shirts and lots of people are freely very nice to you lest you give their band an absolute 'trouncing'! What could possibly be better for an indie kid sauntering into his twenties?

The early doors eye-opening vibe was helped by the fact that by 1989 I'd tired of falling asleep on the N96 home and waking up five bus stops too late in Chingford, so I left C86 Forest Road and moved lock, stock and very small indie barrel into Jayne Houghton's back room on Cephas Avenue in Stepney. Jayne was a brassy northern lady who took photographs for the *NME* on her way to running PR campaigns for the likes of Happy Mondays and New Order, and her other lodger was another northern lady who wrote for *Sounds* and was called Mary Anne Hobbs, so I was about to get many a bonus out-of-working hours lesson in the basic machinations of the music industry.

The first lesson was that as a freelance music journalist there were no out-of-working hours. Pretty much every waking moment was spent either watching bands, listening to bands, writing about bands or thinking and indeed drinking about bands in a bid to make enough money for that last kebab home. In short, on Cephas Avenue I found myself thoroughly lost in music. To wit, barely a week went by in Stepney without finding all of the Inspirals crashed out on the front room carpet, or Mark Gardener from Ride lurking in the back garden, or

John Robb moulding his mohawk by the Moulinex mixer in the kitchen.

At the height of the rave scene, Jayne decided to throw a dance party that involved stripping her own front room of all furnishings, including various stray Inspirals, and her entire carpet, and filling the room with mad lights, big drugs, big, mad people from Creation and Heavenly Records and big bad sounds from Ibiza and beyond.

I immediately twigged that as both a lady and a professional music photographer, Jayne was not to be messed with, and as an ally on the *NME* frontline she was armed with a bolshiness and bravado I was so sorely lacking. The fact that she is the only person who has ever consistently referred to me as 'Simes' only adds to my recklessly rose-tinted view of those times. In essence that twenty-fifth-floor open plan office was a sky-high world of half-broken typewriters and untypical writers smoking and drinking, joking and thinking, poking and stinking. Steven Wells storming around shouting at himself. David Quantick being cryptic in the corner. Andrew Collins and Stuart Maconie making up stories about Bob Holness's saxophone prowess for the 'Thrills' page (no, Bob did not perform on 'Baker Street'). Terry Staunton tearing up stories on the news desk. Dele Fadele smoking and fretting in the review room. Gavin Martin fretting about the smoking on the film desk. Roger Morton posing in his leather trousers. Paolo Hewitt polishing his loafers. Danny Kelly raconteuring happily in the middle of the chaos.

In many ways I very much felt that I was the runt of the literary litter. But I was diligent and disciplined. And I was frequently in the office, hanging around, making a useful nuisance of myself. I worked out you could basically get work just by loitering casually in the eye-line of a commissioning editor. There were live reviews, album reviews and features to nab. Plus, back when the *NME* represented some kind of pan-cultural arbiter of taste, there were film reviews and book reviews and TV previews, and interviews with comedians and actors and authors like Terry Pratchett and Martin Millar and famous people like Michael Palin and Eric Idle and Eddie Izzard. One day I interviewed Harry Hill in a Marylebone hotel and after the interview I got into the lift with Paolo Maldini and some other AC Milan giants in town to play the Goonies and then I went to a no doubt super hoopla gig. The following lunchtime I went to the Brunswick Arms to be interviewed by two students from my Latymerian alma mater, and I pretended that every day was like the day before just to make myself look cooler than I never could be.

Being in the eye of the editorial tiger had its other floppy fringe benefits, too: Danny Kelly can't be arsed to go to Paris Olympia to review James tomorrow? James Brown can't be arsed to go to Cambridge Corn Exchange to review the Fall tonight? (Curiously, I bumped into the Farmer's Boys at the bar of that show and they were very helpful with more obscure tracks. I looked like a total fucking genius when I handed the copy in. Or maybe I just looked like a twat if I'd put in any of their joke titles.) Helen Mead is off ill so we need someone to do the letters page and run the Live section? Up stepped the wee fanzine boy. One week I earned 777 squids just by pretty much hanging around looking slightly confused, rolling around the floor and answering the phone to even more confused press officers on the Live desk.

The big boys weren't totally lacking in advice for the young at heart, however. One day I went to Rugby with snapper AJ Barratt to interview Pete Kember, aka Sonic Boom, formerly of drug muling drone kings Spacemen 3. No press officer, just a day trip on the train. Pete was at his parents' very nice house and he was on some very nice methadone treatment. This meant he had a tendency to doze off mid-conversation, which was a bit of a problem when it came to the *NME* interview, which relies quite a lot on verbal communication.

Lacking a middle ground press officer to give Pete a nudge, while Pete dozed, AJ gave me a 'what the fucking fuck' stare across the cosy Kember family lounge while I shrugged my bewilderfuddled shoulders. In the end our hero managed to rouse himself from his slumbers without us having to poke him awake with a poker, and we snapped out a photo session with him lounging on an E-Type Jag lounging in the drive and scuttled back to the South Bank.

At this time I saw myself as a writer of immense culture and restraint: a sophisticated scribe who was thoughtful, possibly even a touch aloof. The non-rioting writer putting the 'pen' into 'pensive'. At around pretty much the same time editorial lynchpin Danny Kelly saw my Sonic Boom feature as being a touch too heavy on the restrained thoughtfulness and cultured aloofness. In fact, Danny thought the piece needed a bit of va va voom to spice everything up. In fact, he told me so in no uncertain terms. And so I reached for the wordy fireworks and threw in sparky things like 'Sonic couldn't go boom if you shoved a stick of dynamite up his arse!!!' or something like that.

I suspect that Pete might have been surprised at this turn of literary events after hosting such a convivial afternoon in his parents' lounge. He may well have got around to sending me an irked letter were it not for the methadone snoozings getting in the way. Either way, I wasn't proud of myself, but it set the standard for the next decade. From that point on, with the exception of roughly one Arab Strap album review, no metaphor was too phorced, no pun too punny, no artist above a dose of piss-taking, no matter how sly. All with added exclamation marks!!!

This wild-eyed wordage frenzy reached its apogee in what we can tentatively describe as my breakthrough moment, i.e. the first time any of the grown-ups openly complimented me on my scribblings from the other side of the office. Back in these fun times one of my very favourite creative indulgences were On the Road live features, where you would literally go on the road with bands and hang in their dressing room and at the back of their touring vehicle and in hotel lounges over the course of two live shows. Antics roadshow. Kind of.

At that time, the Mission were at the peak of their neo-Gothic fame, headlining Birmingham NEC and Manchester Apollo on the muscular back of 'Tower of Strength', so I was duly commissioned to hit the road with them. But this was a job with a difference, because not only was I expected to hang with the band, I was also ordered to infiltrate their hardcore fanbase, the Eskimos, who diligently followed the band from gig to gig, and report back on their hardcore activities. This was a commission with a serious Mission mission.

Curiously, I discovered that those hardcore activities didn't actually seem to involve the Eskimos ever watching the Mission play live. They seemed to have much more fun hanging out with each other far from the stage, swapping tales about the last tour when they hung out together and never watched the band they were following around on tour with their big boots and their army bags and their crusty demeanours. Nonetheless, my non-chalant hanging out in the foyers of the NEC and the Apollo paid off across the resulting double-page Live spread and, as a bonus, the shows were accompanied by my first ever proper hotel room experiences. Now all I had to do was work out just what this room service thing was.

Back on the South Bank the nonchalant hanging about was paying off. The first time I reviewed the singles for the Singles Page it was brilliant. You had to go through all the post and stagger home with a giant IPC carrier bag bulging with 7-inch and 12-inch vinyl releases and press releases. My first ever Single of the Week in the spring of 1989 – and permit me a wee blush here – was 'Made of Stone' by the Stone Roses. They'd been knocking around for a few years, evolving from murky goth-pop roots and snotty Manc rumblings to something a bit shinier and slicker and groovier. 'Made of Stone' was, and still is, brilliant and it proved that they were on the cusp of breaking through.

'The Roses? They'll never happen!' scoffed features editor James Brown when I dared to suggest it might be time we did a proper feature on them. By the end of the year half the staff writers were chewing each other's ankles to get to the top of the flared mountain and tell the world they were the best band ever. Except me and Jack Barron – he was the one who managed to give the Roses' debut album a moderately dismissive 7 out of 10. Mind you, it has been statistically proven that roughly 70 per cent of album releases are actually worthy of a 7 out of 10. In our *NME* reviewing world, there should really only be one 10 out of 10 review a year, and 5 out of 10 was an average record. I hated the marking system because no matter how positive you were about a record people always saw 5 as meaning the record was very boring indeed, and they only wanted to read reviews that gave the album 9 out of 10 or 2 out of 10, and it has been statistically proven that only 2 per cent of albums ever warranted a 2 out of 10.

Anyhooo, before the mountains and the madness, I had my moment in the Stone Roses sun, or the pub at least, when James

PANDAMONIUM!

decided to agree with me and commissioned a one-page feature on the band. Myself and Kevin Cummins took a day trip to Manchester and he pictured the Roses in a local park behind a Perspex sheet daubed with John Squire's artwork. We had some drinks and they squeezed lemons in their hands as a tribute to some tear-gassing incident at a Paris show and, while not exactly hitting the high notes in terms of ricocheting quotability, they were very pleasant and not at all like the snarky ogres they were portrayed as in their home city. I had a very pleasant snooze on the train home.

Not long after that, I was offered my very first front cover feature. Thrilling! Following the success of the on-the-road piece with the Eskimos this time I was to spend some quality off-the-road time with the Mission appearing at *Top of the Pops*. Well, not exactly *at Top of the Pops*, technically it was more like I was spending off-the-road time with the Mission watching the Mission appearing on *Top of the Pops* in the Mission's manager's front room in Fulham. The endlessly recurring glamour! Three thousand words of thrusting gothic grooviness, you say? We may be some time . . .

A couple of weeks later I go into the office on a Tuesday lunchtime, when the hot-off-the-press new *NME*s arrive, stacked full of alternopop palavers. Pick up a new issue to see . . . Guy Chadwick skulking on the front. Me and Wayne Hussey had been hustled off the cover. And nobody had bothered to warn me. In fact, nobody ever bothered to sit me down and explain what had happened. I'm realistic enough to realise that perhaps my overview of the Mission's manager's domestic furnishings was not going to blow Lester Bangs out of the water, but a wee heads up from the eds would have helped. This *NME* office was decidedly not a 'house of love' for me all of the time.

67

In COVID lockdown, an old Fraggle Rock compatriot called Pete Cole started rolling out old *NME* cuttings on Facebook. In Steve Lamacq's book, *Going Deaf for a Living*, he says looking back at his journalistic endeavours he sounds much more sarcastic than he remembered, and similarly looking at Pete's cuttings, away from my Mission submissions, there was a surprisingly tetchy edge to my early words as well. I suppose in the context of Barbara Ellen's glamorous contempt, Swells's manic diatribes and Quantick's deadpan dismissiveness, I was still a literary lightweight, but there is no doubt that a degree of bitchiness seeped into the most feeble fanzine kid's musings as I flattened the Flatmates and ripped the piss out of the Pastels. Especially the Pastels.

In the post, as well as things like records and fanzines and T-shirts us showbiz journos would frequently be sent letters. One day I got a letter written in very lurid green ink that turned out to be a very furious bespoke poem from Pastels singer Stephen Pastel, in which he concluded that I was 'a dumb cunt'. This followed a series of unfortunate events whereby I'd reviewed one of their singles in a slightly unflattering manner, and followed that up by not being entirely flattering about their album.

By the time Helen asked me to go and review the Pastels' live show at ULU, I realised we were entering dangerously lurid green ink territory and I explained that after the single and the album reviews a live kicking really wouldn't be a hat trick to cherish for either me or the band. But Helen was so desperate to find someone to do the gig – perhaps the fact that nobody else wanted to touch their ULU show with a bargepole that night was a bit of a giveaway – that she pleaded with me to go to appease the band's press officer. And so I relented and I went and I duly slagged off the live show to complete the set and presumably pissed off that very same press officer, not out of spite or malice or any malevolent attempt to sabotage the Pastels' career but because I was naive and honest and I just thought they were quite a bit shonky, even for a shabby indie kid like me.

So I have massive regrets about the unfortunate series of events and thirty-something years later I shall take this opportunity to most profusely apologise to the Pastels and their colourful friends. I have no regrets about receiving the pop tart poem, however, because if I had been in Stephen Pastels' brogues in Scotland watching my musical output being single-handedly dismantled by what I could only presume was some spiteful indie twat in that there London Town, I would have been raging at the injustice and unfairness of it all and would have indeed posted myself a pop tart poem calling myself a totally dumb cunt.

Still, if you didn't suddenly end up going to Paris or ULU or Cambridge or Manchester or the middle of the Midlands to hang out with Eskimos, you could just go down to the Stamford Arms with Lammo and have a relaxed drink with the actual *NME* editor, Alan Lewis. Bloody loved Alan. Proper old-school journo and total charmer. He'd invented *Kerrang!*, was destined to do likewise for *Loaded*, and, for a man in charge of the 'world's best-selling music weekly', was a sensationally relaxed character full of words of wisdom and pints of lager, facets I tried valiantly to comply with in the years ahead.

And, if Alan wasn't there, it would be just me and Steve, the Fraggle Brothers-in-arms standing tall in the Stamford. Or slumped in the corner, at least.

31 DECEMBER 2019, 6.02 P.M.

I slowly make my way out of Leroy House: down the long, silent corridor; past the empty, abandoned offices; out through the fire doors, down the stairs, through reception, out of the main entrance, out into the fresh early evening. Outside in Canonbury, real life goes on. I haven't walked this cautiously since a freaky acid trip in E17 during the '88 Olympics – you've never seen rings like it, whirring out of the TV screen.

Over the lights. Careful, careful. Creeping past Bobby Gillespie's snakeskin house . . . slowly past James Bay's non-bay windows . . . and to the sanctuary of number eleven. A slow knock on the door. Russell lets me in, immediately looks concerned. Concerned enough to call an ambulance.

I am now slumped over the living-room sofa. This is becoming a habit. I try to rouse myself to tell Russell not to tell my wife exactly what I've done. He can't hear me – he is back in the kitchen busy on the phone to Liann telling her exactly what I've done. He says she says just keep trying to keep me awake, don't let me drop off to sleep because then I'll pop off for ever. This is actually an urban myth, but by now delirium is kicking in. I haven't had the greatest of days.

Russell is consternated but, crucially, calm. The perfect man for an imperfect situation. There'll be no hysteria here. The ambulance arrives. Questions. Tests. Decisions. The crew mull over where to take me, it now being New Year's Eve. The Whittington in Highgate and University College Hospital at Warren Street are both mentioned in dispatches, but both are close to Camden, so could well become overwhelmed with drunk revellers later on. So they choose the Homerton in east London.

While I'm being belted up in the back, I look around dozily at the emergency gear and the medical facilities and the oxygen tanks stacked up on shelves and in cubbyholes and say, 'This is like a perfect camper van . . . for festivals.'

The ambulance crew man stops taking notes, looks at me strangely and says, 'I thought you were going to say Camper Van Beethoven then.'

That's weird.

The ambulance glides away in the darkness, towards the hipsterlands of Dalston and Hackney. It is 6.47 p.m. We may be some time.

8

NOW TIME

One day I knew I'd made it in some very small but significant way because I was in a posh bar on the South Bank with a few of the big old grown-up writers and David Quantick said, in his casual, but not entirely uncaring way, 'We like you and Steve because you go to all the gigs so we don't need to.'

This then was the essence of our role at the *NME* for three raggedly glorious years as the self-proclaimed and briefly bylined Legendary Fraggle Brothers, aka Steve Lamacq and Simon Williams: we were the wild boys on the frontline, heading out to live all the live shows nobody else could be arsed to go to. Topping 200 gigs a year (each) was a regular occurrence, back in the days when decent gigs had four indecently good bands performing and pretty much only occurred on Wednesdays and Thursdays, as at the start of the week venues were normally given over to poor-quality demo bands and the end of the week usually to groups who could guarantee coaches of fans from Colchester, regardless of musical merit.

By the start of the 1990s, Steve had sneaked across the *NME* office from the news desk to replace Helen as Live editor, and had also convinced new editor Danny Kelly to let him build an entirely new editorial outpost called the 'On' page. Before then, interviews with new bands were generally tossed into the comedy chaos of the 'Thrills' section, but now the 'On' page would be devoted to the very best two or three bands of that minute, complete with its own wee weekly top-ten chart.

Now controlling not just one but two self-contained sections of the *NME* we battened down the hatches, stacked up the sandbags and had the time of our tiny little lives, launching band after band after band from the merry indie gutter. Many of those groups made one great single or played a few smashing gigs and vanished. Some of them stuck around through our time together at the *NME* and beyond, releasing a couple of admirable albums and building cult followings. A few of them we took flushed from their first successes on the toilet circuit and their very first live review right through to the *NME* front cover, sometimes in north London, sometimes in North America. Sometimes we even got the chance to write that front-cover feature ourselves. But not always.

The scenes, much like the seasons, came and went: '89 was prime time for Baggy and Madchester. Grunge then took over the world, Camden Lurch took over the World's End, Shoegaze smouldered in the Home Counties. We danced to the still-bubbling-under Stone Roses at the ICA on the Mall, within swaggering distance of Elizabeth, my dear, on the day of a Tube strike. Years before 'OK Computer', I did Radiohead's 'On' piece in the Stamford Arms. Years after 'She's So High', Blur told Steve that our enthusiastic *NME* support had – quite literally – stopped them from being dropped by Parlophone.

When Lamacq was bored by the mad lack of gigs in the New Year, he came up with the idea of the *NME* 'On' live nights, which took place at the Venue in New Cross on the first weekend in January with PJ Harvey, Suede and, of course, Fabulous playing. And, after the gigs ended, there was always midweek fun to be had as the clock struck midnight: Tuesday was Feet First at Camden Palace, Wednesday was our own Club Smashed! night at the Powerhaus in Islington, Thursday was Syndrome on Oxford Street, the indie basement club where 'The Scene That Celebrates Itself' would merrily and very drunkenly celebrate itself with Blur, Ride, Lush, Swervedriver, Chapterhouse, Moose and a bar full of PR people and hacks from *Sounds*, *Melody Maker* and *NME* would put the world to rights.

In many ways, Steve and I were equals, almost eerily so: two lonely only boys (take that, Andrew Gold), born eleven months and 60 miles apart, both having to make their own way in the musical world, intrigued by what was on offer but always searching for more, forever digging deeper and deeper underground to uncover nuggets we thought deserved some kind of crack at the mainstream. Steve was brought up in Essex, me on the outskirts of east London, both of us the outsiders breaking in, loving gigs, the counterculture, pubs, smoking, DM boots. We bought our favourite records at Ugly Child and brought our finest pint-swilling, pen-scrawling, pun-spilling instincts to the grubbiest depths of the toilet circuit. And very often we skipped tea.

Thing is: Steve always took it to another level. I quite liked going to gigs to see new bands and going to pubs before going to the gigs to see those new bands. Meanwhile, he'd be off seeing Teenage Fanclub soundcheck at the White Horse in Hampstead, or zooming around the M25 on the old school A&R circuit with Ben Wardle from eastwest or Tony Smith from Chrysalis or

Mike Smith at EMI publishing, scouring Bedford Esquires or Oxford Zodiac or Tunbridge Wells Forum in heated pursuit of some cheeky new sensations to enthuse about.

My idea of a nice holiday was a fortnight in the sunshine lying on a Naxos beach. His was a midwinter week in the back of a tour van selling merch for Bleach. I quite liked popping onto the radio, doing the gig guide or some such for Gary Crowley over the weekend. Steve would be there in the studio splicing recording tape together, learning the broader textures of the broadcasting trade from the inside out. For a while, he would commute to the South Bank from his small gaff in Harlow in his Mini Metro, the overheated car stereo chewing through dozens and dozens of demos and record company promos. In many senses, he was ahead of the curve. In one other sense, he was way ahead of Curve.

Hanging out with Steve was not so much like work experience as a workaholic experience. Infamously, he once broke his foot kicking a stubborn *NME* piece of furniture in some sort of editorial rage. In a less literal sense, he didn't only kick down doors for the likes of me, he built those doors in the first place. Then he hung them very carefully and glossed them to a lovely sheen. And then he kicked them down again. It's already been made plainly obvious the main reason I got any work at all at the *NME* was down to Steve's influence. Later on, I would take his empty seat behind the Live desk, fill his vacated chair at Xfm and watch Fierce Panda bands Scarfo, Placebo and Idlewild all move on to his Deceptive Records. Even my fervent relationship with live promotions was kickstarted by his smashing Mean Fiddler booking mate Neil Pengelly inviting him, me and fellow indie hack Ian Watson to DJ at a new venture called Club Smashed! in 1991.

So I kind of followed his path, but more in an oh-that-looks-interesting kind of way, a maybe-I'll-have-a-go-at-that kind of way, rather than attempting to blatantly rip him off. In fact, in many other ways I often felt like I was the Wise to his Morecambe, the Emu to his Rod Hull, the John Pratt to his Steve Perryman.

By this point in time, I'd left the Stepney domestic rave scene and ended up living back in Walthamstow, this time in a nursing home, but not of the convalescing kind: this was a terraced house on Orford Road and it was full of nurses from nearby Whipps Cross, scene of my fine boychild vacation circa '74.

The house was called the Doins, as in the do-ins. There were four nurses in residence, plus various other nursey comings and goings, plus a studio engineer called Dave, plus little old me, who was by now stepping out with one of the nurses called Sarah, who had arty beads in her hair and a hearty love for Morrissey. You can only imagine the knitting sessions and quiet card games. It was a riot of colourful medical tales and night shifts and lurid stories about exploding catheters. Colostomy bags of fun, you could say. I won't follow the usual cliched line about nurses knowing how to party, but it was a little bit like living on the set of *The Young Ones* with the really pissed cast of *Casualty*, not least when spontaneous food fights erupted.

None of these food fights would ever involve sausages or spam because these people were hardcore vegetarians who occasionally spent a hearty winter's eve watching blurry bootleg films smuggled out of abattoirs. You can only imagine the subtle rom-com twists. Still, at least hanging with a load of Smiths fans gave me the chance to realise I was the crummiest vegetarian of all time. Lacking any appetite for cheese or beans, the staples of any veggie diet, I took a Tigger-like journey through the darkest recesses of the Sainsbury's health-food aisle: Marmite disagreeing with me was scarcely unusual; Linda McCartney pies tended to taste terrific first time round, then appalling after five; and imagine my alarm and surprise when, having briefly existed on a diet of tins of Postman Pat pasta shapes, I realised they contained cheese. Little wonder then that when I was surrounded by beef avoiders and pork swervers I often felt the urge to sit alone in a darkened room with my old friend Mr Ginsters. Yes, I needed some meat time.

It was, inevitably, intense, and sometimes when the entire household decamped to Reading Festival, in tents as well, because the bloodied nurses bloody loved their music, and the more alternative that music was the better. They went to gigs to see our old bud Nicky Cave and the Bad Seeds, the Cure, John Otway, Kitchens of Distinction, the Young Gods. They went dancing at some indie club in Stratford called Pigeons. Aidan and Andy were in a hardcore band called Juice. Aidan went so straightedge he got rid of his The Wedding Present records because 'they were too slow'. Gorilla Biscuits ruled his world.

The whole musical world got much weirder when a couple of tough-looking American ladies called Christy and Mary-Jane moved in with a battered old van parked out front. They were experts in European tours of punk rock squats. American bands would fly in, work out their jet lag on the Doins sofa, and then head off on a six-week jaunt of the least salubrious undercarriages of Amsterdam, Hamburg and Bergen. One time, we had Christ on a Crutch staying. Another time, some new band called Green Day. It really was a life of surprises.

One day Nigel from Ugly Child was ambling, if not quite rambling, through Epping Forest, when he found a football pitch. A proper one. With goalposts for goalposts! True, the posts were rusted and lacking in nets. And the pitch itself wasn't so much a Premier League carpet as a ragged old rug rescued from the nearest skip. But for several glorious Sunday lunchtimes it was a proverbial hotbed of indie footballing fun. Sometimes we took along some of our touring band friends, which is how on one sunny Sunday afternoon we happened to hit the green turf with Green Day, who didn't embarrass themselves by picking up the soccer ball and running 57 yards for a touchdown, and crucially nor did they embarrass us locals in the home of Blighty by secretly being Kasey Keller or Eric Wynalda and whomping our indie butts by five scoreballings to zero.

I'd really like to tell you a lot more about this sporting glory, enough to turn into a film, perhaps, but that's about as much as my memory can muster. Maybe we would have paid more attention if we'd known back then that our earnestly enthusiastic soccerballing colleagues would go on to headline Reading Festival and generally rule the punk rock world, but, then again, you could say that about a lot of bands who have amazed everyone by how well they've done against the litany of hyped bands who rather less amazingly crashed and burned. At that time, it just seemed like the most normal thing to try to nutmeg Billie Joe 'Georgie' Armstrong in the middle of Epping Forest.

There was a properly meta Walthamstow moment, when I interviewed Tony Mortimer from local boisterous boy band scallywags East 17 quite literally in E17, specifically in the Nag's Head pub, and where I found that he really liked Michael Jackson and George Michael – which made a spectacular change from the usual blah blah bonus indie interview blarney – and he was very good at pool.

And, on 11 February 1990, the day that Nelson Mandela was released from prison, I saw Carter USM in Hull Adelphi. This much I know because Jim Bob and Les came around the Doins on that Sunday morning and we drove up to Hull in a Mini Metro.

The night before they'd played the Fulham Greyhound, which was a gig I was supposed to review, but there was a small problem in the sense that the venue was totally sold out so we couldn't get in. And for anyone who ever went to a Fulham Greyhound show back then, they'd know that a total sellout really did mean you literally couldn't get in through the door.

In many senses, this was the start of the Fraggle Rock wars, with Lammo and the boy Williams fighting side-by-side-by-cider in the Fraggle Rock trenches. Fraggle what? Fraggle Rock, my friends. Indiepunkpop music with various twists, turns and sub-sections, but driven primarily by loud guitars played by proud, literate, leftfield-leaning indie scallywags.

Carter the Unstoppable Sex Machine, Mega City 4, Senseless Things and Ned's Atomic Dustbin were the headline acts but there were others lurking just behind – the comically berserk hardcore snufflers Snuff (a favourite memory is of them coming onstage at a rabid Kilburn National Ballroom to the sound of the *Match of the Day* theme, booting footballs into the audience); the cannily feline Family Cat; the caustic gruffery of Leatherface, Scorpio Rising, Frank & Walters and my old schoolmates BOB. There was another new generation of indie labels and fanzines – Big Cat, Damaged Goods, Too Pure, Decoy, Fear & Loathing, Snakebite City, Food, Lust & Guitars. And, as it morphed from piss-bottle battles to the sounds of Uriah Heap and Status Quo, there were some sensationally indie-centric Reading Festivals, where 98.9 per cent of the punters wore band names on their chests.

For this was a world of baggy T-shirts and grubby big shorts worn by the grebos, the crusties, the pop kids and the goths. It was tatty, ragged, punky, homegrown, and it was ours. We knew the fans, we knew the fanzine writers, we were on first nickname terms with the roadies. We were one of them. Well, two of them. We felt that burning DIY-hard sense of community running around the gigging nation, from the Bull & Gate to the Bullring, from the Aldershot West End Centre to Syndrome, the Borderline, the 100 Club, the Marquee and, of course, the mighty Astoria in the epicentre of the West End of London Town.

Even Manic Street Preachers came through that toilet-circuit-training scene, albeit in a predictably dysfunctional way. They shared bills with the bands but didn't seem to share the other Fraggle tropes, the humility, the normality, the guitarist-at-the-bar chumminess. Theirs was a rash, brash car-crash approach with talk of outgunning Guns N' Roses and a love for Public Enemy that initially made them public enemy number one to the perplexed Fraggled generation.

Unsurprisingly their manifestos and manifestation of artistic terrorism were catnip for half the *NME* office: the *Generation Terrorists* debut got a trembling ten out of ten. But for some bands and our wee cabal there was something a little bit off about it all. It seemed so forced, so much . . . effort. I wrote a brilliantly outraged review of the Megas' and Manics' releases together in the Singles page, frothing about the horrific injustice that one of these bands was about to sign to a major label, and it wasn't Mega City 4. Proper journo wanker.

The Fraggle Rock face-off reached its zenith with Richey Edwards carefully carving '4 real' into his arm in front of an aghast Steve at Norwich Arts Centre (again). I was in the office the following morning when Ed Sirrs brought the gig pictures in. The Richey snap really is extraordinarily horrible – he's holding out his left arm to show the bloodied flesh wounds, the image weirdly offset by the guitarist smirking coyly at the camera lens like a small child being admonished for being naughty. Which, in a way, carving '4 real' into your arm very much is. To the

NME's eternal editorial credit it was decided to print the shot on page three instead of putting it on the front cover. But it was close.

The most telling time was at the peak of our so-called success, when one afternoon we found ourselves in the Stamford Arms. The Fraggle Rock machine had struck again and it had struck hard. It was March 1992 and Senseless Things had got onto the *NME* front cover, following in the saggy, baggy shorts of Carter USM and the Neds. A success, in every possible sense. The pop kids skulking in the corner had come up top trumps again. Time for a celebratory pint or three, surely.

Still Steve wasn't satisfied. Even though three of 'our' bands had made it from the backstage of beyond to the front of the *NME*. Even though the year had been kickstarted by another couple of his obsessions – Teenage Fanclub and Kingmaker – starring on the first two covers of 1992. He pulled out another Silk Cut and scowled darkly at his lighter. 'The Megas haven't been on the cover yet,' he muttered into his cider.

Barely six weeks later Mega City 4 duly pogoed onto the *NME* cover, completing the Fraggle Rock set. But that call to arms in the Stamford was proof that for Steve Lamacq the fight was always there to be fought, a war was always waiting to be warred. In short, Lammo always needed more ammo. And, luckily, a bloody giant bomb was about to crash-land into the middle of the twenty-fifth floor.

31 DECEMBER 2019, 7 P.M.

Behind an easy-clean curtain in a cubicle in the A&E department the medics and psych team are taking stock of the wreck sitting quietly in front of them. As ever, at the absolute extremes of madness there is jocularity and gallows humour. We are in the calm after the storm, with a potentially bigger storm on the way. This is our time.

One doctor looks supercool, all short dreads and wired specs, like a young David McAlmont. This relaxes me even more. He is asking me questions. How am I feeling? Do I know why I'm here? Can I tell him what I've done to myself?

I am becalmed. I tell him the exact overdosages of painkillers and the precise three times I took them. He sets up a saline drip to start flushing me out, removes the Tavistock toilet roll from my wrists, cleans the wounds as best he can. Too late for stitches, not too late to ask if I'm okay with everything that's happening around me, if I'm feeling okay in myself.

Russell says, 'Yeah, this is pretty normal for Simon.' I catch the doctor flashing him a look from behind his McAlmont-esque specs that shouts, 'This is NORMAL??'

The slashing hasn't worked. The hanging hasn't worked. But the painkillers are still very much in me. There is no sudden moment of panic when I go 'Fuck!' I'm comfortably numb. I know I need the hospital. I just don't know how much.

The specialists calculate that from arriving at the Homerton at 7 p.m. on Tuesday evening, with the painkillers in my system left to their own devices, I am on target to achieve total liver failure within eight hours. By my calculations, this means I will be dead by Wednesday morning, 3 a.m. The flying A&R man, lying dying in A&E. How poetic.

9

NEW YORK CITY IN SPACE

One of those little curios that used to blow people's minds into tiny smithereens was that those deadly music papering rivals the *NME* and *Melody Maker* were both owned by IPC Publishing. Not only that, but they were based a floor apart, with the *Maker* just a fire escape scamper up to the twenty-sixth floor. The weirder thing was with the *NME* and *Melody Maker* a single floor apart, and with Stamford Street not entirely overloaded with decent boozers, you might imagine some kind of geeky blinders-style running rivalry between the two magazines, with hacks spitting split infinitives at each other in the King's Reach lobby.

For sure, some *Maker* writers held their counsel and stared at their shoes even when I generously held the lift doors for them, and some of the *NME* teamsters were a bit sniffy about the competition upstairs, but among the journo lags in the Stamford Arms there was generally a convivial bar-room ambience. Chris Roberts, Ian Gittins and Ian Watson were super friendly, and the Stud Brothers were excellent drinking company. Editor Allan

Jones always had a nod and a smile for the *NME* enemy, and his assistant Steve Sutherland likewise.

So what happened next was even a bit weirder than the weirdness highlighted before: Steve Sutherland wrote a hyperbolic front-cover feature on the up-and-coming Suede band, where he took the opportunity to suggest that the *NME* was a bit rubbish and *Melody Maker* was very fabulous because they were writing hyperbolic cover features on Suede, a band we had already covered extensively. In fact, he used the words 'dogshit' and 'diamonds' in that very context, which, it has to be said, did not go down entirely well in the *NME* office. In the general scheme of things, it was a petty poke from a rag that sold half as many copies as us and, in terms of creating some kind of rivalry between the two papers, an entirely justifiable action that was quite probably applauded by the publishing overlords.

The feature was to come bite many an arse, however: *NME* editor Danny Kelly had rather abruptly jumped ship to some monthly magazine thing called *Q*. No problem – Danny had replaced Alan Lewis and continuing a smooth editorial theme the *NME* office was full of plausible replacements. In actual fact, you could say there was a 'Q' of ideal candidates to fill Danny's swivel chair. It was slightly surprising therefore to see all those possible *NME* candidates canned in favour of a certain Mr Steve Sutherland from *Melody Maker*.

Rumour has it this was an inhouse IPC fait accompli – I heard that Allan Jones had planned to move out of the *Melody Maker* hot chair and Steve Sutherland had been promised that very vacant hot chair. Then Allan did a U-turn and decided not to leave, leaving the publishing overlords in a fruity pickle. Then when Danny Kelly sodded off to *Q* magazine, some publishing overlord on the floor above put two and two together and came up with nineteen and the frankly preposterous notion of Sutherland taking the *NME* chair, dogshit et al.

The announcement of Steve Sutherland's appointment in October 1992 went as well as can be expected, if the publishing overlords expected a clutch of key writers to instantly resign and for the entire paper to be hurled into complete disarray. Steve Lamacq, Mary Anne Hobbs and Andrew Collins all walked out, and Stuart Maconie wouldn't be far behind. There was an excruciating introductory meeting with a predictably bolshy Sutherland trying to salvage a disastrous situation, but after his infamous Suede feature the core of *NME* wouldn't be swayed.

In *The History of the NME* by Pat Long, Johnny Cigarettes says: 'I remember being in the pub with all of them just sitting there with their heads in their hands, acting as though World War Three had been declared, My thought was, *It's only a fucking newspaper. It's not Rwanda, is it?*' The Boy Cigs had a point. But to be perfectly frank, this tiny wee editorial altercation altered everything for little old me. IPC had become a glowering inferno, and amid the smouldering ruins of the *NME* office Steve S and I had a tense, private little chat. I was on the cusp of the precipice of following Lammo, Mary Anne and Andrew right out of the door, into the lift, down to the ground floor and out onto Stamford Street into a bright new dawn, or into the darkened pub at least. I told Steve S this and he gave me an irked speech along the lines of not giving a toss about boo-hooing indie boys crying sobby wobby tears because their bestest matey wateys had left the paper and we disagreed to disagree and he made me an offer to stay on as a freelance lackey, which I could very easily refuse – and refuse I did.

Luckily for the future of the *NME*, chief sub editor Brendan Fitzgerald, a man who out-rock 'n' rolled most of the writers whose work he subbed, took me to the pub and told me what I should ask for and I went back up in the lift and asked Steve S for what Brendan told me to ask for, and got it. All of a sudden, from rolling around the office carpet waiting for 'God Fodder' I was the brand-new editor of the Live pages and the 'On' section and on the *NME* staff-writing payroll in charge of the polite brigade. When I say 'luckily for the future of the *NME*', by no stretch of the imagination am I suggesting that I saved the *NME* from completely imploding. But I knew some people who did, and they basically rebuilt the paper from the ground up. Because if the Fraggle Rock wars were distinguished by some judiciously placed sandbags and a reckless disregard for our own personal safety, this new era was to be based on more organised warfare.

First, I used lessons learned from my early days of being a freelance writer: my Live desk ran a tight ship, there would be no spiked reviews or spooked reviewers being called dumb cunts by irked Scotsmen on my watch. If the running of that ship was sometimes so tight that sometimes we were short of a live review or two when pages needed to be put through to the sub-editors, then no sweat, I'd just rustle up 200 words on whatever small wonders I'd invariably witnessed out and about the night before.

Second, and somewhat typically, Lammo's legacy was strong: Johnny Cigarettes was already on board, John Harris had been rescued from oblivion in the Maker files upstairs, Ted Kessler came in from Our Price, Mark Sutherland was wheeled in from his *Food, Lust & Guitars* fanzine via *Smash Hits*. Later on, we went out as a gang, five or six or 361 of us: Ted, Mark, Johnny H, Cigs, John Robinson, Dele Fadele, Paul Moody. Mark Beaumont and James Oldham would join the fun a bit further down the line, sometimes John Mulvey as well. It's bloody marvellous phoning up a perplexed PR and asking for a plus-six for the guestlist at a venue that holds forty-six punters. Sometimes we even let girls come along – Gina Morris or Sylvia Patterson or Angela Lewis or Sam Steele or Susie Corrigan or April Long, or any other female of the species who took enough pity on us to come along and watch us make absolute arses of ourselves watching achingly desperate wannabe superstars onstage.

I always suspected people thought I was pretty militant about the whole gigging vibe. Like, if you don't salute the Sir George Robey then I won't respect you, if you don't grab the Bull & Gate by the horns I will think much less of you, and if you don't go to twenty-eight gigs next week I will feel so horribly let down I will stop giving you work. True, there was the odd writer I felt didn't fit in, but being my drinking buddy was never a pre-requisite of getting work, and the mighty likes of Roger Morton and Johnny Dee were always worth a cheery review or two in spite of their admirable reluctance to join us in the boozer. Truth is: I wasn't militant at all – as much as I liked small, slightly smelly gigs I totally understood that some people could tire of the dubious delights of the toilet circuit pretty quickly. And, while I could see that others were blatantly just using them as a stepping stone to bigger and better concerts and features and ultimately careers, I just somehow contrived to use them as a stepping stone to smaller and slightly bitterer things.

What I do know is that that generation was the greatest free PR the *NME* ever had. While the smoke from the editorial chaos gently dissipated, we had what I considered to be a squad of sharp, sassy writers eager to please and even more eager to create high art. These were the writers on the frontline, selling the *NME* message better than a million publishing overlord white-boarding sessions ever could. Press officers could find us in the pub at lunchtime, bands would bump into us out and about in Camden or the West End or some other grubby postcode in the evening. We were excitable, accessible and often to be found crushed together around the corner table of your favourite venue. One day we even decided to answer the Live desk phone every time it rang and actually communicate with the free world. Fifty-seven telephonic conversations later we went to the pub. For lunch.

A form of peace broke out across the office as everyone settled into their new roles, albeit with the odd unexploded bandmine near the editor's office as Steve S tried a bit harder to settle in than anyone else. Before his alarming arrival I'd indulged in a rather splendid journalist trip up and down the US Eastern Seaboard to interview Daisy Chainsaw in Boston, the Boo Radleys in Manhattan and Mercury Rev in upstate New York. It featured a fabulously empty solo train journey from Boston to Grand Central station. Steve Sutherland did not seem to appreciate the joys of my Eastern Seaboard transiting, insisting that all three features be cut in half to make the paper. A bit annoying on a personal level, in terms of lost words and wasted effort. But a moderate disaster on a professional level as the trip had been carefully pieced together with three indie labels – One Little Indian for Daisy Chainsaw, Creation for the Boo Radleys, and Beggars for Mercury Rev – paying for various hotels, flights and empty train journeys they could ill afford. Not a good look. Definitely not good PR.

Kurt Cobain from the Nirvana band shot himself on 5 April 1994. We had a Very Important Emergency Editorial Meeting in Steve Sutherland's office. I stood by the window staring down at the Thames while tribute ideas were thrown about. It was decided I should write a special *NME* think piece about what life is like for you after your dad kills himself. I wasn't so sure. It was decided that Martyn Goodacre's seminal picture of Kurt with guyliner would be the front cover. Everyone was very sure. When the meeting was over, I collared Brendan and said I couldn't do it. I'd spent the entirety of the meeting wondering if Blackfriars was the very bridge my dad had jumped off. Brendan was very sympathetic and had a discrete word in Sutherland's shell-like, and he was very understanding.

It wasn't the only time he showed his compassionate side: one afternoon in the Stamford Arms Steve S revealed that now I was on the staff I could claim overtime. Wow, really?? Yeah, but there was one catch – I couldn't claim overtime for all the gigs I went to, because I went to *too many*. IPC didn't pay over-overtime, it seemed. Still, these were the best of times, not least when Britpop blew in from Camden and whipped the sales into a frenzy. Such good times in fact that one day I sat down with Steve Sutherland and asked to become assistant editor of the *NME*, working on the basis that virtually every front cover act had come through either the Live pages or the 'On' section or both, and I really quite liked nurturing new writers and encouraging them to be much, much better than me. To be fair, for the first time ever in my life I didn't get an instant rejection. If memory serves, I didn't get any answer at all.

My list of achievements is not entirely long. I came up with the Brats, aping the Brits, as a name for the *NME* awards shows that had evolved from the old 'On' nights to a zillion shows at the Astoria. I reviewed Oasis at the Water Rats, Suede at the Falcon, went to Paris with Green Day and met Catherine Deneuve on a TV show. I went to Japan with Ned's Atomic Dustbin, to Australia with Garbage, to LA with Rage Against the Machine, to Milan with the Cure, Iceland with Ash, Derby with the Wishplants and to New York again with the Prodigy, with Chapterhouse, with Bob Mould.

I once described Idlewild as 'sounding like a flight of stairs falling down a flight of stairs', which was actually on their Facebook info last time I looked. (In fact, when we recycled the slogan for Fierce Panda's twenty-fifth celebrations and slapped 'the sound of a flight of stairs falling down a flight of stairs since 1994' on a glossy backdrop, we rather sensationally got accused by a punter of ripping off the band). I made Radiohead's 'Paranoid Android' Single of the Week and said that 'it sounds like "Bohemian Rhapsody" being played backwards'. I also compared quite a lot of bands to furry critters, which they really didn't like – the Sundays were Wombles with teeth, Spiritualized were angry rabbits – and I know this because us journalists talked about our interview experiences to each other back in the office.

One time, Johnny Cigarettes admitted to one weird interview tick he had. 'When I get nervous it makes me yawn,' he said. One day he interviewed our old friend Nick Cave. A tough assignment, for sure. One where you'd expect to be a bit trepidatious, if not downright fearful. Cigs sat down with Cave. He yawned a lot. 'Am I boring you, mate?' asked our concerned old friend.

Apart from being irked about the various mammalian metaphors, most bands were really nice in the flesh. Even the likes of the Levellers and Chumbawamba, who weren't necessarily at their most comfortable in the company of music journalists, could see the funny side after an ale or three in Prague or Belfast, and I enjoyed a most convivial afternoon in the pub with beyond-goth-shockrats Christian Death. True, interviewing the Divine Comedy in the Seven Dials in Covent Garden for the 'We Could Be Eros' front cover, I couldn't get Neil Hannon to admit a soft spot for Scott Walker, not even after four lovely afternoon pints of Guinness. Mind you, over at Scott Walker's manager's house in Notting Hill, I couldn't get Scott Walker to admit to a soft spot for himself, every carefully judged question pertaining to the Walker Brothers '60s pop chaos gleaned from the *A Deep Shade of Blue* biography being rebuffed by a polite 'I really can't remember that'. Scott did take his sunglasses off thirty-seven minutes into the interview though, which I took to be a good sign.

One of the magazines I really admired was *The Word*. It's no longer with us, inevitably, but I recall a great piece in there, possibly by David Hepworth, about how, far from stitching bands up, most music journalists actually protected musicians and made them sound more rounded and interesting in print than they could ever be in real life. I know this to be very true. I could list the flagrancies and vagrancies of bands that remained unreported in ink, especially on the road, where what went on in room 245 of a mid-price hotel in Sheffield generally stayed in room 245 of a mid-price hotel in Sheffield: the accidental affairs, the bathroom blow-outs, the backstage blow-ups, the drug binges, the drunken hissy fits, the bearded indie frontman who said, 'I follow girls home', the female-fronted Britpop band who merrily apologised for their shabby demeanour because they'd been 'chasing the dragon', the ethereal boy band who said, 'We're not shoegazing onstage, we're cleavage-gazing!'

Actually, we did print that last quote in their front cover feature – an ashen-faced apologetic ethereal boy singer later saw me outside the Astoria and said, 'I'm never going to drink during an interview again' – because sometimes some things are just too alluring to resist. In a similar vein, I interviewed the Jesus and Mary Chain in the middle of the afternoon in the corner of a pub in Farringdon. The psychotic *Psychocandy* years were long gone and Jim and William Reid were comfortably good company, happily baiting the establishment with the carelessly irreverent 'Reverence' single. But halfway through something hit me – their gentle Scottish brotherly banter was fiercely reminiscent of the bickering pandas in the Aardman electricity adverts, and I told them so.

'Hey! Don't fucking print that!' snapped Jim. Okay, okay, I said in the *NME* two weeks later. No need to get so animated.

And then there was Oasis. Or should we say Oas*s?

31 DECEMBER 2019, 8.22 P.M.

There's been panic on the streets of Suffolk. Liann and Scout have rushed down from home, throwing Willow and Spirit, the pups, in the back of the car and trying not to freak out in the front. Hurdling over the horizon on the M11 near the junction with the M25 they will see the illuminated London skyline, watching the New Year's Eve explosions in the sky.

When they finally arrive at the Homerton they're fearful of what they might find behind the easy-clean curtain, then tearful when they find me, all things considered, compos mentis, if not even a little bit chirpy. The A&E psychiatrist isn't fooled. 'This is all an act,' she tells a weeping Liann. 'We'll get through to him.'

The drip starts making me violently, profusely, apologetically ill. Saline does that to you, apparently. But there is one other thing, one really big other thing nagging me: Russell isn't supposed to be here. He's supposed to be up in Leicester with his wife, Sarah, at her mother's. Owing to a series of unfortunate incidents he was in Sainsbury's instead, picking up a curry for a manly New Year's Eve feast-for-one when he answered Liann's emergency call.

What if? What if Russell had been marooned in the Midlands? What if he hadn't been stalking the Islington supermarket aisles on a one-man quest for a one-man feast? Liann says she would have called another friend, Martin, who lives just a little bit further away, in Highbury. Too far for me to walk to in my state. Then she would have called the Tavistock Hotel and perhaps the receptionist would have called housekeeping and they would have said well, actually, since you ask there was this trail of bloodied towels left in his room. Then she would have called the police and told them about the telephone silence and the Tavistock's trail of bloodied towels.

Somehow, some way she says, someone would have found me, and found me in time.

I'm still not so sure.

10

LET'S MAKE SOME PLANS

In 1993, three *NME* music journalists took a great leap into the unknown. That great leap into the unknown took place in our third office – King's Reach Tower was first, the Stamford Arms the second – which was the Blue Posts on Tottenham Court Road, a characterful old-school corner boozer within honking distance of the Dominion Theatre. The Blue Posts was a West End curio in the sense that rather than making any attempt to engage with thirsty tourists with a hearty appetite for some Oxford Street treats, their pub jukebox played Motörhead at such a mighty volume even the most adventurous traveller would take a few steps through the front entrance and exit immediately through the side door on to Hanway Street, sped on their way by 'Ace of Spades'. Excellent work, obviously, although in terms of running an orthodox business it wasn't far off total commercial suicide.

Speaking of which, after a few fruity Darling Premiers one night we decided that the scene known as New Wave of New Wave deserved a tribute single, and we were the most sensationally unqualified people to release it. By 'we', I refer to John, Paul and Ringo, aka John Harris, Paul Moody and myself. John and Paul were both excellently passionate *NME* compatriots, with musical knowledge aplenty and writing skillings in abundance. John was to later suggest, slightly sniffily, that New Wave of New Wave was a little bit like 'Britpop without the good bits', and it could be said that NWONW wasn't the most deep of musical scenes to be mined. In these invigorating early days, the likes of Elastica and even Shed Seven were associated with NWONW, but truth be told at this particularly excitable juncture at the end of 1993 the scene revolved around S*M*A*S*H and These Animal Men, two bands whose trashy, punky take on adidas chic and amphetamine peaks was a wide-pupiled diversion from the mainstream.

Propelled onwards by the force of nature that was Caffy St Luce from Hall or Nothing PR, the lady who did the press on both S*M*A*S*H and These Animal Men, the core NWONW bands were gobby, verging on controversial and seemingly surviving on drugs, but actually quite nice underneath it all – absolute catnip for music journalists. The odd bug-eyed *Top of the Pops* appearance aside, their impact on the general populace was fairly minimal, but their legacy was strong – within six months Camden Town was awash with bands who'd studied the model and found themselves in the midst of the Britpop masses. And, three decades on, it is very safe to say that Fierce Panda would never have existed without it.

The morning after the Blue Posts toasts the night before, we gathered together our hangovers and our hairstyles in the *NME* office and laughed heartily and said 'Hahahaha. What on earth were we going on about? We're music journalists, we don't know how to make records, they just arrive on the back of the IPC postboy like magical musical Royal Mail sack beans! Hahaha!'

And this, dear reader, is why 97 per cent of the greatest record companies known to indie-kind have never got off the ground – there they lay, draped over the smouldering starting block, because most people simply didn't know how to make records, which, pre-streaming services, was a pretty key component of releasing music.

Luckily, in this rare instance I did know a man who did know how to put out records. He was called Ian Ballard and he ran Damaged Goods, a very punk rock label in east London who had launched in 1988 by licensing 'Where Have All the Boot Boys Gone?' by Slaughter & the Dogs, a punk relic lurking in the Decca vaults. He'd spent the previous five years releasing further records by Adam and the Ants, Billy Childish, Helen Love, Wat Tyler and the *New Art Riot* EP by Manic Street Preachers. He was therefore more underground than an agora-phobic mole. We had a mutual friend in Nigel Ugly Child, who was his beering gigging buddy. And Ian had a cheery disdain for poncy music journalists – he certainly wasn't seeing this as his chance to sneak his Melons band onto the 'On' page. It was a suitably formal start to the business relationship. Ian remembers me shouting 'D'you wanna out a record with us?' across a power-crazed Powerhaus bar, and we were off and lurching.

The world, it has to be said, was not in dire need of yet another chipper indie label releasing compilation EPs, or any-thing else perky on pink vinyl for that matter. In fact, the early '90s witnessed some kind of vinyl boomtime and you couldn't move for indie labels: there was Cheree, there was Chemikal Underground, there was Cherry Red, and they just represented the 'che' alphabet of indie labels, like the tip of a giant under-ground indie fatberg. These cheeky tykes lined up alongside

Laurel, Ankst, Nude, Domino, Wurlitzer Jukebox and dozens more dangerously optimistic music fankids.

Staggeringly bravely into this boomtime hurricane, we decided to call our label Fierce Panda. This is partly because we only intended to ever release one single and call it a day, so it didn't really matter what it was called because nobody would remember us in three months, let alone three decades' time, and partly because I like pandas, and generally they aren't fierce, apart from when they attack goats. On a more subtle level, you could say that Fierce Panda was a knowingly pithy reaction to the serious stalwarts like Creation, Factory and Mute, and the new generation of multi-syllabled companies like Deceptive, Dedicated and Indolent, but that might be giving us a touch too much intellectual credence. Either way, if I'd known back then that Fierce Panda would still be bumbling around thirtyish years later I might have put some more thought into the name. Might.

We had four bands we planned to be on our one and only 7-inch single release. But then word got out, and another two bands wanted to be on our record. We asked Ian if we could get six tracks on one seven-inch single. 'Of course you can't,' he shouted back across the Powerhaus bar, probably. But we could get those six tracks across two 7-inch singles, and so the legendarily seminal Fierce Panda double-vinyl EP release was born.

In the end, the debut one-and-only *Shagging in the Streets* EP featured suitably shaggy tracks by S*M*A*S*H, These Animal Men, Blessed Ethel, Done Lying Down, Action Painting! and Mantaray. Not all six of the bands may have completely adhered to the NWONW doctrine (two white lines, three black stripes, one-two-three-four-oi! melodies), but they were all at least sufficiently bold and bolshy to make the package stand on its own two feet. 'Shagging in the Streets' was given a catalogue number of NING 01. This was immensely exciting as in my mind 'NING' was a tribute to the knights of Monty Python's *Holy Grail*, which very much fitted our gently anarchic take on this whole record releasing malarkey.

Each package came with those six songs spread across a pair of 7-inch singles in a wraparound sleeve slipped into a clear plastic bag. Each EP also came with an A5ish-sized paper insert, on one side of which was the label copy with the relevant band information and on the other side of which was some monumentally irrelevant but heartfelt indie wibblage. The back of the sleeve had a chunk of poetic hoopla and a French quote.

Ian's influence immediately ran deep: we gave him half a dozen DAT cassettes given to us by the bands and some mentally Pritt-sticked paper artwork, and he went off and sorted mastering, printing, manufacturing, distribution and essentially everything else we had no idea even existed in our sad, naive journalistic little brains. It turned out that with an RRP of £3.99 the EP would actually break even – once you take any sense of profit and loss out of the music industry the music industry becomes much easier.

Hence *Shagging in the Streets* required 2,000 7-inch singles, 1,000 wraparound sleeves, 1,000 inserts (essentially 500 sheets of A4 chopped into two) and 1,000 clear plastic sleeves. It also required three blokes to put the singles, the wraparound sleeves and the inserts into the clear plastic sleeves, which obviously couldn't be done down the pub or at the Powerhaus.

By now I'd left the wonders of Walthamstow for the fiftieth time and ended up flat sharing with John Harris at 136 Pitfield Street in Hoxton. With my usual impeccable timing this was pre-hipster Hoxton where the pubs closed at the weekend when the Liverpool Street City Boys were safely locked up back in Essex.

In actual fact, Charlie Wright's International Jazz Bar around the corner was pretty much the only local place I can remember being able to get a drink in – for all other live entertainment it was a case of Camden or bust.

Anyway, we commandeered the front room of 136 Pitfield Street, and set about stuffing. Eventually, the *Shagging in the Streets* EP was released on 24 February 1994, which we call Fierce Panda's official birthday, and it sold all 1,000 copies in a week. We threw a launch party at the Powerhaus, which was sold out as well.

Not everyone was as overjoyed at this turn of events as us. We know this because Mute Records printed up some very special 'Fuck the New Wave of New Wave' T-shirts and sent them to us. Mute Records! Home to our mate Nicky Cave! Maybe this was all his idea! With a classic sense of media empathy John and I took those 'Fuck the New Wave of New Wave' T-shirts and put them on and we got our pictures taken modelling them in the Stamford Arms toilets and then we printed those pictures in the *NME*. Proper journo wankers.

But by now we were having fun. Might as well do another release. So, pissing very much on our hi-falutin one-release-only ever principled chips, we did. NING 02 was a celebration of teenage angst, bringing together the sound of youth in the form of a slew of new-to-'94 teenies called Supergrass, Ash, Gorky's Zygotic Mynci, Credit to the Nation, Noise Addict and Tribute to Nothing. The EP was called *Crazed and Confused* and the art-work featured a collage of youthful tykes, one of whom ended up wearing a T-shirt that said, with enormous gravitas, EAT YOUR PARENTS.

It sold out. Might as well do another three. And so we each took a concept and ran with it in our own sweet way. NING 03 was Paul's labour of love, which was called *Return to Splendour*. It featured six bands of a mod-ish hue, fronted up by the Bluetones and the Weekenders and wrapped up in a picture of the Hotspurs' victorious double-winning team of 1960–61. NING 04 was my pet project, *Build to Blast*, which brought together our soccer-balling chums Green Day, Understand and four other acts of a frantic punk rock bent. Julie Andrews was on the front, playing the music in *The Sound of Music*. And NING 05 was John's responsibility, which was called *From Greer to Eternity* and fittingly starred six bands of a feminine bent, including Lush, Ivy and Splendora, and I seem to remember the cover was a picture of John's mum's school hockey team, because if you can't use a picture of your mum's school hockey team on the sleeve of a record on your own record company, when can you?

For avoidance of many doubts, these EPs were cobbled together on a ning and a prayer back in the corner of the Blue Posts. We tried to ensure that each one had a Bluetones or an Ash or a Green Day to hold the release together, but other than that we allowed ourselves to put on whoever we wanted, and indeed whoever wanted to be involved, and virtually all of these acts we'd seen play live before, so there was a vague degree of quality control, even if a lot of that quality was actually completely out of control.

Some of these bands were never heard of again. A few of them were barely heard of even at the time. Some of the tracks we used were precursors to future hits, some were live versions, some had already been released elsewhere or were about to be re-released somewhere else, some were demos – we weren't choosy and, working on a steady budget of nothing, nor could we afford to be. Like the compilers of *C86*, we had to go with the indie flow. Nonetheless, we released the latter three EPs over the course of three weeks – a searingly monumental effort considering the number of bands to organise and the thousands of records, inserts and clear plastic sleeves that needed stuffing not-in-the-pub and carried back and forth across north London, a heap of pristine records escorted by Ian Damaged.

All three EPs – *Return to Splendour, Built to Blast, From Greer to Eternity* – sold out immediately. We'd started 1994 with a vague idea and ended it having shipped a grand total of 5,000 EPs, which equates to an even grander total of 10,000 7-inch singles slotted into 5,000 wraparound sleeves and stuffed into 5,000 of the clearest of clear plastic bags, along with 5,000 slightly deranged inserts accompanied by quite possibly 5,000 tinnies of liquid lager. The accidental label had accidentally got itself a following.

Having accidentally got ourselves that following, you might think that what we did next was sit down and think long and hard about how to keep that audience engaged. In fact, what happened next came as a bit of a surprise, because we didn't really know what we were going to do next as we were a little bit sleepy after releasing thirty bands over five EPs and because we were still actually supposed to be proper music journalists. We could have quite easily called it a day at that point and carried on with the proper musical journalism. Indeed, Paul and John started drifting away from the panda coalface on to bigger and better things – Paul to get fried in the Regular Fries, John to get riled writing for *The Guardian*. And, perhaps if Ian Damaged had drifted as well, here could well have been where the Fierce Panda story ended.

But the surprise that happened next – and much to my absolute bewilderfuddlement – was that in 1995 people started approaching *us*, asking Fierce Panda to release songs that weren't destined to be on any six-track EPs. First up were some nice music-biz promoter people from a company called MCP who said they wanted to do a Fierce Panda tour – a Fierce Panda tour!! – with Geordie punks China Drum, Kentish punks the Flying Medallions and brotherly crazed and confused punks Tribute To Nothing. It was a good sell, it was a great idea, it was pretty in punk.

So NING 06 was a split 7-inch single with 'Riot' by the Flying Medallions on one side and China Drum's chundering version of 'Wuthering Heights' on t'other, and NING 07 was a Fierce Panda tour T-shirt flagging up all three bands and the tour dates. The split single came in a plain white bag with a panda stamp on the front and all copies were numbered from one to 1,000. This was an infinitely easier manufacturing process than packing up all those six-track EPs, and that easiness was only usurped by the breezy ease of taking delivery of a box of lovely warm Fierce Panda tour T-shirts. Discogs tells me that the *Evening Session* were involved in some kind of giveaway with the singles. My name made the tour poster as 'Xfm DJ', which sold precisely minus three extra tickets across the nation. A success, in several ways.

To celebrate this success, in May of 1995 we released *Nings of Desire*, our first album that was a compilation compact disc collecting together a lot of the bands from those first six vinyl releases, albeit with a lot of those bands giving us completely different tracks. The artwork out-shonked everything we'd scrabbled together before with little more than paper, glue and the odd tongue poking out in intense concentration, and the cover featured a picture of two pandas shagging, but not on the streets, because pandas are reclusive creatures who avoid dwelling in urban conurbations.

The *Nings of Desire* compilation was released with a catalogue number of NONG 01, because I thought NONG went very nicely with NING, not least because my previous presumption that NING was a tribute to the Python's *Holy Grail* was absolute bobbins – they were the Knights Who Say 'Ni!', whereas we were stealing from another source, that source quite obviously being Spike Milligan's 'On the Ning Nang Nong' poem. Honestly, we were so anarchic we couldn't even figure out which comedic legends we were nicking stuff from!

No less surprising to me was the fact that NING 08 was our first ever standalone single, 'Skinny' by jittery agitpop cats Scarfo. Why did they get their own single? Because we really liked them and, more importantly, their manager asked if they could have their own release instead of sharing the vinyl platter with anyone else. That's how easy it was to seduce us. NING 09 was a standalone single as well, 'This is the Life' by brassy Manc indiepop dreamers Pullover, who had found their way south to the end of York Way and presumably asked the same surprisingly sensible question as Scarfo's manager had, and presumably got the same surprisingly sensible answer.

Scarfo. Pullover. Knit the north! Etcetera.

By this point I had started courting an American lady called Lisa, who seemed to be running Sub Pop's UK outpost in somewhere called Aberdeen House on Highbury Grove. This ostensibly meant working releases by brand-new American acts like Jale, Pond and Velocity Girl while trying to keep the Sub Pop brand relevant in the crazed post-Nirvana haze at the precise point that grunge was being expunged by Britpopper action. This meant digging deeper than deep to find that indie spirit, which meant setting up her own label called Love Train.

One day I was reading the *Evening Standard* and in it was the headline 'Suzi Quatro Lives in Chelmsford'. Wait, the leather-cat-suited glam goddess had a gravelled devil gate drive in the middle of Essex? What more of an excuse does an indie chump need to make a record? So the *Suzi Quatro Lives in Chelmsford* EP was born as NING 10, a three-track 7-inch split between Fierce Panda and Love Train with a young Suzi on the front and Scarfo, Joeyfat and Ligament on the grooves. And there was obviously a Suzi Quatro Lives in Chelmsford tour T-shirt, which was NING 11. And so there was obviously the Suzi Quatro Lives in Chelmsford tour to coincide, which didn't actually get to Chelmsford, but did go to Colchester, which is pretty close on the Norwich mainline, or perhaps the A12.

We chose to travel up the latter, firing up the Quatro coach outside the Good Mixer in Camden Town as the bands and various glad-handlers joined us. The bus drove out of London via Walthamstow and went right past the front door of C86 Forest Road, which gave me ample time to enthral the Scarfo rhythm section by pointing out the various ways in which E17 had gone to hell in a handcart, all the way from Tottenham Hale to the Waterworks roundabout. The touring party descended upon Colchester's the Twist, where Joeyfat threw breakfast cereal into the crowd and we raised several glasses of liquid lager to salute Suzi Quatro's devil gate gravel drive lurking somewhere back down the Essex highway.

These were excellent times. The bestest, the brashest, the shoutiest and the most innocent of times. Having launched Fierce Panda on the back of the likes of the Bluetones, Supergrass and Ash, just as Britpop was girding its loins and ambushing the mainstream with zingingly radio-friendly tunes aplenty throughout 1995, we were doing the exact opposite and heading right away from the commercial pleasure zone. It wouldn't be the last time.

I don't know if my enthusiastic record-releasing ineptitude brought Ian and Lisa down to my level, or they just indulged me, but in terms of learning curves having Damaged Goods and

Sub Pop as ersatz indie label mentors did Fierce Panda no long-term short-sleeved harm whatsoever. I certainly suspect that this was the year that cemented Ian Damaged's . . . not respect, not admiration, let's call it gently quizzical enthusiasm for giving Fierce Panda a massively helpful helping hand, partly because Paul and John's drifting meant that he and I were working more closely together, and partly because a few of those tracks by China Drum and Scarfo would have been pretty good fits on his own Damaged Goods label.

We would never be this punk rock again.

31 DECEMBER 2019, 11.59 P.M.

I am sitting in a wheelchair, slumped like a ragged Guy Fawkes doll, gliding along beneath clean, bright white lights. I am being transported from the A&E department to the acute ward of Homerton Hospital. I have a belly full of painkillers. I have fresh bandages wrapped around my wrists. I am still accompanied by a saline drip pumping me full of fluids, trying to wash away the poison.

The wheelchair comes to a squeaky halt. Double doors swing open to reveal a ghostly room full of midnight shadows and mumbled slumberings, soundtracked by the chirpy chirpy beep-beep of monitor units and illuminated by the eerie glow of computer screens.

'You're our first patient of 2020!' beams the welcoming nurse. Congratulations, everyone.

Outside the deep black windows fireworks explode across Hackney, thunder-clapping through Clapton, throwing shattered showers of light over the land of the battered hipster.

So this is the New Year.

And I don't feel any different.

11

GUT ACHE

I have no idea quite how I ended up being the drivetime disc jockey on Xfm. In 1994, I couldn't even drive. What couldn't be denied were the twenty years I spent getting the best possible experience for being a DJ – listening to the radio. Do you remember lying in bed, with the covers pulled up over your head? I do. I remember Ed Stewpot's *Junior Choice* with its weekly request diet of Terry Scott, the Wombles and Rolf Harris; the ever-genial Diddy David Hamilton soothing our teatime pain in Whipps Cross; the Tuesday lunchtime chart rundowns with Paul Burnett, huddled around the transistor in the school playground. The Jam have gone straight in at number one? What the . . .?

I remember the cavalcade of pre-*Evening Session* early evening presenters on Radio 1 – Mike Read, Kid Jensen, Annie Nightingale, Janice Long, Richard Skinner, Simon Mayo, playing the Smiths and Prefab Sprout and REM and the Farmer's Boys and being company for lonely indie boys and girls across the land.

In fact, having been within 47 yards of Peter Powell's bomber-jacketed radio radiance at a Radio 1 roadshow in Porthcawl circa 1979 I can safely say that I actually get more starstruck by disc jockeys than I do musicians.

One day at the *NME* in the early '90s, I went to the old Capital Radio tower at Euston with Spinal Tap – it's a very long story. As Nigel Tufnel, David St Hubbins and Derek Smalls prepped to spill the beans about their *Break Like the Wind* album, we bumped into said ex-Radio 1 lunchtime chart rundown presenter Paul Burnett lurking near the office filing cabinets. 'I'm currently residing in the "where are they now?" file at Capital Gold,' he gurgled, sadly.

A few years ago, we went to one of the accurately titled Radio 2 Live in Hyde Park days out. Our Longfellow band headlined the BBC Introducing tent, while the likes of the Corrs, Bryan Adams and Rod Stewart played the main stage to prove to 55,000 sunburnt punters it really was 2015. Backstage meanwhile was a cavalcade of showbiz fantasticness where ruggedly wealthy radio pluggers rubbed shoulders with Radio 2 royalty – any environment where you have to swerve to avoid spilling lager over Moira Stuart's skirt simply has to be experienced by every wide-eyed indie nerd in the known world.

And over there, with the queue of admirers and the heroic pate glimmering in the afternoon sunshine like some kind of mental stardust in the desert? Why, it's Ken Bruce. Big fan of Ken. I joined the cluster until my turn came.

'Hi Ken, I'm Simon from Fierce Panda Records. Big fan of PopMaster.'

'Oh, hello Simon from Fierce Panda – I've *heard* of you.'

Thrilled at this showbiz acknowledgement, I turned away, back to my sad life.

'Hi Ken, it's Bob Freeloader from Flangebucket Promotions,' said the next fanboy. 'Big fan of PopMaster.'

'Oh, hello Bob Freeloader from Flangebucket Promotions – I've *heard* of you.'

(Repeat to fade.)

Even Enfield and Whitehouse's comedic savagery of Smashie and Nicey couldn't dent my enthusiasm. I bumped into Alan 'Fluff' Freeman at a film screening in the West End, in one of those weird wee cinemas on Wardour Street. He'd been accidentally reactivated by Smashie and Nicey's sensationally puntastic, bomber jacket-mungous piss-take of old school Radio 1 DJs. Seeing a massive legend like Fluff at the tiny bar in the weird wee cinema, I totally panicked. 'Tell you what there, mate,' I said, 'I'm having a lot of trouble getting hold of a copy of "You Ain't Seen Nothin' Yet" by Bachman Turner Overdrive.'

He could have taken the opportunity to give me a right old biffing, but Fluff was lovely. He listened carefully and made a note. A few weeks later, wading through the jiffy bags in the *NME* office a cassette tumbled out onto the live desk. No note, no packdrill, just a C90 with some tidy handwriting that said, very simply, 'BTO x 7'. Proving that we really do play everything we get, no matter how challenging or cryptic, I put the cassette into the office stereo system. And blow me down if the mighty sound of Bachman Turner Overdrive didn't blast right bloody well out of the speakers. Seven songs deep. A gift from the Fluffster himself. Not fucking 'arf.

And have you ever read any DJ's autobiography? A sincerely strange experience because if you read an autobiography by a DJ you inevitably read it in their radio voice. This gets even weirder when it comes to Simon Bates's masterfully titled *My Tune* opus, because not only do you hear Simon Bates reading his life story inside your head, you hear him reading it over the soundtrack of Nino Rota's weepisome 'Love Theme from *Romeo and Juliet*', which used to have hundreds of lonely house-wives clutching empty milk bottles to their hearts listening to 'Our Tune' every morning.

Anyway, the world was not lacking in alternative DJs in 1994. Oh, hang on a minute, it was! For all of John Peel's relentlessly downbeat exuberance and the perennial joys of Radio 1's 7 p.m. slot, alternative music remained very much an alternative to the standard radio chart fodder. Even most of the evening presenters were just passing through on their way to daytime popfoolery.

There was no 6 Music, no Amazing Radio, no Radio X, no underground sounds on Hoxton or Soho or Joyzine or Boogaloo Radio. But the radio times were a-changing: Steve Lamacq and Jo Whiley had kickstarted the *Evening Session* in 1993 with their peachy Doctor Martens boots, and a mad radio enthusiast called Sammy Jacob had teamed up with the Cure's Robert Smith and his manager Chris Parry to create an American-style indie radio station called Xfm.

Inevitably, Steve was involved in the early days: his DJ appren-ticeship had been spent in a semi-detached house in Leyton on Xfm predecessor station Q102, steady with the leftfield tunes but always ready to scarper out the back door if any official-looking types came a-knocking, for this was modern-day pirate radio, two minutes from the Baker's Arms rather than adrift on the high seas. I was sufficiently aware of the set-up to make the odd guest appearance with Nigel Ugly Child, reviewing records or guiding the kids through the gig guide or some such, but it never occurred to me to try my luck behind the mic.

When Xfm was in the process of trying to get a pukka licence, my journo friend Ian Watson and I were asked to come along to test for a show. Both of us DJ'd out at Club Smashed! at the Powerhaus in Islington, so we had mastered the art of turning the faders up and down at the right time with one hand, a fag in the other, and cueing up a 12-inch single after six pints of Holsten. But this radio DJing malarkey was another thing entirely. Unscripted and under-prepared, we bumbled around for an hour or so together in the studio without much of a clue, realised pretty quickly that I was pretty useless and didn't think anything more of it.

And then a few weeks later I got the Xfm gig. It was a genuinely astonishing moment, and one presumes either Sammy Jacob was desperate or crazy or genuinely thought I had something even I couldn't see. Or maybe I just brought a handy *NME* association with me. Or perhaps there was just a petite Lammo-shaped DJ chair that they thought was so easy for me to fill. Again.

Either way, in between incredibly hi-falutin business meetings with Chris Parry and the broadcasting authorities, Sammy was a wee perambulating pixie, a minxy minx forever scuttling around the studio giggling at himself and cracking jokes. He wasn't the only one – in the early days, Ricky Gervais would also pootle around the station making himself hilarious, and it is testament to Xfm's relentlessly fun-filled atmosphere that the David Brent character in *The Office* is eerily similar to Sammy Jacob in his pomp, right down to the 'I'm the best boss you'll ever have' schtick.

The Xfm building was on Charlotte Street, Fitzrovia. One studio – quick seat change for the DJs handing over between shows. Proper set-up. Professional sounding. The ever-excellent engineering guru Fraser Lewry secretly ran the station, made the dials swing, made the speakers sing, seemingly tempered Sammy's madder moments. This was alternative radio with commercial breaks, the adverts and jingles stacked up on cartridges. Touch me, I'm slick.

Sammy had got together an amazing radio crew, too: Janice Long, Gary Crowley, Claire Sturgess and John Kennedy were all on board, Mary Anne Hobbs and Keith Cameron joined me from the *NME* ranks. At one point I swear I was the seventh-best DJ on the station – at least. The shows took place during month-long RSLs (Restricted Service License), the test runs where the Radio Authorities who – quite literally – controlled the airwave spaces would judge if the aspiring stations were fit for purpose. I took part in two RSLs. This was not pirate radio.

As predicted from the test event, I had absolutely no natural talent for being a disc jockey. I detested the sound of my own voice, I hated the 'performance' angle of it all and I was also terrified, so far out of my depth I couldn't see Seafood on the seesaw with the seashells on the seashore any more. And I absolutely, furiously, sweatily loved it. Before each and every weekday drive-time show (4 p.m. until 7 p.m., pop kids) I would leave the *NME*, cross London Town and go to a nearby Fitzrovia pub – either the Blue Posts or the Carpenters Arms – and plot the show. The lonely boy with his double Dutch courage with three hours of pure airplay to fill, mixing in the day's must-play playlist tracks, scripting all the links, timing it all to perfection. Totally in control with my boring old drinking partners, Diligence and Discipline. Hold steady.

I brought my own radio-tastic angles: What's the Year, Bongo?, where I'd play three classic indie tracks from one wunnerful year back-to-back-to-back and listeners had to guess what that wunnerful year was. Then there was Flopping Around Five, where I'd segue together two lushly laidback leftfield tunes, maybe something from Afghan Whigs into the Orb, and give the listening dozens ten blissful minutes off from hectic reality. In short, my live-time drivetime show was the least spontaneous activity known to mankind.

After the first week, I stopped being quite so utterly petri-fied, although you had to be on your toes at all times as I swiftly realised that live radio was always alive with danger. Forgetting to line up the needle on the next 7-inch record. Accidentally playing sweary Green Day album versions of sin-gle tracks. Eating a giant bag of beefy Monster Munch with the mic open. And real-life chats with bands – especially real-life chats with bands.

One time, I interviewed Justine Frischmann from Elastica live in the studio. They were prepping to play a Shelter benefit for a release project put together by Lisa Sub Pop. As Sub Pop in the US weren't really pulling up any screaming trees at that time, Lisa tried to spark some A&R fires – with a little bit of help from yours truly – by releasing immaculately packaged 7-inches by UK bands like Elastica, Gene, Supergrass and S*M*A*S*H, all in a swanky box set. The bands were playing together at the Forum, with proceeds going to homeless people – not necessarily Justine's specialist subject, I suspected.

'So how did you get involved in this project then?' I asked Justine hopefully.

'Because you asked me to, Simon,' she responded sweetly.

Righty ho.

The RSLs worked splendidly. Xfm got a licence and permission to become a full-time radio station. Celebrations all round. A brilliant result, and totally deserved for the relentless work and effort Sammy Jacob had put in over the years. My *NME* bags weren't quite packed, but the taxi was on its way to prepare for the launch on 1 September 1997.

Sammy phoned me at the *NME*. This was it. Primetime drive-time, here we come. Prepare the leaving party canapés. No more journalism, no more Fierce Panda. From IPC to Xfm, and all thanks to ELO.

'How would you like to do the evening show, say seven 'til ten?' he asked.

Silence. Stunned, astonished silence.

Deep breath. Don't panic.

'Ummm. Well, snag is I'd be going right up against Steve on Radio 1.'

'Yeah, I know! Perfect, right?'

More astonished, stunned silence.

'Ummm. Well, not really. I'm kinda like a rubbish version of him, so nobody is going to listen to me. And I wouldn't be able to go to gigs, which kinda defeats the object of my show, which relies on seeing new bands early in the evening.'

With my brain buzzing like a freaked-out fridge I can't remember the conversation carrying on much longer. Sammy mentioned something about me doing a show on Saturday night. I rebuffed that by saying the last place I'd want to be on a Saturday night was the West End. This was not going as planned for either of us. An unhappy situation.

I was beyond devastated. To be fair, Sammy had once again astonished me.

Paul Anderson got the full-time drivetime gig. Total radio pro. Totally nice guy. Totally passed on his apologies. 'Mate, I cannot believe you didn't get the slot full-time,' he said, totally gutted for me, blushing with sadness, too nice to bullshit.

Sorry to embarrass you.

1 JANUARY 2020, 9 A.M.

All is quiet on New Year's Day. I'm still here. Easy-clean curtains swished around the bed. I'm reappointed in cool hospital pyjamas and wired up to ECG. A lovely new nurse found us sandwiches in the fridge, a mighty midnight feast, my first food since leaving home thirty-six hours earlier. Not that anyone is counting. Russell has taken Scout and the pups back for a Canonbury sleepover. Liann is sleeping over in the chair by my bed. She isn't going anywhere.

After twenty-four hours, it is decided that I should be transferred from the Homerton to the Royal Free. It's pretty clear I won't be getting the bus. The medics at the Homerton have been speaking to the specialists at the Royal Free about my case since I'd made my glamorous entrance in the close-to-death throes of 2019. The Royal Free have now decided the Homerton's medical prognosis warrants closer specialist attention.

In a nutshell, it's not looking great. The doctor kindly explains everything to Liann about the liver, which, like the Moog, is a complicated organ. Thanks to the fistfuls of painkillers mine is on the brink of failing. There is a 70 per cent chance I'll need a new one. The Homerton has excellent facilities but the Royal Free specialises in transplants. Everyone is very worried. I definitely need an upgrade. Even in my addled state I am appalled by the idea of a transplant. Not for surgical reasons — I've been stitched up more times than a favourite old teddy — but the thought that someone way more deserving on a waiting list would be queue-jumped by such a self-destructive cretin.

The cretin is told not to be frettin'. I'm seriously ill, they say. I'm as deserving as anyone else, I'm told. I'm still not sure. Cry me a liver indeed.

At one moderately un-fuzzy point, I work out that I was born very near here. The Salvation Army Mothers' Hospital, quite literally fourteen minutes' walk away on Lower Clapton Road. The Sally Army hospital shut down in 1986, but its remaining equipment was shipped to the brand-new Homerton, where I'm lying now. Ipso facto, in fifty-four years I have travelled a grand total of 0.9 miles.

The ambulance crew turn up at my Homerton bedside to facilitate the move. It is the same paramedic team who brought me in forty hours earlier. Weird. 'I've been doing some research on you, Simon,' says one of them. He has as well. Turned out in the '80s he had joined the army and was based in Dorset. He would train it into London for the weekend and go to Klub Foot to go mad with the psychobillies. We talked about The Wedding Present, the Raveonettes and the very essence of indie rock 'n' roll as the ambulance glided down the Holloway Road, back past the old house.

My wife, who has endured twenty-plus years of total strangers gleefully handing me their demos in venues, pubs, shopping centres and holiday resorts, rolls her eyes and sighs when I tell her.

12

GULP

In true hapless Fierce Panda style, if I'd had my way, our most infamous release would never have happened. Sound City, Glasgow 1994. Midnight chaos at the Forte Crest Hotel bar. Bands and journalists and press officers and hangers-on every-where, drinking and puffing and drugging up. I'm gabbling to Karl Hyde from Underworld after their heroically haphazard headline set when John Harris appears through the schmoozy fug. He's come up to interview Oasis, who themselves are appearing at Sound City, for the *NME* front cover. Mad for it. Only trouble is, we've only just put Oasis on the front cover.

It was the one I did, with the snap of Liam from Oasis stand-ing in the Oasis bar in Newport. It was part of an on-the-road trip taking in Portsmouth Wedgewood Rooms, Newport TJs and, for me, the added bonus of Derby Victoria Inn. Their first proper tour with the buzz building and the dates selling out. Just the band: no roadies, no tour manager, no hangers-on, just five blokes in a mini-bus. Nice blokes. Very efficient, very polite. At breakfast the morning after the TJs show they are suffering, but it's Guigsy and Bonehead who entertain, acting the hungover clowns while everyone else looks on, laughing through the lager fumes. Cool. Mad for it.

Over that same south Wales breakfast in Newport, they slightly kidnapped me and took me with them to Derby Victoria Inn, the five blokes and one journo in the mini-bus. Bonehead was driving. Leastways, he was when he wasn't stage diving into the back of the van in the middle of a motorway traffic jam. Our road trip ended with drinking supersonic gin and tonics with Noel in the bar of the Britannia Hotel back home in Manchester. It was quite the journey.

Now we were interviewing them again? This was proper journo madness, publishing overkill – the worst thing you can do with a new band is over-write about them – you overwhelm the readership and sicken them. Then they won't believe the hype. Words were shouted by me to John. Words were shouted back by John to me. John duly interviewed Liam and Noel. It would be the last time they would ever be interviewed together for the press. They basically had a massive mother-fucking fight on tape. Swear words were shouted. Swear words were shouted back. Turns out John and I had had an argument about doing an interview that was going to turn into one of the most famous arguments in the history of rock 'n' roll.

John knew he had solid cassette gold. Back on the South Bank, he played the interview in its entirety to the whole *NME* office. Everyone was aghast, enraptured, howling, howling, howling as Liam and Noel traded insults in a Glasgow hotel room. We hadn't had this much fun since Frank Sidebottom read out the football results. It was our generation's Troggs tape. Oasis were back on the front cover of the *NME*. Word spread.

'This should be properly released,' someone said, fatefully.

If only we knew someone who put out records.

Oh, hang on a minute . . .

At this point I would like to say that, as debonair reprobates, we sallied forth into the release-o-phere with nary a carey in the world. Truth is: we were as scared as the Postcard Records drumming cat. We had what I considered to be a decent relationship with the Oasis team at Creation Records, but Creation went through Sony, so this had the potential to go seriously legally awry. It took quite a while for us to convince ourselves to put it out, let alone anyone else. Over a year, in fact.

In the end, between the three of us – Ian Damaged, John and myself – we decided to go for it. Cross your fingers and hope to die. We carefully listened to the tape and worked out the most coherent chunks of profanity and pithy points of debate. Then we took it off to a top-secret radio producer man who fed it into a computer and trimmed it down to fourteen minutes of verbal mayhem.

Now we had to cover our furry legal arses as much as possible. There is no direct reference to the band – the release is by Oas*s, the front image is of the Kray Twins. Classic Fierce Panda cover. The title, 'Wibbling Rivalry', is a great bit of punnery on sibling rivalry and a nod to the Gallaghers' very bothered brotherhood. The 7-inch had a Liam side and a Noel side. Sue us if you dare. Took a deep breath, sodded off to a nice beach in the Cyclades, but not before I bumped into Noel Gallagher sitting in the Xfm green room.

'I hear you're releasing our interview,' he said.

'Yeah, yeah we are,' I said, trying very hard not to look busted, or indeed, like anyone in Busted.

'Good stuff,' he nodded, chuckling. I think. I was a bit fuzzy.

'Wibbling Rivalry' came out. It was the sweary talk of the town. By which I mean it caused serious fucking chaos.

A fraught moment: Sony's lawyers are on the phone. Uh-oh.

'We've just heard the single is really funny, so we wondered if we could get a copy?'

Christ.

Another fraught moment: the Official Chart people are on the phone. Uh-oh-oh.

'It looks like 'Wibbling Rivalry' will go into the top forty, so we need some track details.'

Double Christ.

A third fraught moment: a 'representative' of the Krays phones up the *NME* news desk. Uh-bloody-oh.

'The boys are not 'appy about being associated with a pair of reprobates like the Gallagher brothers.'

Triple Christ on a crutch.

In the end, the world did not end. The Sony lawyers were laughing, in so many senses. 'Wibbling Rivalry' only entered the charts at fifty-two – still the highest ever placing for a spoken-word release, so we heard. And the Krays' 'representative' was appeased with a payment to their favourite charity.

So much was right about that release. The timing, the vibe, the cussing, etc. I honestly think that, paradoxically, Oasis had such momentum that 'Wibbling Rivalry' could only help their cause. It's not like they needed any more support from the *NME* per se, and it's not like a number fifty-two chart position was going to amaze them. I suspect it just added to the band's Manc street mystique, made them seem more alternative and real at the precise point they were cracking the mainstream wide open.

I'm still not quite sure how we got away with it, although we certainly wanted to do more releases like it. With the slightly spurious Oasis v. Blur wars around the corner, the thought did occur that I'd done a pretty hilarious interview with Blur for the previous Christmas issue – even Steve Sutherland liked that one – but sometimes what ends up looking great in print doesn't make for ace listening because quotes are chopped, changed and chopped again to keep the flow going on the inky page.

The stories from Alex James are still pretty damn good though. As we had an early Christmas dinner in Groucho's he explained how one year he was so poor that he simply wrapped up the groceries – bread, sugar, teabags et al. – and put them under the tree for his girlfriend.

Still, could be worse: 'Last year I bought her a broom,' the bassist said happily, blushing.

No, what really worked with 'Wibbling Rivalry', the nonchalant brilliance of it all, is the way that John nudges the brothers along, just rolls with it. He's not goading them à la Grundy grunting at the Pistols, quite the opposite – he makes them feel so comfortable in that fuggy, foggy, F-bomb-strewn Forte Crest hotel room, they could let themselves be their sweary, shouty, hilarious selves.

I mused about talking to John about an anniversary reissue of 'Wibbling Rivalry', it being twenty-five years old in 2020. But I thought better of it. I wasn't sure if he, let alone Liam or Noel, would appreciate the gesture this time around.

Time flies. Let sleeping fookin' dogs lie.

3 JANUARY 2020, 11.21 A.M.

All around me in my new Hampstead home are unfamiliar faces, worn-out faces, sympathetic faces. Royal Free's very bestest medical experts – Professors and Sirs and Misters and Doctors and Lords and Ladies – scurry through in scrubs and suits, swishing the curtain around the bed, bowties a-whirring, spectacles a-sparkling, clipboards clip-clopping, assistants assisting, keeping time. Keeping my time. Poking, prodding, referring, cross-referencing. Notes are taken. Decisions are made. Doses are upped. Drugs are downed. The easy-clean curtain is unswished. It's all such a rush and a hullabaloo I think they should call us all impatients.

I'm also involved in a one-to-one nursing situation. To quote a passing medical procedural, 'The aim of one-to-one nursing is to provide continuous observation for an individual patient for a period of time during acute physical or mental illness.' It is, in essence, a trained health professional sitting at the end of my bed throughout the day and night making sure I don't do something stupid. Or, in my case, anything more stupid. In another essence, I am on suicide watch.

Earnest personnel from the Royal Free psychiatric team pull up fake plastic chairs to practise their cheery mind techniques. The same questions, day after day. Testing, testing. One-two. One-two-one. One-to-one.

To be fair, I have given this suicide thing a damn good go. Liann does say I'm very stubborn. But the fact that I had kind-of-allowed Russell to save me has given me a giant get-out-of-jail card. If I had been found turning purple on the orange office sofa, there would be a totally different take on my situation, especially from the psych team. This is unbelievably crucial to the whole recovery process: if those Leroy House security doors had had to be broken down to save me, I would be looking at being sectioned before teatime.

'Are you relieved you're still alive?' the Psychiatric Forces ask.

'Well, seeing as how I've spent the entirety of the year thus far lying in bed dressed in little more than a pair of regulation NHS jim-jams I'm not actually quite sure if I'm not already dead and this is all some kind of hyper-surreal residual dream taking place in Hospital Heaven, or indeed Hell,' I reply.

'Hmmm.' They frown.

I'm not sure if I'm helping.

Liann's best friend Sarah pours some lemon squash and says, matter-of-factly, 'You're not mad, you're just sad.'

This makes me wearily glad.

13

A PROPHECY

'Wibbling Rivalry' was Fierce Panda's twelfth release. I often stop and think if we'd just stopped right then we'd be at least a twelfth as cool as Postcard Records, who themselves ground to a halt after a dizzying dozen singles. Maybe we *would* have stopped if NING 12 had just been a whacked-out indie release, or a.n.other box-fresh tour T-shirt, but 'Wibbling Rivalry' was a few giant steps up for us. By releasing what we thought was some meta journalistic in-joke and treating it with even more fear and caution than our normal releases it actually got the Fierce Panda name into nooks and crannies we'd never nooked or crannied our way into.

Plus, come 1996, we were young, we were quirky, we were carefree – we were almost a walking, talking, drinking Supergrass lyric. These were our very own teenage kicks, and we took that spirit into the heart of our releases. NING 13 was 'Bruise Pristine' by Placebo. NING 16 was 'Come Out 2nite' by Kenickie. NING 17 was 'This Is My Hollywood' by 3 Colours Red. By the time we'd hit NING 29, 'All You Good, Good People' by Embrace, we'd squeezed out fruity debut singles by Dweeb, Tiger and the Pecadiloes, all of whom signed to majors, as well as terrific records by Formula One, Chewy and lovely old Kitchens O.D., aka Kitchens of Distinction. All of a sudden we were on some kind of roll. A shonky, badly constructed roll with too much limp lettuce and not enough hammy ham, but a roll nonetheless.

We were real, we were genuine, we were often really, genuinely drunk. If a band happened to excite our scouting synapses, we would immediately seek them out after the show, perhaps backstage, perhaps under the bar, perhaps desperately trying to start up the van and drive off before we caught up with them at the traffic lights at the bottom end of Camden Parkway. And we would say, 'Hello, that was fun. Would you like to do a single on Fierce Panda?' because 'Would you like to do a single on Fierce Panda?' was our catchphrase. Quite often the bands were so taken aback they said 'yes' without actually thinking about it, or realising what madness they were agreeing to, or even noticing that the traffic lights had turned green. It was the least complicated procedure known to indie A&R kind.

Now, one thing that sticks in my craw as much as it must do with anyone else who knows their A-ha from their Elbow is Fierce Panda's tag as 'the label with the golden ears', as 'discoverers' of 'hitherto unheard-of talent'. Truth is: people were just very nice to us. Placebo came from the live agent Steve Strange, who'd just seen their third ever gig supporting Catherine Wheel at the Underworld, and were managed by our old WAH 17 trooper Dave McLean. Kenickie was a tip-off from Mark Bowen at Creation, and they'd already been released on Slampt! in Sunderland. Mighty Lemon Drops manager Cerne Canning took me to the Brunswick Arms to tell me all about this grrreat new band he was working with called Tiger. And so it went . . .

In fact, out of all those early Panda releases the only time I can recall 'discovering' a band was going to see 3 Colours Red play first on at the Water Rats simply because I liked their name, poncy French arthouse misery and all that. Bloody great they were, too, really chunky and low-slung and melodic. But still, being credited with 'discovering' a band like 3 Colours Red playing the Water Rats to loads of people . . . when Ben Harding the guitarist had previously been in Senseless Things. I dunno, it's a bit cringe, innit?

While we're talking about Kenickie and 3 Colours Red, what is worth noting here is that they come from opposite ends of the indie spectrum – 3CR being punky rocksters arrowing towards *Kerrang!*, Kenickie being cheery indieglampop sprites embraced by Peel. But we could do both, and we did do both, back-to-back. This defined us by making us indefinable, which is another way of saying we were committing commercial suicide from the very early days by not sticking to one obvious style or specific genre like, say, Sarah Records or Spinefarm Records. In 1996, Kenickie supported the Ramones at their last ever UK show, at Brixton Academy, and went on to sign for Bob Stanley and Pete Wiggs' EMIdisc label. 3 Colours Red moved on to Creation, where Alan McGee took all the pressure off them by announcing the arrival of the 'new Sex Pistols', whereupon they took even more pressure off themselves by supporting the old Sex Pistols in Finsbury Park.

Another change here was that after happily putting out whatever we were given by the bands through the first dozen or so releases, once we clocked that we were becoming some kind of haphazard launchpad for the next wave of acts we would gently suggest that they give us one of their best songs to release because a) they might split up tomorrow, or b) they might get run down by a bus next week, or c) slightly more optimistically, they could well sign to a bigger record company for whom they will re-record the same track in six months' time and perhaps even have an indie schmindie hitto with it. Which is certainly why Placebo, 3 Colours Red and Embrace impacted so speedily, because they pretty much used their very bestest songs at that time. To emphasise the point, Kenickie's 'Come Out 2Nite' was number one in Peel's Festive Fifty – and we didn't even vote.

So if we weren't ever kingmakers, we were certainly ningmakers, creaking open the back doors of the mysterious out-of-town music industry industrial unit for new bands to sneak through. We were monumentally naive, so we were entirely natural. We put out a lot of stuff simply because we saw a lot of great bands and heard a lot of ace music. Plus we enjoyed helping people, we quite liked being quite liked – always a mightily dangerous feeling in the music industry. I look and listen back and some of those early records sound as they appear, i.e. gauche, clumsy and cobbled together, and that's primarily because they were. Everything was in the moment and totally instinctive. The records weren't necessarily designed to sell out within a week – we didn't want to tease the record-buying public that much – but a few of them did, which only seemed to add to what I delicately describe as our nascent credibility.

The release turnover became manic. It was almost like being a freelance journalist at the *NME*, where you couldn't turn anything down. Like some weird transformative creature of the night, you'd wake up in the morning covered not in lipstick or blood or fur, but demos, flyers and hairy bass players' phone numbers scrawled halfway up your arm. It was quite possibly the unsexiest alarm call known to mankind. It used to drive some people mad – Ian Damaged would find out about new signings before I'd had the chance to tell him because while I was ambling into the lovely new top-secret Walthamstow Village Damaged Goods/Fierce Panda office (just on the corner by the Labour Party HQ) the morning after a night of A&R chaos, some over-excitable manager was already on the Panda hotline telling him how delighted his band, who Ian had never heard of, was to be on his Fierce Panda label.

It would be hopelessly disingenuous of me to suggest that the *NME* connection didn't help attract new bands and hairy bass players' phone numbers in some sweet way, but in my innocent mind it was no more enticing than an invitation to fill a slot at Club Spangle or a daytime spin on Xfm, and the most obvious talent-free chancers got short shrift. Did people agree to be on Fierce Panda for fear they might never get in the *NME*? I do hope not – I might have still been attempting to run the Live section and the 'On' section while I was running Fierce Panda, but consider that in an average mid-'90s year the *NME* would have covered 150 new acts on the 'On' page and run hundreds more live reviews and it can hardly be said that Fierce Panda releases, no matter how mentally numerous, were dominating the editorial agenda. Besides which, a lot of the second wave of Britpop bands who were getting a heap of coverage in the paper were so bloody awful even the Panda's enthusiastic bargepole was poleaxed by them.

Plus, by this point, things had gone really weird with other writers at the *NME*: Keith Cameron had become embroiled with Costermonger Records, who put out Gene; Iestyn George got himself similarly involved with Townhill Records, launch pad for 60ft Dolls; and James Oldham had set up 4M Records on his way to setting up Loog Records on his way to successfully infiltrating the major label system. Throw in the various dance releases emanating from the Vibes desk and at one point there were about half a dozen labels being run out of the *NME* office. Indeed, there were rumours of a record shop out west, possibly in Bristol, who had a whole release section devoted, not entirely charitably I presumed, to releases by music hacks.

In our defence, we made some excruciating attempts to try to avoid looking entirely corrupt: new Panda singles would be sent to me at the *NME* by Ian, and then I would send a box over to Sarah Neve at Press Counsel PR, who would then post them back in individual packages to the writers at the *NME*. In the general scheme of things it wouldn't have made that much of a difference to outsiders, but at least my conscience felt moderately assuaged by not actually going around my colleagues' desks plonking down new Panda releases with a nod and a wink like some total nodding record-company winker.

To add to the hapless business insensibilities, we rattled through all these one-off singles because we were never trying to tie bands down for the long term and steal the years away from them – quite the opposite, we were trying to give them that extra crucial six months when they had time to build a fanbase, time to hone their craft, time to try to begin to understand how the music industry works, time to become the band they so desperately wanted to be before the major label tried to turn them into the band they so desperately *needed* them to be, which are two very, very different things. It sounds sickeningly conceited, but we thought we were doing A Good Thing. We were certainly having a grand old time with the bands, when they were playing their first gigs with crowds, reading their first press reviews, hearing their first radio plays. Those first six months are usually the funnest, fruitiest, frothiest months – even if you don't get an ounce of radio or press you push on in expectation rather than deflation, you're so caught up in the excitement. Then most of the bands left.

The thing is: this is just what I thought all bands did on labels like us: from the Cure's 'Killing an Arab' debut on Small Wonder, through the Farmer's Boys on Waap! to virtually the entire Postcard roster. Aside from the rarities like Depeche Mode and New Order, who stuck with Mute and Factory over here at least, it's hard to think of a single significant band, from Buzzocks' 'Spiral Scratch' through to Coldplay's 'Brothers & Sisters', who didn't move from an indie label to a major or a mandie, aka major label indie.

Hence, when it came to our prodigious output, we thought that's just what bands do, and that's just what indie labels do for the bands, which is help them on their way with a fruity Fierce Panda single and a cheerily tearful wave from the front step of the Dublin Castle. So they came and went: Llama Farmers signed to Beggars, Campag Velocet to PIAS, Toaster to Creation, Magicdrive to Mercury, the Regular Fries to V2, Ultrasound to Nude. Could we really moan when bands we really wanted to stay for a cup of tea and a cuddle still fucked off in the morning and left us with little more than a creased hangover and a sense of howling spiritual emptiness?

Yes, yes, of course we could. But, by 1997, we had made a rod for our own back. Or, in the case of 'Chandelier' by Idlewild, we'd made a Rod, a Roddy, a Colin and a Mad Bob for our own back.

4 JANUARY 2020, 7.50 A.M.

Reassuringly, the hospital meals are uniformly awful and inedible. Quickly realising there is no point in waiting in salivating expectation of a lavish lunch, I make sure I always breakfast heartily at 8.10 a.m. on two slices of toast and jam and one strong cup of tea. Evening platters are similarly drab and inedible, wheeled up as they are from some central gulag kitchen. Custard, however, we discover is made on the ninth floor, which is quite possibly why it tastes nice, so the puddings are generally lovely, so I generally subsist on fruity pies and tarts and sponges, always getting my just desserts. Throw in the gallons of Robinsons squash I'm knocking back and it's little wonder I'm redeveloping the primitive taste buds of an eight-year-old from 1974.

My new best friend is Tony Robinson, happily striding across the land as he walks back through history each and every lunchtime. Fresh air! Rucksacks! The real world! The sun really is shining on TV. At some point in between Baldrick's rambles and ramblings, news comes through about some flu thing in China. A disease nobody has ever heard of is infiltrating a city nobody has ever been to. Weird. Not the kind of thing that happens in places like this, eh? On my wanders I've seen the room just around the corner, which is designed specifically for containing contagious diseases. Lots of black-and-yellow stripy warnings. Very creepy, even when very empty. Beep calm and carry on.

Speaking of creepy, late one night the Royal Free's free hospital radio is playing to the ninth floor's trapped lost spirits down a distant empty corridor. You honestly haven't just-about-lived until you've heard 'Fix You' floating through the crushed medical ether at half past two in the morning. Still, at least nobody here knows what I do for a living. Oh, hang on a minute . . .

'I was actually a big Death Cab for Cutie fan,' one bashful doctor tells me shyly one bright morning. 'Their Transatlanticism album soundtracked my time through med school in Edinburgh.'

Liann sighs and rolls her eyes.

I successfully refrain from writing 'Death Cab for Acutie' down on my acute ward notepad.

14

THE ABSENT GUEST

Having agreed to disagree to agree with fried little scamp
Sammy Jacob I ended up with a Sunday afternoon slot on
the freshly radiant full-time Xfm when it launched properly
in September 1997: 2 p.m. until 5 p.m., or something. Or was
it 1 p.m. until 4 p.m.? A specialist show on a specialist station.
Another fine example of the endless recurrence, but niche even
by my recherche standards. The problem with Sunday was
that I had a full week between shows, enough time to get really
nervous all over again.

Another problem with Sunday was that it was a dead day for
industry, so nobody I knew was listening out there in Radio-
land. Yet another problem with Sunday was that it was a dead
day, even for Xfm. No staff. No buzz. No Fraser Lewry. No
frippery. No more carefree laughter, silence ever after. The
flickering dials and the fucking dead day DJs could take care
of themselves. Let yourself in, let yourself out, just don't let us
down. One time, nobody bothered to tell me the new entry

security code to the studio, with hilarious locked-out panic-stricken pre-show consequences.

I was fully aware that Sunday afternoon was dead airtime because American DJ Eric Hodge had got the daily breakfast show, and every Thursday morning I would slink into the shiny upgraded radio headquarters to pick up my post and it felt like one giant big radio party. Amid all the excited daytime buzz and bants and Fraser Lewry frippery I'd pop into Eric's studio while he was on air and enthuse about the bands I'd seen play live that week. One day, with a bit of off-mic priming, we had a spot of radio-tastic airplay-mungous fun.

Eric: 'Morning, Simon – seen any great new bands this week?'
Me: 'Nope.'
Eric: 'Thanks a lot, Simon – see you next Thursday!'

One joke, nine seconds. It was probably my greatest single appearance on Xfm, which says everything.

I used to listen to the daytime shows, loyal to the end. And there was one great shiny silver sun lining to my whole cloudy Xfm sky – they would be playing Seafood, Campag Velocet, Llama Farmers, Fierce Panda releases aplenty. Had I still been revving up in the drivetime chair merrily spinning my own singles each and every day between 4 p.m. and 7 p.m., after the dubious delights of running a label from the corner of the *NME* office, this could well have been a conflict of disinterest too far for the music industry polizia, and quite rightly too.

So it was absolutely amazing – if meeting DJ people is easy then hearing your record on the radio is beyond thrilling. It's the whole point of the exercise, even to this very day . . . and you get paid for it! The year 1997 was kabooming boomtime for the nascent Fierce Panda and it transpired that Xfm was my most perfect radio station. Ipso facto, it was doomed to fail.

The main problem wasn't actually me arsing around on Eric's breakfast show; it was the fact that the RSLs ended in 1995, when Xfm got its licence, and by the time it made it to air in 1997 the world had already changed, in so many ways. Launching the morning after Princess Diana's deadly car crash was unfortunate timing – it most certainly wasn't an okay time to play 'Alright' by Supergrass. But, no less damagingly, the station had been off-air for the entirety of 1996, the year Britpop broke. Come the end of 1997 the adidas chic peak had already peaked. Where were we while you were getting high? Backstage at the Oasis Knebworth blowouts, DJing in a portacabin to the festival crowd instead of a festering nation.

Also, one thing I learned early on in my ill-fated daytime career is that most music radio output – certainly in weekday-light hours – is driven by stark raving airplay terror. Fear that the listener is losing interest, is being beguiled by a.n.other station, is having their heartstrings tugged by Heart FM, is sitting with their fingers micromillimetres away from the tuning dial, waiting for any excuse to make their excuses and go listen to something more interesting instead.

'Are we losing listeners?' is the constant, playlist-clutching cry. We are! They're going to switch over! QUICK!! PLAY SOME OASIS!! Phew! 'And after the break we've got the Chili Peppers, Green Day and more Oasis – stay tuned!' I personally despair of radio where they tell you the next three records coming after the break, because it means they have killed the element of surprise, which is why I despair of so many of what purport to be vaguely 'alternative' radio stations nowadays. I'm not asking to hear a new 'Birthday' by the Sugarcubes being birthed on air every day of the week – I actually have a soft spot for Steve Wright's Non-Stop Oldies at 3 p.m on Radio 2 when a listener chooses half an hour's worth of their favourite music, because while sometimes it's awful, at least it's always awfully surprising.

To be fair to Sammy, we possibly clashed over the fact that he fretted about the listening figures and I favoured a more eso-teric approach to broadcasting. I wanted much more madness, he wanted complete control. I wanted Kenny Everett, he wanted Everclear. So for me the really great thing about my Sunday show was having free rein. After me was Tony Smith's request show where he played the Stone Roses, Green Day, Red Hot Chili Peppers, stuff that people actually wanted to hear, which I reckoned gave me carte blanche to honk the heck out of whatever I wanted to play.

So I put my best DM-booted foot forward, even though for some infuriating reason my show started at 1 p.m. or 2 p.m. with a news blast at 1.05 p.m. or possibly 2.05 p.m. Obviously the big stations got the on-the-hour news slot. Instead of the previous show overrunning to fit, I had to find a five-minute track to fill the gap before switching over to the bulletin. Happily, Ipswich's symphonic gothic metallists Cradle of Filth – not naturally Xfm listening, to be fair – had plenty of tracks that fitted the bill on their new album, *Dusk . . . And Her Embrace*. Cue the music. Then screw the music.

(Note to any prospective alternative disc jockeys out there: if you are going to use a link like 'That's "Funeral in Carpathia" by Cradle of Filth, and now it's time for a slice of cheeky news pie,' please do make sure the newsreader isn't going to open the bulletin reading news headlines about a terrible plane crash in Bucharest or Budapest or somesuch dark eastern European portal.)

I had so much free rein that one Sunday afternoon I was play-ing a track by Free Kitten, the side project from Sonic Youth bassist Kim Gordon, who presumably thought that the band's *Washing Machine* album was such a shallow corporate sellout she had to get back to creating some seriously leftfield noises to appease her supercool conscience. It was, it's fair to say, pretty challenging stuff. It was also a 12-inch remix, roughly about six minutes long.

Halfway through the freeform alt.rocking Free Kitten remix experience, the studio phone rang. Exciting! Probably a fan! I picked it up!

'Ahoy oi oi?' said I.

It was Sammy on the line. This was becoming a habit!

He had a question for me, a question that simply couldn't keep until Monday.

'Are you deliberately trying to lose us listeners???' he bellowed.

It is to my eternal credit, and also my perpetual regret, that I didn't patch him through so he could continue his rant live on air. Although weirdly, he never once complained about Cradle of Filth.

I was about to become an ex-Xfm presenter.

5 JANUARY 2020, 10.30 A.M.

The liver specialist Dr Rosenburg sits me down one day to deliver a message. Well, I'm already sitting in bed, but he has his Very Serious Face on when he looks me straight in the eye and says: 'Simon, you can never drink again.' And then, begrudgingly, he adds in a mutter, 'For at least six months.'

The strangest thing – and this really resonated with anyone who'd had a drink with me over the past thirty-five pub-table-thumping years – was that, until the avalanche of painkillers at least, the medical team said my liver had been in absolutely excellent condition. Like, really tip-top. Like, so tip-top it totally saved me from eventually tip-topping myself. Problem is the liver count is improving but now the kidneys are struggling to pick up the slack. In fact, they are cracking under the strain. Having sidestepped the perils of a liver transplant my battered innards are now careering towards some seriously diehard dialysis action. In short, we are playing kidney bingo.

The antibiotics are bumped up. The IV drip drips. The wrist wrappings flap. The catheter gets emptied. The stubble itches. Eight days without a shower and counting. I really am quite the catch.

15

MY DAYS ARE NUMBERED

I spent a grand total of eleven years writing for the *NME*. I can't recall exactly when it was the most practical piece of advice for anyone remotely interested in nubile new music appeared, but at some key point in my so-called decade-long tenure there was a key piece of research that the boffiny *NME* publishing bigwiggoes indulged in. They basically got a group of people, possibly students, to read the paper cover to cover for a month and tick some boxes. The results were interesting. On one hand they were bleeding obvious: the news pages and gig guide were the best read, then the singles and letters and gossip pages, then the live and album reviews, then features.

Those surveyed said they had least interest in the 'On' page and the 'Vibes' page, entry points for new indie acts and dance combos respectively. Yet one of the key survey questions was: what do you want to see more of in the *NME*? And the resounding answer was: 'More new bands!' This was perplexing. The

'On' page was full of new bands. Couldn't get enough of them. But the students didn't read it.

In the end we realised that what they actually wanted was new bands, but new bands that they'd *heard* of. Alternatively, they didn't want to read about new bands they *hadn't* heard of. And therein lies the crux of every PR pushing their great new band to press, or every plugger trying to plug something amazingly fresh to radio producers. Even Fierce Panda has had times when we have witnessed total thigh-slapping nonsense from supposed musical experts saying, 'Never 'eard of 'em.' Remember this, pop kids: every band was new once, even the very old ones.

I got to know quite a bit about our publishing overlords in the end. By this time, I had started courting a lovely indiegoth girl called Liann. She worked on the twenty-sixth floor in something called an 'advertising department'. This meant she went out for nice lunches with very important record company advertising people in the music industry, gently convincing them to spend their money on plugging their releases in *NME* and *Melody Maker*. This meant she had a much more important job than any of us writers. And, in the early days of our courtship when nobody else in the IPC marketing departmentals had clocked we were courting, this also meant that she was privy to some excellent top-secret conversations definitely not meant for furry editorial ears, specifically mine.

My very favourite was from a boffiny meeting where a very serious-faced publishing type said, with an ever-so-gentle sense of exasperation, 'It would appear that Simon Williams is running a record company out of the *NME* office.' And apparently everyone around the table sucked their teeth and nodded wisely and decided they couldn't do anything about it because nobody had ever actually started a record company from the *NME* office before, so nobody knew what to actually do about it now it was happening.

So anyway, we really do know where the bodies are buried, publishing boffoes.

Only joking!

We know they're not buried, they've just been chopped up and stuffed into the filing cabinet in the review room.

Only joking again!

It is to the *NME* teamsters' eternal credit that, even as I ran a label, pretended to be a DJ, promoted live shows left, right and in the shadow of Centre Point, and generally investigated the national train network to find entirely new rails to come off, they still indulged me like a favourite young nephew. At one particularly perilous point in my life, then-Live editor Iestyn George said, 'You need a holiday' – which was very true. 'So you're going to cover the Caribbean Music Festival.' And myself and snapper Ed Sirrs were packed off to pack our bags and head to Nassau, the very capital of the Bahamas, for a music festival that decidedly did not have a backstage area full of Mega City 4 roadies.

Joe Strummer once wrote about a white man in Hammersmith Palais. He'd have had a creative field day with two skinny indie blokes in the Caribbean, kicking back with rum cocktails in coconuts in the sea and getting very peculiar side-eye looks from the rest of the official press corps, who seemed to consist of well-dressed professionals from *Echoes* magazine and the like. One day we had so much fun with the rum cocktails we managed to miss the bus to A Very Important Event for the festival at Compass Point studios. Hanging around the hotel foyer, Ed and myself scratched our nicely browning brows and pondered what to do.

'Can we help you?' asked a man in a suit.

'Yeah, we need to get to the studio for this festival launch thing.'

And that's how we ended up in the back of a mighty limousine with the Mighty Sparrow. He was very nice. We had a good chat about his headline slot, what with him being the biggest star of the entire event and generally the calypso king of the world. We were basically cadging a lift off Sir Paul Macca on his way to Glastonbury. On the journey we chatted about the festival, about fame, about rum cocktails. He was the nicest Calypso King we had ever met. The limo pulled up outside the swanky studio, where the entourage waited, lined up by the kerbside. The door opened and Ed and I fell out in our beach bum attire, much to the horror of the entourage who were dressed in their formal meeting-the-Mighty-Sparrow finest. When the Mighty Sparrow stepped elegantly out of his mighty limousine and greeted the masses, the entourage gawped. All of a sudden we were everyone's bestest friends.

Fantasmagorical sympathy trips to the Caribbean aside, I reckon I stayed at the *NME* two years too long. The first clue was that by 1997, after nine years in the typing trenches, I'd totally run out of coherent ways of describing the electric guitar, so I just compared everything to animals instead. The second clue was when I ran out of animals. Another clue was that while my first Single of the Week back in 1989 was that song called 'Made of Stone' by that band called the Stone Roses, my last two Singles of the Week were both by extreme jazz crunk noise terrorists the Monsoon Bassoon. Says it all, really.

There were other problems with bands who I'd previously released on Fierce Panda, primarily down to over-familiarity. I was sent off to Sheffield University, where, weirdly, Jon Fat Beast appeared in full effect to interview 3 Colours Red. Digging out the complex interrogational classic of 'What is the very best thing that has *ever* happened to you?' Chris McCormack said, 'Why, doing the first single with you, Simon.' A lovely sentiment, but perhaps not the greatest pull-quote for an *NME* feature.

It got worse when I went to interview Placebo in Paris, where they were due to support U2. I arrived at the hotel in the afternoon to await a call arranging to rendezvous with the band. Nice hotel, quite chintzy. The band were out and about doing photos. After a few hours, or about six days, Anton the PR man called me to say they were on their way back and looking towards having a drink with me. Then he called me to say they were on their way back but they were too tired for a drink. So after six hours or fourteen days of kicking my heels and licking my pillows in a hotel room I ended up in the nearby Hard Rock Cafe drinking a beer with Anton from Bad Moon, a man who doesn't drink at all. To be fair, it did occur to me just to fuck off to the Gare du Nord that night. But I didn't. Instead I met the band downstairs in the morning in a foul mood. Brian Molko, who'd only ever seen me tipsy and cheery at the Dublin Castle or some other thriving dive, freaked and ran off upstairs to his room. He wouldn't come out, no matter how gently Anton tried to coax him back downstairs or how much I promised to cheer the fuck up.

I called John Mulvey and told him the very person I was supposed to be talking to wouldn't actually leave his room to speak to me. He was very sympathetic and told me to call it quits and come home. So I had one last drink with the PR man who doesn't drink outside a bar by the Gare du Nord and got the Eurostar back to Waterloo. I slunk back into the office from my front-cover trip with no front-cover interview. Not a tremendous journalistic success, frankly.

When did the *NME* die for me? The *NME* died for many people many times, but one key bullet in the head occurred in the 1990s at an editorial meeting when it was decided we would dispense with the new-release listings in the news pages. The new-release listings were where all bands could have a chance of getting their news in the paper; no opinion, no hyperama, no slaggings, just a few words cribbed straight from the press release about your new single or album or upcoming tour, even if you were Dumpy's Rusty Nuts. In fact, *especially* if you were Dumpy's Rusty Nuts.

Someone important said, 'Let's face it, we cover all the important releases in the singles pages anyway.' A little piece of the *NME*'s heart stopped beating that lunchtime. Instead of being a democratic demotape-devouring newspaper, it was the start of the long meltdown into cripplingly cool hipsterdom, where you had to hit a certain level of approval before even being considered for a mention in the paper. The open-door policy was over. Dumpy's Rusty Nuts were never mentioned in the *NME* again. And I wasn't far from the exit myself.

Freed of any deskbound editorial responsibilities, I'd become a hack without protocol. From being a useful piece of the office furniture, a steady Eddie ready to write to order, I felt as though I'd become a marginally annoying ball-bearing bouncing between desks, rolling beneath people's feet, getting in the way. Even the traditional lunchtime pub sessions had been usurped by five-a-side soccerballing action on the concrete pitches over the road or actual, well, lunch in the surprisingly plush IPC magazines canteen, surprising in the sense it had taken us a decade to discover its existence. Otherwise I divided my time between King's Reach Tower and Walthamstow Village. In many ways, I had become half man, half panda.

In this tiny little head at least, it is to my eternal credit that in the last twelve months of my *NME* tenure I still turned in a total of fifty live reviews, big, small and smaller. On my last day, we went to the pub-with-many-names opposite Camden Palace, where our Inner Sleeve band were playing Feet First. We had some lovely farewell drinks. The gang gave me my personalised *NME* cover, a red toy Ferrari and a navy-blue Spurs away shirt, as modelled by Steve Perryman and John Pratt circa 1969. It still fits. We went over the road to see Inner Sleeve play a not entirely excellent set. Those gigging *NME* pop kids, our very own super classy Class of '92, now all grown up and editing sections and running the paper I'd given eleven whole-ish years to, wished me luck. I think they thought I'd really be needing it.

Could I do it now, critique bands and their live shows and their records and their haircuts and their eerie similarities to angry Wombles? Not now that I know what goes on with labels. Not now that I know what musicians go through. A lifetime of spitting out rehearsal-room blood, sonic sweat and melodic tears summed up in 198 pithy, possibly slightly bitchy, words with the vague hope of a hopelessly coquettish punchline. Plus, with that cuntingly dumb-tastic social networking, nowadays I'd be being called a dumb cunt every six dumb cuntingly-mungous minutes.

Time to let go.

6 JANUARY 2020, 7.35 P.M.

Once they have mastered the delights of the London Overground timetable, friends come bringing pies and fruit cordials, books (Wodehouse, Christie, Viz) and magazines (Private Eye, definitely nothing music-related), pencils and notepads and binoculars and comfort and news of the outside world. Not a day goes by without some excellent visitation and everybody is sensationally together and helpful and positive and comforting. Nobody calls me a stupid selfish twat, even if they think it. They don't tut disappointingly or suck their teeth disapprovingly or poke me or ask what the mighty god of holy fuckitude it was I thought I was doing to end up here.

The Pandamonium Festival is occurring in the outside world. A slew of panda bands like playing New Year shows across the Victoria, the Lexington, the Sebright Arms and the Social. The gig reports are good. I feel distant residual satisfaction at being part of the Pandamonium planning and promotion, if not a part of the drinking at the final event. At the same time, I am alarmed by talk of shutting the label down – that was never the aim of the grand malarkey. My death was supposed to revitalise Fierce Panda, not kill it. Either way, I suspect I won't be going to any gigs for a while just yet, but I have no idea how outside forces will dictate just how long that while will be.

It is only much later that I hear how upset some of the crew had been at seeing me in that state, but it is to their eternal credit that nobody lets their true emotions betray them on the ninth floor. There were times when Liann had to stay home in Suffolk. She desperately wanted to be by my side but she also wanted Scout back at school, back in something approaching a normal routine. But friends stepped into the breach. Ian D, Nigel N, Karen K, Russell T, Suzie L, Sarah M, Martin W, Andy P, Chris W all made it in. Part of the crew.

PANDAMONIUM!

There were some good signs though: each floor of the Royal Free has its own picturesque themed decor to distinguish it from the level above or indeed below for befuddled patients or overworked staff. When the lift doors opened on the ninth floor, the casual visitor was confronted by large pictures of pandas. Really.

16

DON'T WORRY

You could say that Liann Armstrong-Williams saved my life not once but twice. If the second time was driven by the wifely instinct of fretting about the pastry-loving husband not dashing home for special pie on New Year's Eve, then the first is a touch more ephemeral, when she was known more simply as Liann Armstrong. Certainly, when we originally met I was not in a grand place. I'd already had my first mid-life crisis, in 1995, dying my hair green, getting a Chinese panda tattoo and buying a pair of leather trousers. The top button pinged off the first time I tried the trousers on. The green, and indeed much of the hair, is long gone. I still have the tattoo. By the time I met Liann I'd departed the burgeoning hipster delights of Hoxton three minutes before it became the coolest place in the country and home was now shared with fellow scribe Mark Sutherland in a battered basement at 39 Balfe Street in the very broken heart of King's Cross.

Back then it was still a haven for hookers and other illicit hookups – not, I can assure you, at our flat, but certainly in the gnarly neighbourhood, with King's Cross station just down there and the main rat run for drug dealers and thoroughly faithless healers thirty seconds away towards Pentonville Road. And I was in no less a ragged place on a personal level, living on a steady diet of nothing but lager and kebabs and tabs and gigs. As lifestyles go, this one was decidedly not sustainable. And this is just a teeny glimpse into the madness lurking behind the flimsily battered basement curtains of my life by 1997.

In many ways, we were hopelessly ill-suited. Liann was an independent success story with her own bijou flat in Balham in south London, while I was fast becoming the illegible bachelor. Embroiled in a hard-boiled world of fleeting indie snogs and heartily rumbunctious relationships, I felt like severely damaged goods. I was a wild card, the runt of the romantic litter. This wasn't a case of low self-esteem, it was a matter of no self-esteem whatsoever. Friends and colleagues were marrying in their hordes in their silky finery, but I was always the drunk guest at the edge of the wedding photo, never the groom on the broom in the middle of the room. This whole engagement thing was an absolute mystery. Asking me to consider settling down with a young lady was like asking a horse for their wife's recipe for ratatouille.

Liann had her own group of non-music industry friends who loved music but didn't feel the urge to see five bands a night and who really liked an Old Red Lion lock-in on a Saturday eve. One of them – Martin – was such a rabid Pastels fan he still has a ticket stub numbered 001 from when they played Highbury Garage. Another of them – Russell – makes the odd appearance elsewhere in this story. But Liann was equally capable of dealing with the average sensitive *NME* dweeb in a social environment, knew how to handle a wide-eyed band of indie kids at a gig and, crucially, she could handle herself while standing smack back in the middle of an A&R bunfight. She was classy, organised, driven, and often found driving around in her IPC company car. And she really loved Suede, which I didn't mind too much, because I liked Suede so much I'd previously interviewed them in the Duke of York pub in Islington. After three months friends said I looked healthier, colleagues told me my clothes smelled nicer. It really was a bizarre, possibly illegal, rewrite of the goth lady and the indie tramp. Two years after our first date, we moved in together, into 39 Tollington Road in the sunshine state of Holloway. After three, we were married, on 12 September 1999. It was quite the spacey year.

With wearying inevitability, I would have happily got hitched in a dark drunk den in Camden and held our wedding reception at the Bull & Gate given half a chance. Luckily, Liann was in control of marital proceedings, so we ended up getting married in a very nice hotel and spa rocking in the rolling greenery of Surrey. It was called the Nutfield Priory and it was a very respectable affair, so respectable in fact that I didn't even feel compelled to roll out the usual scuffle of squirrel puns. It was a very nice posh day with lots of Panda teamsters mixing with our northern family people. Steve Lamacq was best man and did a very good roving speech with a joke involving Ian from Damaged Goods as the punchline. Seafood were getting drunk on table six. Clint Boon from the Inspiral Carpets was the wedding DJ. He played lots of Mega City 4 to keep the old punkstas happy. One time, I glanced up at the DJ booth and was surprised to see it was unmanned. It was unmanned because Clint Boon was sliding through the middle of the dancefloor on his knees in the middle of one of his own songs. I didn't do a speech, too shy. I don't think anyone missed it.

Funny thing was each of our geographical family roots ran deep across Durham, Washington, Chester-le-Street. Indeed, it turned out Liann was born in the very same hospital as my cousin Kim – from Langley Park to Metal Bridge indeed. Another funny thing was, we almost never met in a previous life. Back in the north-east half a decade earlier, Liann used to hang out with people from Kitchenware Records. She talked to them about perhaps becoming a music writer. They suggested writing a gig review and sending it to the Live editors at *Melody Maker* and *NME*. They gave her a couple of names, which she jotted down on a piece of paper. Andrew Mueller for the *Maker*. Simon Williams for the *NME*. She wrote the review. But she only sent it to Andrew. Didn't think there was any point in sending it to the *NME* bloke. Probably wouldn't give her the time of day. She was delighted to rediscover that bit of paper when we moved in together half a decade later. She still has it. Safe and sound.

So those two extra years at the *NME* towards the end of the '90s weren't entirely wasted. In fact, while I seemed to be treading water and dreading bedtime as a music hack there were enormous changes taking place in a very subtle nothing-to-see-here kind of way with the surprisingly durable Fierce Panda record label. Once Idlewild left us after the 'Chandelier' 7-inch and signed to Deceptive for the terrific *Captain* mini-album, on their way to signing to Parlophone for the excellent *100 Broken Windows* album, one of those interesting external things that seemed to happen to Fierce Panda every now and again started to happen again to us. People I liked and respected and stood with outside the Falcon, the Water Rats and the Dublin Castle in between bands shooting the breeze and sipping the beers started saying things to us like, 'Why don't you do a deal?'

'Do a what now?' we said.

'Do a deal, you know, with a major,' said they. 'The Panda keeps finding all these bands and they move on to bigger labels. So why not do a deal directly with a bigger label and then you can get some money and then you can keep hold of all these bands instead of watching them sign to someone else.'

Interesting. Having casually burned my disc-jockeying bridges at Xfm and carelessly concussed myself on the glass ceiling at the *NME*, perhaps it was time for a serious career rethink. I sat down with the most furiously independent punk rock anti-major label person I knew, Ian Damaged, and asked him what he thought. We then embarked upon a low-rent A&R chase with those major labels, with us doing most of the chasing. Like a fifth-rate new band, we were not wined and dined, just invited for faraway meetings in faraway places like Putney and Fulham at the crack of dawn or at the end of the day, the Panda spiel competing with the early-morning coffee machine or the cleaner's squeaky Henry the hoover wheels.

Still, most A&R people we met were quite nice and did lots of nodding as we shouted over Henry's shrieks, even if they didn't do a tremendous amount of out-bidding each other for the glory of our A&R services. In the end, Korda Marshall at Mushroom/ Infectious seemed nicest and noddiest of all, and the timing seemed perfect. He'd got some money off Rupert Murdoch and was on a signing rampage: Infectious had Ash and Garbage and some new band called Muse; Mushroom brought in the Aussie dollar with Peter Andre; Korda then did a deal with Rawkus to bring the hip-hop hoopla from New York, and Perfecto with Paul Oakenfold for the dancey 'Vibes' vibes, while Fierce Panda brought the indie glamour.

Only jesting.

It was a big old crew squeezed into a very full Fulham office: Pat Carr and Wez were on the organisational frontline. Stuart Camp and Nigel Adams were our creative points of contact, and very good they were too. Stuart Bridgeman was radio plugging over there, Uncle Bob and Andy MacIntyre were A&Ring over there, various other inventive marketing and distribution and international people were lurking everywhere else. Nigel and Wez would later set up Full Time Hobby records. Stuart Camp would end up managing Ed Sheeran. Stuart Bridgeman would carry on being very much Stuart the plugger until the end of indie time. But for a while there was fun to be had in the shadow of Stamford Bridge and elsewhere.

One Christmas they took the entire office horse racing in Sussex followed by some hoary drinking in Brighton. It pissed it down and I was delighted to discover that my patented Hundred Reasons branded anorak was about as waterproof as a Yorkshire tea bag. There were other less damp excursions to be had though as we signed a couple of bands to the Fierce Panda/Infectious set-up, those bands being guitar-rattling indie tykes Seafood and exuberant Icelandic quintet Bellatrix, who consisted of four girls and one boy drummer called Karl, who was either the luckiest boy drummer of all time or a sensationally unfortunate individual, or perhaps a bit of both.

Then the madness really began. After some stridently authentic releases in Iceland – one early band name translates into Black-Ass Hookrider, and the Icelandic version makes little more sense – Bellatrix had bounced up through the Camden venue scene armed with their *G* album on Global Warming Records. They blended the pixie-lated passion of their homeland with a shiny bright pop sensibility that I realised a tiny bit too late didn't work when trying to entertain the glum masses supporting, say, Gene at the Shepherd's Bush Empire. It did work a treat though when band manager Anna Hildur did a deal with Icelandair to fly a hackery of music hacks from various publications to up Reykjavik for a jamboree of interviews and photo sessions and some fruity drinking action. Bellatrix mustered a couple of top 100 singles and smashed in at number sixty-five with 'Jedi Wannabe' for one special week.

Seafood had come right through the Fierce Panda A&R circus, as evinced by the *Messenger in the Camp* mini-album that collected together their early classic singles like 'Porchlight'. We'd got a tip-off to go see their fourth gig upstairs at the Garage. Legend has it we could have seen their third gig but the Panda representative had got too pissed at the *Kerrang!* awards to make it along. When I say 'legend has it', what I mean is this is what Wikipedia tells me happened all these centuries later. The luck was never entirely long-lasting for the Seafood band, who consisted of three boys and one girl drummer, Caroline, who was either the happiest girl drummer of all time or totally ground down by indie boys fond of six-minute pedal-punching cascades of sonicness, or maybe a mix of the two.

Days before a key slot at Reading Festival in 1998, guitarist Charles badly cut up his hands in an unfortunate glass-dealing incident at a party. Lacking time to train up a replacement, Seafood opened up the *Melody Maker* stage as a three-piece and showed their gently berserk side by dousing a little bit of Berkshire with a nine-minute rendition of 'Walking in the Air', which made Sonic Youth sound like some kinda batshit Kim Gordon side project. Seafood managed a pawful of top 100 singles and hurtled in at number seventy-one with the 'Cloaking' single for another singularly special week.

PANDAMONIUM!

So we had some great fun. Bellatrix and Seafood headed to New York together to showcase at the Mercury Lounge. Bellatrix would go on tour with some band called Coldplay. Seafood went on the road with Jimmy Eat World and headlined a tour with labelmates Wilt and Turn in a hearty attempt to show solidarity with our Mushroom/Infectious overlords in SW6. We had a roster – a small roster, but a roster nonetheless. All we needed now was to align ourselves with some future world beaters and try to sign them for ever. Easy, eh?

7 JANUARY 2020, 12.12 P.M.

I warrant constant nursing attention, apart from one time when I am taken down to the ground floor for an ultrasound scan to sort out the latest mystery to afflict my innards. One thing you quickly learn about hospitals is that the porters are very adept at taking you Somewhere Else, but not so entirely efficient at organising the return journey back from wherever that Somewhere Else is. The ultrasound department is about 100 yards from the hospital entrance. This much we know because on the way there we glide right past the main doors.

The scan is prompt and swift and makes me feel a little bit like a pregnant ladywoman, after which I am wheeled out to a holding point down the corridor and lie there for what feels like an hour but is probably actually three days waiting for the porter to come back to fetch me. All alone, and 100 yards from the exit. Ample time to consider making a run, or at least a slow hobble for it. Maybe it's a test. Maybe I've seen too many episodes of The Prisoner. *Maybe if I make it out, I'll be hunted down by a Red Bus Rover. But in my heart of aching hearts I just want to get back to my bed.*

Funnily enough, my bed has been moved again, this time to the ward right by the nurses' station. This new room is as bad as things can be for its four inhabitants, hence its proximity to the staffing area, I presume. If you're not planning on leaving here on your own slow two feet, then the next step is the ICU. I slowly struggle to judge my position in the patient pecking order: one day I think I am the healthiest person on the ward, the next I guestimate I am the sickest. It is a fluid situation. Quite literally, in several senses.

We inmates don't actually sit around merrily comparing war wounds. But the impression I get is that the mysterious, twitchy bloke next to me is a recovering junkie and alcoholic judging by the mutterings about liver damage and the regular bedside deliveries of methadone. The jolly chap over there had a transplant last year but the new liver rejected his body – or vice versa – so he had to have another liver – a trans-transplant? – and during his extended stay in hospital over Christmas inevitably picked up the usual motley selection of infections and gentle mental traumas. The third of my medical shipmates, slumped in the opposite corner by the door, is so sickly with something mysterious that at one point his tearful partner is actually pleading with the doctors and the medics to take him back into intensive care.

He certainly looks to be in a bad way. But, then again, look who's squawking over by the window, crumpled up with the lukewarm apple crumble.

17

KNEE-TREMBLER

The first time I walked out on Coldplay was 1 April 1999. Out of the Bull & Gate, Kentish Town. This was the launch night for their 'Brothers & Sisters' single, and the evening had started extremely well. There was a queue right along the venue corridor, out through the front doors and down past the kebab shop towards Kentish Town Tube station. Latecoming A&R people were pleading to be sneaked in, but there was simply no room in the indie inn. We had a packed backroom, the Bull & Gate at its very best — the Bull & Great.

Halfway through their rendition of 'Shiver' I walked out. Well, I actually squeezed my way out through the throng, muttering apologies for any spilt drinks and split loyalties. But either way, I turned my back on that bright-eared backroom because my wee indie heart was about to burst out of my feeble alt-pop chest, because I was feeling so excited, because I was having *too much fun*. So I went to the bar and sat on my own, the lonesome panda buzzing bashfully like a forgotten robot at the bottom of the toy box. This heady Bull & Gate headline was the culmination of six months' worth of work, a tiny pimple on the rear-end of Coldplay's over-arching career, but a pretty significant half-year in the Panda's slightly less glamorous history.

Interestingly, 1999 is seen by some musical experts as being one of the worst years ever for music. Not being a musical expert, I actually thought there was some spectacular eccentricity going on. Britpop was mercifully dead and Campag Velocet, Ultrasound and Gay Dad were vying to be the new *NME* pin-ups (and yes, two of those bands had started off on Fierce Panda, and no, neither of them were Gay Dad). The music industry had previously been overrun by sub-Oasis wannabes who'd found it as easy to rip off Noel's tunes as he had with the Rutles and the Coca-Cola franchise, but away from the weird spectacles of the Gay Dads, Ultrasounds and Campags there lurked a new cabal of immensely capable bands who'd been building up at a slower pace, primarily because they'd been sitting in their bedrooms working out just how the bally heckington Jonny Greenwood got those sounds on 'OK Computer', or just sliding away to listen to something other than 'Slide Away'.

And so it was in this precocious space, 1999, that Doves, Elbow, Coldplay and Muse all really made their mark on the public consciousness. We'd actually already put on Doves at Club Panda at the Bull & Gate in the spring of '98 when they played the loudest gig ever after handing us what we presumed to be a joke guestlist featuring Barney New Order, Neil Pet Shop Boys and someone from *Coronation Street*, all of whom actually turned up. We offered to put out 'Catch the Sun', but they said they already had an agreement with Rob Gretton to release a single. I saw Elbow at Upstairs at the Garage and was enthralled by their mellifluous melding of Prefab Sprout, the Blue Nile and

Talk Talk – their 'Newborn' single was my single of the year two years running. I once met Guy Garvey on the Lock Tavern veranda to talk about some Fierce Panda release action when they were in between proper record deals and have fond memories of being merely £100,000 short of what the band needed. And I never once 'got' Muse, but Korda Marshall did. Which, for him at least, was very fortunate.

The first time I saw Coldplay was at the Falcon, Camden, in October 1998. Our mutual lawyer Gavin Maude at Russells had suggested I toodle along in an informal, oh-you-never-know and only-if-you're-in-the-area kind of way. In the area? I spent so much time at the Falcon back then I was on first-name terms with the lavatorial fungus. Gavin had been tipped off about the band by Caroline Elleray from BMG, who was looking to sign them for publishing. In turn, Caroline had been tipped off by her A&R friend in Manchester, Debs Wild, who is now marked down in the annals of melodic history as the original industry person who first took notice of the Coldplay sound and actually told them they sounded genuinely great. In fact, I suspect Gavin was a bit baffled as to why they weren't already signed – they'd played the A&R showbiz pick-up fest In the City in Manchester a few weeks earlier, after all. I think he'd reached the end of his tether, or at least reached the end of his list of sensible prospective labels.

For Gavin, who also had Idlewild on his books, Coldplay certainly weren't an obvious indie-punk-ish fit for his Fierce Panda client: they were gauche, geeky, nerdy. The singer wore a tank top and had a mop-pop of hair. He sounded posh, cracked cringey jokes, played an acoustic guitar. Nobody outside of the Wurzels wore tank tops, cracked jokes and played acoustic guitar in 1998, leastways not all at the same time or outside of a Travis soundcheck

in the West Country. If those weren't sufficient crimes against
industry humanity, on the surface the youthful Coldplay sound
was fundamentally a raggedly fruity combination of Jeff Buckley's
swirling grace and Radiohead-height intelligence. Cribbing from
the udders of one sacred musical cow was one thing, but to do
it twice was downright gold-topped sacrilege. Then again, there
was not much industry to be seen that night in a Falcon that was
overflowing with good vibes and a lot of happy faces I didn't know.

'Got some fans there,' I said to the beaming singer afterwards.

'Oh, they're not fans,' said the singer with a shrug, beaming,
'they're just mates from uni.'

'Well, mates from uni don't often sing along to all the songs,'
said I, thinking I'd forgotten something really quite important.
Oh yeah. 'By the way, would you like to do a single on Fierce
Panda?'

Word from the corridors of University College London was
that singer Chris Martin was an utter, utter, utter pain in the
arse, forever going on about his bloody sodding band, giving out
bloody flyers, working the sodding students. Then those same students would go and see the Coldplay band play live and go, 'Wow!
They are really good!' And those songs really were great – light of
touch, charming of manner, chipper of melody. 'Bigger Stronger'
and 'Shiver' stood out most of all, and there was more to the music
than any angsty Buckley/Yorke axis: there was an understated-
ness to the guitars, a cracked passion to the vocals, a strange edge
to the ebb and flow of the songs that had their peaks and troughs,
but had those peaks and troughs in odd places, like the band still
hadn't quite found what they were looking for, but were having
intensely excellent fun searching for it.

This was the start of a beautiful relationship between band
and label that would last for ever and for ever, or for half a

year, at least. Their location was perfect – Coldplay lived down Camden Road, a fifteen-minute stroll away from the Holloway family home, in a proper student house. I should know, I visited the toilet. They were therefore within staggering distance of every half-decent venue back when most bands would play half a dozen times on the toilet circuit, at the Bull & Gate, the Dublin Castle, the Falcon, the Laurel Tree and the Monarch, so each promoter would have a chance of putting them on and each band would have the opportunity to nurture their sound and build a crowd.

Their timing was perfect at radio as well: I predictably enthused about my Falcon experience to Steve Lamacq, who returned to the same venue in December to check them out and found himself picking his jaw up off the floor after half a set. With the *Evening Session* still in full effect, they gave Coldplay a Radio 1 Maida Vale session, the first for an unsigned band. The press side of things was no less helpful to the band: my days at the *NME* were pretty much numbered by the start of 1999, but the editorial support for Coldplay was furiously strong from the outset as the latest Live desk tiger, James Oldham, wanted to extend the paper's relationship with the A&R fraternity even as I neared the exit. So they got the main picture and some hearty words from a live review of our week-long New Year-busting Pandamonium event, which presented their inaugural Bull & Gate show on 7 January, when they played first on the bill supporting their labelmates Tiny Too and headliners the Pecadiloes. A quiet blast, but not quite pandemonium yet.

As well as their location and their timing, their attitude was perfect. Everything worked because they just got on with it and never argued, not with us anyway. The manager was Phil Harvey, ostensibly an equally lovely mate from college who was so important to the whole story he is now celebrated as the fifth member of the band. Their live agent meanwhile was Steve Strange, an up-and-coming Irishman who could drink for the whole band, fifth member included, and often did. There was no arrogance, no pretence, no bollocking about. We would ask them to do grubby indie stuff and, for the most part, they would do the grubby indie stuff we asked them to do without a tedious amount of deliberating. For all that, they were patently not the new Idlewild, or never, by many stretches of the imagination, an 'indie' band – by the time they started doing full interviews, Chris would happily enthuse about his love of Genesis – there was an authenticity about the band, not to mention a can-do attitude that frankly shamed loads of their supposedly cooler peers loafing their way around the circuit.

Crucially, no band in the history of Fierce Panda has asked Fierce Panda more questions about how the industry works and how they could make that industry work for them. I spent one such evening in the company of Chris Martin in the Camden Eye, the weird Dairylea triangle-shaped pub opposite the Tube and the World's End. In between questions about the workings of the musical industry, I went to the bar for some refreshments. When I asked the barman for a pint of lager and a bitter lemon with ice, he glowered suspiciously, firstly at me and then at my happy-faced curly-haired companion in the triangular corner. Bitter lemon? This was fucking Camden! However, realising that my companion decidedly didn't look like the sort of character who'd stash half a quart of Smirnoff down his pants to mix with the baby blue Schweppes, the barman nodded his satisfaction. You can say many things about Chris Martin, but in those early Coldplaying days you could never say he wasn't a cheap date.

(Oddly enough, a few years later, if that same barman had craned his neck out of the front window of the Eye and really streeeeeetched to look up Camden Parkway on a particular dank evening, he might well have spotted an impressively less gauche Chris Martin standing on a drizzly pavement talking to a still-very-much-gauche Panda boy. Next to him he had a lady called Gwyneth Paltrow. 'This is the man who made us!' beamed Chris by way of introduction. Gwyneth smiled that almost imperceptible Mona Lisa-ish smile that suggested I was the seventeenth person she'd been introduced to in that manner that afternoon. And the sixteenth was quite possibly the sweeper sweeping up outside the Jazz Cafe, a few drizzly yards up the road.)

There was a record, recorded in February '99. The *Brothers & Sisters* EP consisted of a two-track 7-inch – 'Brothers & Sisters' and 'Easy to Please' – and an extra track on the CD called 'Only Superstition'. Unlike so many previous Panda singles, we didn't get a very favourite live track like 'Bigger Stronger' or 'Shiver', we actually got an A-side that wouldn't be re-recorded and re-issued by a bigger label twelve months later (although a version of 'Brothers & Sisters' was to appear on the B-side of 'Trouble'). Like so many previous Panda singles, it cost £450 to record, this time in Station Studios in Southgate, where Tiny Too had made their *Things That I Discover* album, with Mike Beever at the production controls. It was released on 26 April and it soared to number ninety-two in the charts. Chris Martin was beyond excited.

There was one other key difference to previous Panda singles: this time around we had the backing of Mushroom, which meant that for the very first time in our tiny, mousy musical tale we had the resources, and indeed the industry sources, to try to sign the Coldplay band long term, which we very much did. We put on their key gigs, we released their pivotal single, we enjoyed answering their questions and endured the shame of buying them baby-blue bottles of bitter lemon. In short, we felt as though we were an integral part of a storyline that, like Mr Creosote at an all-you-can-eat Chinese buffet, was expanding by the minute.

But did I genuinely feel we stood a chance? It was a new experience, that was for sure. Luckily we were in cahoots with the people who'd signed Ash and Garbage and Muse, experts who had hoisted Peter Andre's six-pack into the toppermost of the top tens. But, rather than pool our sources, and indeed resources, with Korda's crew, we seemed to go for an accidental tactical pincer approach to signing Coldplay, one that saw Mushroom do their grown-up A&R thing and saw Fierce Panda do its thing that wasn't *quite* puerile or purist, but did inevitably involve the pub.

In short, one day I wrote a gauche, geeky, nerdy list of reasons Coldplay should, and indeed *needed to*, sign to Fierce Panda. We'd grow right up from the grass roots upwards and make it massively big together, the dream band on the dreamy label, that kind of thing. Took it to Backstreet rehearsal studios, under the arches of the Holloway Road railway bridge. Took them to the bar with the ever-changing name, the one by Holloway Road Tube station. Gave them my finest spiel and handed over my geeky, nerdy list of reasons. I think there were eight of them, and they were on orange paper. We could do no more.

Some anxious time later I got a call in the top-secret Fierce Panda office on Orford Road in Walthamstow Village, just next to the Labour HQ. It was Chris Martin on the line.

'Hi Simon,' said he. 'Are you around? We'd like to take you Panda boys for a drink.'

'Sure thing,' I said. 'Where are you?'

'Oh, we're in Hammersmith – we're coming over now.'

Hammersmith, eh? Home to Parlophone Records. Didn't take a stout Belgian detective to work out that they'd done the deal, and they'd done the deal with someone who very much wasn't us. And so they drove across London, from the wayward west to the elusive east, and the four of Coldplay, including the singer who didn't drink, took us to the Village pub in Walthamstow Village to buy us a drink and thank us in their slightly nerdy, gauche kinda way for everything we'd done. It actually hurt like hell, but behind our enigmatic Gwyneth Paltrow-esque smiles the sentiment was very much appreciated, as was the free lager.

The relationship didn't end there and then, either. Funny thing was, early on Coldplay struggled to get any tours. The live agent Steve Strange, who also looked after Bellatrix and Seafood, who also wanted to go on the road, was once so flummoxed he came up with what he considered to be a bonzer idea whereby Seafood, Bellatrix and Coldplay would go on tour together, killing three panda chickens with one foxy fox. In the end, once I'd stopped choking on my Yorkshire tea and carefully closed the office coop, Bellatrix and Coldplay went out as co-headliners, starting a theme whereby every band Coldplay played with would be totally fucked for ever.

To wit, were Coldplay really as nice as we thought? They subsequently co-headlined a UK tour with Welsh scrappers Terris. When it came to London on 7 April 2000, a full year on from the Bull & Great, the London show was at ULU, pretty much Coldplay's home university venue, yet Terris headlined the night. Can you guess what happened next, kids? Coldplay played to 800 joyous 'mates' singing along, about 700 of whom promptly left after their set, leaving Terris to rage at a near-empty room.

Accident or cunning? Interestingly, this show was the first time I heard a new song called 'Yellow'. 'That'll never be a single,' thought I, snarkily. 'Chris can't even hit the high notes live.'

So, the next time we crossed paths, 'Yellow' had rocketed up to number four in the pop-tastic chartings, much to the delighted surprise of everyone including, it seems, their astonished record company. Down in the Panda boondocks, there was very little delight. Chuffed as we were for the Coldplay band and their teamsters, on a personal level it was a gruesomely painful blow to my so-called professional pride to miss out on something so thrilling unfolding in front of my very bloodshot eyes. So painful in fact that for one day I decided to freeze Coldplay out of my life: no listening to the radio, no reading of the press, no watching of the television. It was a nice day, walked from the Holloway house up to Finsbury Park Tube. Traffic was its usual wild self, i.e. a riot of colour gridlocked around the old Rainbow venue. Windows were wound down. Time was unwinding in the north London haze. And then from the front seat of a white van I heard a horribly familiar sound, the sound of white van man whistling, the man in the white van whistling the refrain from 'Yellow'. You can hum, but you can't hide.

Funny thing is: I was never especially annoyed by Coldplay signing to Parlophone. Back in 1999 even *I* would have signed to Parlophone, it had such a great roster and reputation. But it was quite the odd six months. And apparently it could have been even odder, as it seems in spite of my nerdy, needy list of reasons they should sign to Fierce Panda, we were the only two labels left in the chase. Whenever I now see Korda Marshall he shakes his head and sighs, 'We should have doubled our offer for Coldplay.' And all the way from 1999 right up until the last time I saw him, alive and very much kicking in the Islington in

Islington in 2019, their live agent Steve Strange would say, in his gently bellowing Belfastian barfly manner, 'Simon, you have *no idea* how close Coldplay were to signing to Fierce Panda.'

I'm not sure that's really helping.

10 JANUARY 2020, 2.31 P.M.

Fluids are vitally important to the recovery plan. I am permanently attached to a drip and told to drink as much water as possible. The inevitable result of this is I end up taking in so many liquids I am fit to burst. The other somewhat inevitable result is fluid on the lungs — the excess has to go some-where, after all. Then of course the problem is the onset of a chest infection, so I'm bombarded with antibiotics. Then the problem is my body temperature, which refuses to drop to a level that makes the medics at all happy.

The other somewhat inevitable result is that the IV cannulas are popping out of my arms like exploding mini-corks. They can no longer get a needle in me to take the vital daily blood tests that tell them how my insides are faring because my entire skin is tauter than Kim Kardashian's ever-ballooning buttocks. A succession of enthusiastic medical experts try to pierce my flesh — they even have a go at my feet — with a variety of increasingly tiny needles, searching in vain for a vein, struggling to get to the bloody point.

When they (mercifully) stop with the fluids, I deflate slowly, like a very sad punctured Spacehopper, and somehow contrive to lose 2 stone over the course of one single weekend.

I'd let my family down, I'd let my friends down . . . and now I'd let myself down.

Boom, and indeed boom.

18

PIMPS

Some people ask me how many gigs I've been to in my loafy little life. Truth is: I have no idea. 4,000? 5,000? 8 billion? By the time I realised I should keep count of the number of gigs I'd been to, I'd already lost count of how many gigs I'd been to; I was too far gone. But I don't really care. I've never seen going to gigs as a box-ticking exercise. It's never been a challenge or a chore. In fact, as someone who possesses all the musical talent of a broken gopher and who used to get stage fright putting up the backdrop at the Dublin Castle – *in a totally empty venue* – I am in awe of pretty much anyone who can get onstage and make some melodies work together in a moderately coherent manner. That's not to say that some of those thousands of live acts haven't been totally fucking terrible, but even at their terribly fucking totalitarian worst, a little bit of my soul still looks up at them and thinks, *These people are better, shinier and more talented than me.*

The other truth is that if any one thing sums up the madness of this entire quiet literary opus it is – quite literally – gigs. With

records, you have catalogue numbers and release dates and artwork and press releases, some degree of context based on actual
fact, which can trigger specific memories. With gigs, however,
it is generally a case of going to see some moderately unknown
bands on some midweek night in some fair-to-middling venue
and letting the muddlesome madness occur before it all starts
again the following night. So forgive me for the general fuzziness
surrounding this subject.

   That said, if this book is woefully lacking in rock 'n' roll mythol-
ogy then this point brings it all home: any 'research' into the
Fierce Panda story has generally involved me going to the pub
to sit and try to remember going to a different pub to see a band
or three ten, twenty, thirty years ago, or rifling through boxes
and boxes of flyers. Now and again I have taken old friends to
the pub, and even stayed with them for a tipple or two as they
tried to remember crucial details about my musical life. But their
memories tend to be as haphazard as mine, so we just get drunk
and promptly forget the few things we've half remembered three
pints before. Still, at least it saved on having to transcribe hours
and hours of mine or anyone else's jib-jabberings – in my opinion, this book is pretty much entirely my opinion. I haven't even
asked any bands, old or new, what they really think of the label.
Ironically enough for someone who runs something as ursine as
Fierce Panda, I simply couldn't bear to hear the truth.

   One thing is for sure: after a decade of happily trotting along
to gigs and perhaps reviewing some of them and perhaps not
reviewing all of them, in 1992 I started to get sucked into the
promoting vortex. Like so many other things in this tale, it was
mostly down to the inspiration and encouragement of other
people, in this case canny sorts recognising that the *NME* was
a pretty useful brand if used in a clever, i.e. cool, credible way.

Neil Pengelly was one of the first out of the blocks. He is generally credited with making Reading Festival cool in the late '80s, which is correct because he took over booking the bands. In 1988, Meat Loaf and Bonnie Tyler were still playing the main stage as Reading very much rocked. A year later, the three festival headliners were New Order, the Pogues and the Mission and the hoary old rockin' around was just a hazy piss-bottling memory as Reading became the indiest event on the planet.

That very same year the Mean Fiddler launched the Powerhaus in Islington, on the site of the Pied Bull. Soon after, Neil set up a brand-new event called Club Smashed on Wednesday nights, with myself, Steve Lamacq and Ian Watson on board, all music journalists-turned-indie-DJs. The opening night was a five-band bill featuring some band called Suede. Pulp played our Christmas show. Radiohead rolled in at one point. Marc Perchard in the *NME* art department made some really quite excellent flyers featuring the old for-mash-get-Smash robot. The Mean Fiddler teamsters delivered a litany of cool bands and made those Wednesdays an essential part of any self-respecting indie tyke's gigging schedule.

Some extended 12-inch mixes take me back, a touch twitchily, to those nights – Stereo MC's 'Get Connected', for one – as we valiantly tried to entertain the midweek midnight masses after the bands had finished. It didn't take me too long to realise the notion of 'breaking' new indie smashes on the dancefloor wasn't going to work – it turned out drunk people didn't want their new indie dance bands to be *too* new. In fact, it was only a first Club Smashed! play of 'Killing in the Name' by Rage Against the Machine that elicited any amazed instant reaction from the punters, who queued up at the DJ booth in their dozens to ask who the fuck it was doing that fucking song with all the fucking fucks in it. Apart from that singular single-breaking moment I realised that spinning discs at indie discos was not my forte.

But, if nothing else, we have worked out that gigs are pretty key to this whole Pandamonium process. I'd say gigs are in fact *the* process. If there was fine synchronicity to the Club Smashed! set-up, our next move led directly to a significant promoting step up, as the beautiful symmetry with New Wave of New Wave continued unabated: on one hand, the scene clearly set the ball rolling for the Fierce Panda label; on the other, it was actually organising the sensationally sold-out *Shagging in the Streets* EP launch party at the Powerhaus that triggered, in me at least, a perverse fascination for not just going to, but actively booking and promoting, live shows – something that has continued non-stop to this day. From 24 February 1994, the gig was the thing, the night was even more alright, and the releasing of a Fierce Panda record was almost an excuse for putting on yet another launch party. *Almost.*

Later that same year, three Bull & Gate refugees, Chris Myhill, David Laurie and I, set up Club Spangle, mainly because we liked bands and we liked beers and we liked each other, so we thought this would be a good way of bringing all those things together in a very tidy weekly way. It took place every Monday night at the Dublin Castle in Camden Town and accidentally fuelled the embers of Britpop by becoming the place to play, the place to be, the place to be seen *in*. The first show was on 18 April and starred My Life Story and the Weekenders. Across the last ten Spangle shows of 1994, we put on Marion, the Bluetones, Powder, Smog, Gorky's Zygotic Mynci, China Drum, Tiny Monroe, Menswear and Lush. Catatonia were in there as well. They turned up a) late, b) drunk, and c) wearing sunglasses. In November.

If that booking snapshot implies that we knew what we were doing, then I would suggest that David and Chris were very much the organ grinders at this particular funfair, although I certainly wasn't resting on my laurels in the Laurel Tree with Howard Gough from Laurel Records, or not very often anyway. I just ambled along on their coat-tails infused by a heady cocktail of bravery, pissed instinct and blind optimism. One Thursday lunchtime the three of us were sitting in the Water Rats bar casually mulling over the fact that we had very little entertainment booked for next Monday's Dublin Castle gig, i.e. we didn't actually have a headliner in place. Ash were playing the cheerily rebranded Ashtoria the following week. Perhaps they needed a wee warm-up? Good thinking. Call Tav the manager on the mobile telephonic device. He's on a video shoot with the band. Hang on a minute. Muffled shouting. Tav's back. 'Yeah, they'd love to do it.' Great. Now for a support band. Who was that group the agent Steve Strange mentioned the other night? Placebo? Yeah. Okay. Give him a call. Book them in – 24 July 1995 then. Ash + Wormhole + Placebo. As you do.

Funny thing is: Ash never actually played the Ashtoria shows we helped them get warmed up for – drummer Rick McMurray's grandma took ill and he had to fly home to Northern Ireland. Another funny thing was Placebo's supple blend of sexual ambiguity and super frenetic melodies earned them a Panda single release on that very night, their fourth ever gig. Was there any cunning logic involved amid the chaos? Of course – in this case we could just put our own bands on at our own gigs and not have to deal with any other promoter squabbling over availability, guestlist or fees. If we wanted to piss away money, we could piss away our own very tidily, thank you very much. With Club Spangle we could be on top of the advertising, on top of the bands, on top of the bar staff, sometimes even on top of the bar. We nicked the Cardigans off the Borderline and put them on with Pullover. We put Kenickie and 3 Colours Red on together in a seminal joint Fierce Panda launch party. We set up a spin-off night called Club Spongle – but of course! – downstairs at the Monarch, and then moved to a new live room upstairs, where Chris proved he was so devoted to live promotions he actually lived above the venue. We set up Spangle Records – but of course again! – and put out our own cheeky 7-inch EPs, which then needed their own launch parties, which we then promoted, in some kind of relentless promotional recurrence.

Obviously, if you put on hundreds of bands then eventually a few of them might have been significant enough to resonate with the general populous a few decades later. Luckily for my genteel research sessions, I went to the pub armed with NING 50b (to give it its official catologue number – NING 50a was a T-shirt), which was a fanzine by a young indie enthusiast called John Banfield. I think (and indeed hope) it was for a college course. It was called *How Long Is a Piece of Ning?* and it was certainly an in-depth cataloguing of the first forty-six Fierce Panda singles and associated gigs. As mentioned before, the record releases are fairly self-explanatory, but there is a comprehensive list of Club Spangle shows that even I can scarcely believe I was involved with. We did Rialto? Grandaddy?? Lloyd Cole??? By the time you get to the end of 1996 and we see Travis and Stereophonics headlining consecutive shows at the Monarch, even I start to suspect we're taking the piss. Fair play to John. Without *How Long Is a Piece of Ning?* all those live nights would have just become a blur. Or, in the case of one night at the Dublin Castle on 18 May 1995, it would have become a Blur, as they played a special wee Club Spangle show.

The remainder of the '90s were no less vampish and vivacious and very often spent in doomy, often soon-to-be-doomed back rooms, but wisely Mr Banfield didn't hang around to catalogue the next multitude of live shows. At some point some sussed promoting cats involved in the Splash Club and the Fly followed Neil Pengelly's model and got us on board to start co-promoting *NME* 'On' nights, firstly at the Water Rats, then at the Falcon. Embrace played one night, which I remember very well because Danny McNamara sidled up to me at the bar and said, 'We're gonna be bigger than Oasis,' before gliding off again. These gigs were full of fanzine writers, industry sorts, indie hangers-on. It was a world of ticket buys by major labels, tick sheets for the door people, being ticked off by over-worked sound engineers. So much tick-tocking along years before TikTok. It was mad, weekly chaos, gig after gig after gig . . . and then I met Andy Pointy. At a live show by Tiny Too at the Falcon. Of course.

As well as bonding over berserk all-girl Anglo-Nordic outfits, Andy and I modelled the same trainers (adidas Campus, blue with yellow stripes) and shared a very weird fascination for *Midsomer Murders*, the flames of which were fanned by Andy frequently seeing DCI Barnaby's wife Joyce in his local coffee shop in Highbury and texting me whenever one of those sightings was occurring. He and his girlfriend Sarah had a promoting sideline called Club Pointy, and luckily for us they had the stamina and chutzpah to keep up with Fierce Panda's ever-restless release schedule and increasingly raffish promotional ideas.

And 'increasingly raffish promotional ideas' were fast becoming Fierce Panda's middle names. There was the Panda in a Vanda tour, with Seafood, Billy Mahonie and Tiny Too touring the nation, including a headline show at London School of Economics in Holborn. There was a canny rebranding of Camden

Dingwalls with Five Go Mad at Ningwalls, a five-band bill promoting the *Listen with Smother* EP, which saw the likes of Chest,
Tiny Too, Kidnapper and Ultrasound covering the Bee Gees,
A-ha, the Shangri-Las and Neil Young, while guests Lo-Fidelity
Allstars buffed up 'Diamonds Are Forever' and set fire to the
drum kit. We were back at Ningwalls five minutes later when a
Campag Velocet/Regular Fries double-header launch night for
their Panda split 7-inch was bounced out of a dodgy West End
venue roughly five minutes before soundcheck and the entire gig
was moved up Tottenham Court Road.

It was instinctive, carefree, packed full of madness: we had
Club Pointy v. Fierce Panda nights at the Water Rats and the
Falcon with Idlewild, Placebo, Babybird and anyone else who
needed a Panda single launching. By the end of the century, we
had set up base camp back at the Bull & Gate under the flag of
Club Panda where, as we may well have intimated before, we
put on monthly shows by bands with names like Coldplay and
Doves and Seafood.

But the one regular night that everyone – simply *everyone* –
remembers us for is Tuesday at the Dublin Castle. Exit sighing,
enter Club Fandango.

12 JANUARY 2020, 4.32 P.M.

Good news. I no longer have a special medical friend sitting at the end of my bed watching over me all of the day and all of the night. I'm off suicide watch and in between sweet, sweet sugar rushes I am keeping myself as busy as I can. I'm determined to be independent and, breathless pre-dawn panic attacks notwithstanding, not be a bother to the staff. In short, I never want the nurses to have cause to wipe my ever-diminishing, distinctly un-Kardashian bottom. Even if it takes an entire twenty-seven minutes to amble to the bathroom just to brush my teeth, which will exhaust me for the next three hours.

Even when I run out of water with which to dilute the by-now frankly dazzling array of Robinsons cordials, I disentangle myself from the wires and weariness wiring me to the bed and take myself off for a wander to get a fresh jug, wheeling my friendly drip alongside me down the corridor. At the time what I didn't realise is that someone in scrubs was still always watching my every move and judging my efforts and, presumably, poised to pick me up if I fell over. But the logic is simple: the more I do for myself in here, the more chance I have of getting myself out of here. Just keep moving, just keep improving.

19

JUST TOO BLOODY STUPID

In spite of the screaming white-van-man agony, spending six months sipping bitter lemon with Coldplay was actually very, very good PR for Fierce Panda. It put us even more on the map, gave us an extra degree of gravitas and respect no company called Fierce Panda possibly deserves. Far from representing a professional catastrophe, it seemed like losing out to a Parlophone label on top form was no disgrace in the A&R firmament. True, it wasn't great for our relationship with Mushroom, which came to a grinding halt, perhaps because of Coldplay playing hard to get (and winning), perhaps because they were hoping Bellatrix and Seafood would storm into the charts slightly higher than sixty-five and seventy-one respectively.

Not only did Mushroom split with Fierce Panda, but Ian from Damaged Goods also chose this moment to bow out. Another trawl around the A&R circuit with the Henry hoovers and espresso machines in fulsome effect was not something his punk rock sensibilities could contemplate. To this day I'm still impressed by his patience and professionalism in the face of the walking corporate corpse. After some intense discussions over a pint of lager we agreed that he'd keep on managing Seafood and I'd get the Fierce Panda label, with the mighty added bonus of Ian's right-hand man Philip Ingles becoming the Panda's label manager.

Thanks to Coldplay and the canny post-Mushroom release of 'Take the Long Road and Walk It' by the Music we were still in the eyeline of the majors. Just had to keep on keeping on keeping on, gigging in the rigging and pigging out on new bands. What else were we supposed to do?

It's a Friday night at the Monarch in Camden in 2001, seeing some band called Keane. Word has it they're connected to Coldplay in some way. Like them, it's a guitar-tonking fourpiece. The singer blushes a lot, which is a little bit unnerving. They're okay, but I'm distracted by meeting Paul Adam at the bar. A very nice man, I'm aware of his '90s endeavours at Polydor, working with the likes of Gene and Ian Brown. Turns out he has just been made head of the Universal Records imprint (rather than the Universal Music universe). He's looking at bringing in some cool developmental angle to his A&R team. He's fresh off judging some telly show called *Pop Idol* and inventing something called 'Busted'. 'We should talk more,' he says. And so we do. And then, eventually, we talk to the actual main Universal man Lucian Grainge in the grumpy headquarters glowering over the Hammersmith flyover. He shows me pictures of Ferraris on his computer screen. We do a new deal.

My suspicion with our first deal was that the Mushroom crew, already dealing with releases from Rawkus and Perfecto and Infectious, couldn't quite work out who were the priority, i.e. potential crossover, Panda bands and who were just myself and Ian Damaged's flights of indie fancy, primarily because we didn't tell them and so they worked absolutely everything from Astronaut to Seafood. This time there would be no similar mistake because we created an entirely new label called Temptation (after the New Order song – a heaven, a gateway, a hope) to keep the regular Fierce Panda nonsense away from the ever-spinning Island spokes. Do it clean.

You couldn't fault the set-up. There were design boards for Temptation logos. There were Temptation postcards, cribbing from the infamous Tory-powered Tony Blair devil-eyed posters, the alarming New Labour New Danger slogo transposed to New Label New Danger. There was a glossy Temptation fanzine called *Tempted?* And somewhere along the way there was a record company.

It was the polar bear opposite to the Mushroom relationship, and it was light moons away from the haphazardly spontaneous origins of the Panda. In fact, if the A&R approach had been half as diligent as the laying of the Temptation foundations, I'd be so rich I would have just paid someone else to write this book. It wasn't like I didn't know my role either: after we'd signed the Temptation Records deal, Paul Adam and his boss, Nick Gatfield, the head of Island Records, took me to a bar on Chiswick High Road one blustery afternoon and they said: 'What we want you to do, Simon, is bring us the next Coldplay.' At which we all laughed heartily and supped up our beers and collected our fags.

Another suspicion I had with the first deal was that Fierce Panda was slightly too distanced from the Mushroom crew. This time around we wondered if we should hot desk at the Island HQ, maybe once a week, once a month perhaps. It scarcely fits the indiepunk image of us crawling around the Holloway Road HQ honking like mad alternative geese and mocking our corporate overlords, but one thing you learn about being in the music industry is that if you are out of sight, you are out of mind, which can in turn send you out of your own mind. Anyway, that hot-desking idea. 'You're right, Simon,' enthused Paul Adam. 'You're absolutely right.' It never happened.

In fact, despite my weary enthusiasm for week-long Tube journeys on the District line to Turnham Green to try to turn them green with envy at our A&R skillings, occasional meetings and gig assignations aside, we were kept very much at arm's length. Island were welcoming, but not *too* welcoming. Always said the right things, said they loved working with us, loved the Temptation spirit, the demon-eyed vibe. Usually they did the right things as well, it just took them quite a bit of time to do those things in the right way.

I'd heard the warning shipping tales – how the major labels were giant-arsed tankers who took months to turn around releases while the indies were the nippy speedboats popping out pop nuggets by the minute, and this very much seemed to be the case. Did we honestly think we could still change things? Of course we did. We were indie on the inside, in every sense. And there were moments of great optimism. We swiftly signed crunchy Northamptonshire quartet Medium 21, who came armed with a clanky sound, kinda like fusing Idlewild's intensity with Elbow's melodies. We got on really well with the manager, Jamie Johnston, and took pickled eggs to the band in the studio.

Crucially, Paul Adam loved our signing and then gave us one of his Universal signings, the Rain Band, a swaggery Manc trio with a drum machine who were managed by Steve Harrison, who also looked after the Charlatans. So we had a roster – a small roster, but a roster nonetheless. We had a launch party with Medium 21 and the Rain Band and free beer at the Metro.

And we had backing for our Temptation label, and we still had a separate, entirely independent Fierce Panda ticking along – a glance at a lovely orange paper newsletter from 2003 reveals that we were putting out records by Death Cab for Cutie, the Polyphonic Spree and Six by Seven. Not untidy, and it gave us a good, steady start to hold onto as we bedded in and learned the corporate ropes.

Along the way I was even invited to an Island Records A&R powwow in some posh-nosh gaff on Portobello Road, an all-day affair where the talent-spotting team sat around riffing about who was good on the roster and who was good to kick off the label. In true arm's-length logic I wasn't actually invited to the whole day, just the afternoon session, by which point they were ruminating upon getting excellent new haircuts, or otherwise, for PJ Harvey, Pulp and Puressence.

I got my chance to update the roomful of experts on my sweet Panda journey. I said, 'Well, we're looking at signing these punk scamps from Stoke-on-Trent called Agent Blue for the *NME* vibe, and we're looking at signing these Rotherham emo kids called thisGIRLfor the *Kerrang!* vibe, and we want to sign Keane for the big massive radio vibe because they are the new Coldplay.' And I did my little bit with a little bit of blushing, but everyone nodded sagely and after I talked about Keane and Agent Blue and thisGIRL, Nick Gatfield told us how they'd just signed this girl from Finchley called Amy Winehouse, who they thought had some potential.

And then at the end of the conflab most of the people in the room piled into a mini-bus and headed off to Bristol to go and see a frantic pop band called Chikinki, which I was exceedingly impressed by because for all the tales of self-absorbed major labels' bozos spending all their spare time reading haircut styling magazines, it was honestly lovely to witness genuine A&R enthusiasm for a lager-fuelled hoik along the M4 first hand. Indeed, in the months ahead we would release a Chikinki single as they moved onto the Island roster, and did the same for some jabbering American combo called the Features, who'd been signed in the US.

We didn't get to sign thisGIRL to go alongside Ms Winehouse, but we did get to sign Agent Blue, who Paul Adam loved as much as, if not even more than, Medium 21, but probably not as much as Busted. If Agent Blue were purely on Fierce Panda, they would have made an indie-as-fuck punk rock album in Stoke-on-Trent for thruppence and a crate of crazy juice. As it was they made a Major Label Punk Rock Album with songs called 'Sex, Drugs and Rocks Through Your Window' in some residential studio with dinner at a dinner table and tennis courts. Dinner! Tennis courts!! What the fuck were we thinking??

We were thinking, 'Well, this is what major labels do, so best just let them get on with it and do what they do best, which is spend money on nice producers and nice studios and nice tennis racquets.' Because – and feel free to quiver along here, dear reader – Temptation was a proper major label indie, aka a mandie, i.e. a record company signing new alternative acts and spending old school major label cash on them, which is generally as sensible as building deck chairs out of very expensive cheese. In other words, we were making the same old mistakes as every other major label imprint since time immemorial, or at least since *C86*. Did Alan McGee and Tony Wilson make these same old mistakes, I pondered? It's weird being in a situation where you know you're heading for a fall but there is nothing you can do about it, because you don't have total control. In fact, you don't have any control whatsoever.

Re-enter the New Coldplay. Keane, the band we'd seen at the Monarch all those weeks back and thought were, y'know, okay. The New Coldplay tag wasn't actually designed to be that dismissive of their melodic efforts, as they were friends with them – apparently Coldplay once asked pianoman Tim Rice-Oxley to join their line-up. And Caroline Elleray was a key cog in this wheel as, on the back of her success with Coldplay, she had already taken Keane into the BMG publishing bosom. She was the direct link in the love train running from the Panda to the banda.

By this point in 2002, Keane had been rejiggled, reshuffled, reshaped. The guitars were gone, it was now a three-piece with vocals, drums and keys . . . and no guitars. Stripped back, but somehow thunderous and uplifting. The manager Adam Tudhope sent me some new demos. They sounded amazing. The key was seeing the new line-up at the 12 Bar on Denmark Street. Funny little venue with a normal-sized stage next to a tiny floorspace, with an overhanging balcony. I spent the gig squeezed in at the back, beneath the balcony hanging over me, so I could see Richard sitting down drumming and Tim sitting down playing keyboards and Tom's legs. I couldn't see his blushing face. And that changed everything, for the blushing boy squeezed in at the back. Within five minutes of the end of the set we were in the bar shaking on a Fierce Panda single deal.

Like Coldplay before them, Keane went down a gently putrid indie gigging route that was incongruous to say the least. Certainly, when it came to the traditional toilet circuitry gear share there wasn't a tremendous amount of Keane backline to be shared out. But again, no matter where they were on the bill or who they played with, they just got on with it. We started with a half-empty Club Fandango support slot at the Metro on Oxford Street and popped out a single called 'Everybody's Changing' and the world went a little bit berserk and the gigs got fuller and fuller and the band became hotter and hotter.

There was only one tiny, teeny-weeny problem – Paul Adam didn't like them, no matter how hard they and I tried. And God, I tried. As the radio plays increased and the shows got busier, he came along with me to see them at a bulging Bull & Gate, a rammed Water Rats, a crammed Dublin Castle, all stuffed wall-to-wall-to-Paul with A&R souls, but he didn't budge. There were things that puzzled people about Keane, for sure: the lack of guitars, the stack of keys, singer Tom Chaplin looking like a furious Aled Jones. And true, Tom hollering 'Hello Kentish Town!!!' to 148 punters at the Bull & Gate might have felt a bit over the top. But when he was hollering 'Hello Kentish Town!!!' to 2,000 people at the Forum a year later it made quite a lot of sense. Maybe Paul just didn't trust them.

In so many ways, it ended for us at a Club Fandango show with Keane headlining the ICA. From a dirty dozen at the Metro to 350 on the Mall in less than eleven months. I thought Tom looked a little bit Bonnie Tylerish with the fan blowing on his blond locks, a total eclipse of his art. Our second single, 'This Is the Last Time' was on the Radio 1 A-list. It was a pyrrhic victory. We were already out of the chase. To be fair to Paul, he got me a bonus meeting with Nick Gatfield, who told us he didn't want to sign Keane either. Eventually Caroline BMG told me at one point the band were sitting in the pub choosing who else to sign with. From being turned down by every record company, after a couple of singles on Fierce Panda they had twenty-three offers on the pub table. And I couldn't even think of twenty-three other record companies. Good luck, chaps. Really wish I was there.

One day soon after, Nick Gatfield phoned me up in the Holloway Road Panda office with some Very Important News. 'I'm doing a bit of a U-turn here, Simon, but we're going to sign Keane,' he said, brisk as a brusque talking broom. 'Ferdy's just come in with some new demos and they sound amazing.' New demos? Amazing?? Ferdy Unger-Hamilton??? Really? That's quite a bit annoying.

And so Island Records signed Keane. And so here is where I made my 435th mistake. In spite of being cut right out of the deal like a bruised slice of watermelon, I still honestly, stupidly, cretinously thought, 'Well, they won't forget me. We didn't just casually mention Keane alongside thisGIRL and Agent Blue at some A&R powwow on Portobello Road – with the two singles and the handful of gigs, we literally changed the entire course of their career. They'll make a mint on this lot, get their Temptation postcard investment back in spades and I'll be seen as "The Man Who Did What He Was Asked to Do" and delivered them the hot new Coldplay on a nicely warmed plate. Job done.'

Sadly, instead of being carried shoulder-high through the Island Records mentally departing market with pie-tasting ticker tape tumbling from the salt-and-vinegar sky, as the weeks rolled by, it became pretty apparent that the Panda was being erased completely from the Keane future script. Even more sadly, it ended as these things always seem to do, with me slumped on a sofa. This time I was in the Island Records reception, the lonely Panda boy in the leather jacket, creaking politely while the entire staff of Island Records trooped through the foyer on their way to the Big Meeting Room to discuss the brilliant promo campaign they were going to run on their amazing new signing, Keane.

Have you seen them? I caught them at the ICA! His hair was so lovely, wasn't it? Yes, I heard his lovely hair on Radio 1!

So breezy! Clipboards a-clipping, lips a-licking, spectacles a-sparkling, the occasional half-embarrassed glance or semi-guilty smile thrown the way of the lonely boy slumped on the sofa who'd brought them the sodding band in the first place. For me, it was a little bit like being a corpse at someone else's really fucking marvellous funeral.

So I went on through the deserted corridors to the Universal Records bunker to see Paul – we were pretty much the only people left in the entire building not in the keen-as-mustard Keane meeting. And I said to Paul, 'Well, Paul, we brought you the new Coldplay because that's what you asked for, but in the end you didn't want the new Coldplay, so I don't really know what I'm supposed to bring in any more, so I'm not really sure if there is any point in me bringing in anything whatsoever any more anyway.' And he nodded his sympathetic head and said, 'You're right, Simon, you're absolutely right.'

It was all very civilised and respectful and we very much agreed to agree and I walked back along the deserted corridor and through reception and out the front door, the front door by the meeting room, the big meeting room with the big meaty window through which you could see people departing the Island building, and every keen person in the Keane meeting could see me take my final bowed head walk. Don't look back. Walk away. Burn the past. Live today.

14 JANUARY 2020, 11.21 A.M.

Things are looking up. The numbers are beginning to go down. Enough for me to not warrant occupying this acute bed any more. At one point they want to move me back over to the Homerton for further recovery – they presume I live in London simply because Russell had called the ambulance from an address in Islington. After I remind them I actually live in Suffolk they decide they want to move me to a hospital in Ipswich or Bury St Edmunds, possibly a mental home. Much easier for the family to come visit, but I tell them to be perfectly honest the best place for me to recover is in Stowmarket with the girls and the pups. Home is where the heart is. Hospital is where the hurt is.

At one point in my heroic recovery, the psych teamsters are adamant I should start brainiac medication while I am still in the hospital so they can start balancing out the dosage before I go home. At the same point the medics are adamant that the kidneys aren't up to fending off any more drug invasions right now. It's a moot point anyway – I've already decided that I wanted to go home clean, as clear-headed as possible before starting any meds. For the first time in my surprisingly extended life I crave domestic normality. You wooze, you lose.

20

LOOPHOLES

Number forty-one is always the very, very worst number for a record company. It may all be fun and unipopcorn laughter when you're just an indie fankid scowling on the outside, when you see your favourite bands level out at number forty-two, when that ace new single gets stuck stuck stuck at forty-five. But hell's giant bonging bells, it hurts when it's *your* record. As they say in bingo clubs across the land – 'Four and one? Band on the run.'

By 2005, the top 100 was not an alien terrain for the Fierce Panda module. As outlined elsewhere, Oas*s rattled the Official Chart bean counters with 'Wibbling Rivalry' wobbling up to fifty-two in 1995; Mogwai were amazed to see their Black Sabbath-themed split single with Magoo get to sixty in 1998; Chris Martin was thrilled to see 'Brothers & Sisters' go in at number ninety-two at the back end of the previous century; and Ultrasound's 'Same Band' thundered in at ninety-nine in '97. Or was it ninety-seven in '99?

Even in February of 2005, hitherto unheralded dark-rock exponents Apartment had soared to number sixty-seven with 'Everyone Says I'm Paranoid'. Yet these successes were generally more by accident than design – we'd never tried to get what would be perceived to be a 'hit' 'single' before. But Art Brut themselves had good chart history: their 'Formed a Band' debut went to number fifty-two just over a year earlier on Rough Trade (I still don't know quite why they didn't sign them. I think James Endeacott was a fanboy but Geoff Travis wasn't feeling it). We'd then got their first Fierce Panda single 'Modern Art' three places higher, at forty-nine in December 2004. So we figured that with a bit of this and a bit of that and a bit of the other we might have a chance of breaking our Fab Forty chart duck.

At this time, the Art Brut band seemed to be in their happy place as well, which always helps. We loved singer Eddie Argos, who was fun and clever and a bit wobbly, the most accidental of could-be pop stars with a fondness for non-accidentally baiting Kele from Bloc Party. They made cranky, quirky, offbeat pop songs that were both restlessly naive and relentlessly knowing, and we took Art Brut to see the Hot Puppies at the Water Rats and Art Brut then took the Hot Puppies out on tour with them. They'd formed that kind of band.

We released their quirky, cranky, recklessly joyful *Bang Bang Rock & Roll* album, which people over here seemed to quite like and Eddie got his cuddlesome belly out for the *NME* to spoof Beth Ditto's admirably fleshy naked cover shoot. The album also did sensationally well in Germany. So well that they got on the front cover of the Teutonic *Rolling Stone* and Eddie was eventually found moving to Berlin. They did well in France as well. So well in fact that EMI France suggested EMI sign the band in the UK, which they did, and the band ended up moving from 'Emily Kane' to EMI/Mute, which, if nothing else, meant they became distant labelmates of our excellent raffish amigo Nick Cave.

★

Anyway, back in our happy place, the Panda family was going on holiday, to Cornwall. No ironically named bed-free Bedford van this time round. Scout was almost two whole years old, so it was time to visit a child-friendly hotel called Bedruthan Steps, on the northside, between Padstow and Newquay. Bunks for the kids, fake plastic chairs and rictus cheers aplenty for the groaning grown-ups. We still have the windbreak we bought to break up the wind on the beach.

Bedruthan Steps was a self-contained world for proper families on a proper family holiday. No sloping off to any nearby live venues for me, and as for local chart return shops stocking Fierce Panda Records I could presumably whistle down the wind, all the way back to Exeter. No worries. When we left the Holloway Road house, the Art Brut single 'Emily Kane' was comfortably in the top-forty midweek singles chart, kicking about around thirty-six. No hype, no bullshitwhangery, just one release on one CD and two 7-inch singles and a load of enthusiastic fans. It was looking good to be Fierce Panda's first ever bona fide hit single: 14 May 2005.

I listened to the chart rundown on wunnerful Radio 1 on my own in our room on Sunday evening, with Scout and Liann dining with the other jolly, and jolly knackered, holidaying families. Just me and the radio with bunk beds in the corner, moons and stars on the ceiling and the Atlantic rolling in and rocking out outside the window. Exciting! For a bit.

By the time they ticked down to number thirty-five, I was disappointed. By the time they hit thirty, I suspected the worst. By the time they were down to Maximo Park at fifteen, I was hoping miracles could happen. By the time they ambled past number eleven, where the Killers lurked, my hopes had died and I was finally, sadly, switching off. To add to the musical misery, Dogs (number twenty-nine), Duke Spirit (thirty-three), Idlewild (thirty-two) and A (thirty-five) had all gone top forty: Roger Morton managed Dogs, James Oldham's Loog label put out Duke Spirit, Idlewild were old Panda boys, the A band I'd enthused about greatly at the *NME*. I was now the runt of the chart litter.

In the end we missed the top forty by two sales. Two. Sodding. Sales. Singer-songwriter Lucie Silvas took 'our' place in the top forty. I have no idea where the nearest chart return shop was. You can't look these things up because they are Top Secret. And I suspect Liann would have taken a dim view of me leaving her with Scout to scoot off to scour the streets of Penzance for shops with the *Music Week* chart winking out of the front window. Besides, if I had nipped off to, say, Exeter Music-Tastic Megastore to buy six copies of 'Emily Kane' to keep us in the chart, then her major record company would have presumably promptly sent a work-experience lackey out to buy seven copies of 'The Game Is Won' to make sure Lucie won the game.

We could try to seek solace in being higher than the Stereo-phonics' 'Dakota' and 'Banquet' by Bloc Party, at forty-two and forty-three respectively, both falling out of the forty, but it doesn't really work. Art Brut never got near the chart again. Apart from October that year, when 'Good Weekend' got to number fifty-six. But, apart from then, they never got near the chart again, on Fierce Panda or otherwise. Worse still, in July of 2005 downloads started being counted towards chart sales. From being a hamster's whisker away from getting into the top forty, within a year we wouldn't even be able to get our hottest platters into the top 200. For Fierce Panda, the game was very much lost.

It really is the hope that kills you. I've seen fellow indie labels virtually bankrupted, if not totally destroyed, by the clamour for moderate chart success, plagued by playing the majors playing themselves at their own crazy game, which back then appeared to be getting their new acts' singles high enough in the chart to attract the interest of the *Top of the Pops* bookers. Hence the multi-formats, the subsidised releases, the loss-leading press adverts, the eye-bleeding tour support, the half-crazed belief that all that time and money invested in a bunch of totally lunatic musicians will somehow pay off.

The other thing is: our chart success rate, or lack of it, was somewhat skewed by the fact that, for much of the '00s, at our supposed A&R peak, we spent more time trying NOT to get in the charts than we did getting into the top forty. With the early limited edition 7-inch singles the commercial limitations were fairly obvious, especially as all the early 'classic' releases by Placebo and Embrace were literally limited to 1,000 or so copies and so could never sell enough to chart. With Keane, the Polyphonic Spree and the Maccabees meanwhile, whose records weren't so limited in terms of pressings, their various managers made concerted efforts to find excellent new ways of getting banned from the charts, primarily because they somehow felt that their band going into those charts anywhere between forty-one and ninety-two would have a catastrophic effect on their chances of getting a major label deal.

As some of my favourite ever records had stalled between forty-one and ninety-two, this was an attitude I never really understood. We certainly had civilised discussions about the issue and we made it clear from our side that we saw getting to number sixty-three on a debut indie single as Really Quite A Good Thing, but the management teams weren't for budging. And, while we've built at least half of our so-called reputation by doing things the wrong way round, even we thought that trying to get the bands into the chart when they didn't actually want to get into the chart, unless it was the top ten, which patently wasn't going to happen, was a perverse step too far, even for something called Fierce Panda.

So while the tortuous specifics evade me now, I believe that the Maccabees' 'Latchmere' was deliberately disqualified by the inclusion of a free sticker with each single, *Soldier Girl* by the Polyphonic Spree counted as an EP and so was discounted from the charts because EPs couldn't count, and I can't even remember why Keane couldn't be counted, although both our releases, 'Everybody's Changing' and 'This Is the Last Time' were single compact disc singles because we thought their politely burgeoning fanbase would be more into shiny CDs than seedy vinyls. So Keane never did a 7-inch with us. As soon as they signed to Island, they released a 7-inch and said it was their dream come true, which was weird. Anyhooo, this means that we spent large chunks of the '00s actively seeking out novel ways to not have hit records, which is another pretty classic Fierce Panda way of doing things.

Looking back at the whole Chart Brut escapade, what is really quite interesting is that our highest ever position came when we were a totally independent indie label – no Infectious, no Island, just indie old us. Which kinda says something.

So does the fact that I've never needed to listen to the top-forty countdown since that stormy night, ruefully sitting on a lonely hotel bed in Bedruthan Steps, with the Atlantic waves rolling in and the Panda hopes flickering out. The chart rundown was forever dead to this transistor radiohead.

16 JANUARY 2020, 3 P.M.

It's time to make good my escape, to break royally free of the Royal Free. I pack up my Viz *annual and my wash bag and my dazzling array of Robinsons cordials, pick up clothes that are certainly not clingy as before, say goodbye to my fellow inmates, to the nurses, to the pandas by the lift. Be seeing you.*

I get back home to Suffolk eighteen days and 20 million lifetimes after that last fateful train journey to London, lockdowned and self-isolating two whole months before the rest of the nation catches up with me. I'm sick just after we pass by Bury St Edmunds on the A14. Old habits never die. All things considered, I think I've held it together pretty well. Mind you, I'm the one who's spent the first fortnight of the year living on bowls of screaming custard, so perhaps I'm not the ideal judge.

21

GUNPOWDERKEG

I'm exceedingly pleased to report that in the midst of all the chart-swerving major label graduates, we kept our feet on the ground and our faces in the gutter by frequently returning to and then relentlessly pursuing the reckless six-track EP concept until it was a wizened husk of its previously glorious self, interspersing the A&R star-seekers with ever-more fistfuls of fresh talent. Sometimes the bands ended up on a six-track EP because we were borrowing them from a happy label home elsewhere. Some of the bands on the six-trackers were perhaps not quite ready or strong enough for their own single release. Some choices were just crazy flights of fancy. Sometimes their name or their nous just happened to fit the lunacy in my head at the time.

There was a French quote on the back of every sleeve. Like most things, it started with the best of political sloganeering intentions. Then we just started to nick lines from 'Fade to Grey' by Visage. From the run-out groove messages to the back of the sleeves these were complete and completely painstaking works of art – very much like creating a fanzine, in fact. Shabby, half-cut art for sure, but art nonetheless. Often I'd cycle in through the deserted City of London to the abandoned *NME* office over the weekend to do the dirty work. Just me and the lights of Hackney shining on the horizon and a scalpel, cutting, cutting, cutting out the words photocopied down to the minute optimum on the industrial-sized copying machine down by the art department.

Once again, in lieu of any worldwidening interweb, I found myself ambling up Tottenham Court Road looking for suitable images to fit the mad concepts. If you look hard enough, you will notice that several Panda images were filched from books purchased at Foyles.

At some point we got flash and the wraparound sleeves evolved into fancy-dan gatefold releases. No more stuffing of plastics! Glorious glossy gatefolds glimmering in the gloom! Heady days! And they started coming out on CD as well! But, whatever the format, whatever the sheen of the sleeve, they were always absolutely excellent fun to compile and design – and, if we were really lucky, we could squeeze not one, but two whole launch parties out of the six bands.

So there was an element of seriousness in the midst of the chaos: beyond the puns there were some terrific tracks by some excellent bands and some even more terrific launch parties. There was also a degree of authenticity lurking behind the punnery. Quip it real good. *Nings and Roundabouts* is still the greatest compilation title of all time (beating *Where the Wild Nings Are* by a furry ear), aided in no small way by cover art featuring pandas playing – yes – on swings and roundabouts. And look very closely on the artwork for our Welsh compilation, our third ever album release, and you will see a dedication to a certain

John Williams: *Dial M for Merthyr* was a tribute to my dead-clever dead Welsh dad.

Ultimately, we stopped releasing the classic vinyl six-trackers because we simply couldn't get the very best bands we wanted. The last six-trackers we did were on CD only in about 2010, which meant we could make them seven- or eight-track EPs, which totally missed the point of the original concept and totally missed the point for people who had lovingly collated the double-vinyl editions.

True fact: the Fierce Panda compilations have their own Wikipedia page.

I don't.

22 FEBRUARY 2020

Having thundered into London virtually every week for thirteen years, I go into the cockney capital just once in the first six months of 2020. The task is to close down the office, on Saturday 22 February, two days before Fierce Panda's twenty-sixth birthday. The panda is going into hibernation. The Leroy House HQ is stripped to its bare bear essentials, with the back catalogue, the tea-making facilities, the orange sofa all taken out for a good packing. I can't pretend it's a fun day out – in fact, it's absolutely horrible – but it has to be done. The Framily is here in full effect. All hands are on deck – especially with regards to the shifting of the boat bar. Two and a half decades' worth of indie nonsense are piled higher and higher into a hire van and driven by Russell and Martin to a lock-up in downtown Chingford. Three trips up and down through Dalston and Stoke Newington and Stamford Hill and Tottenham in a white transit stuffed full of compact discs and flattened furniture and shattered dreams.

Friends have rallied round. There are things like mortgage holidays, they said. Simon is vulnerable, they said. Credit card companies have to take that on board, they said. The timing was perfect. Nobody outside of the hospital visitors knew about the Grand Malarkey. If anyone heard anything at all, it was that I was feeling a wee bit ill. Nothing to see here. I let other friends know on a need-to-know basis, but I did that very slowly and very cautiously and as undramatically as possible. I'm very, very tired. Ultimately what I need is a long stint in a comfy armchair and a year or so off the gig circuit. What hope have I got of that ever happening?

Within weeks all the other top-secret Leroy House offices have been vacated. Mortgage holidays are top of the Google hitlist. SXSW – Fierce Panda's first ever official Austin showcase – has been moved online as the good burghers of Texas decide they don't want thousands of people flying in from around the globe to import the disease. I have no alibi.

22

ALL COMPASSES GO WILD

In spite of our best endeavours in the '90s, after the Britpop battleground had been cleared, Camden lapsed back into old habits and going out to see gigs at the start of the week was like being stuck in a sad-faced loop of poor-quality bands playing to poor-quality crowds, and poor-quality audiences enduring poor-quality live sets. Maybe one in four bands was worth a casual perusal, at best. So we did something about it, and the something we did was take those one in four half-decent bands and put them all on together in one fully formed show. We went to Jim and Tony Bugbear at the Dublin Castle and just asked them to give us their Tuesday evenings. We formalised the relationship by calling the new night Club Fandango, after a very old fanzine in-joke. Panda band KaitO headlined our opening night in March 2001 and off we jolly well went.

I will cautiously suggest that this is where we hit our promoting prime. I say 'cautiously' because beyond sharing identical indie-boy trainers and a residual affection for Richard Briers turning psycho vicar in Badger's Drift, Andy and I worked alongside each other on hundreds of shows. Working on that basis, one would assume that our memories would dovetail in some shape or form, yet, whenever we've been asked by reviewers or researchers to recall what happened at our own shows by, say, the Killers or Coldplay, we come up with entirely different stories. This might well be because, while I was out front in the pub swanning around preparing for the live action, Andy was frequently backstage fighting the good fight, swatting away the A&R roustabouts who'd turned up en masse to see the Arctic Monkeys' soundcheck or placating bands who were fuming about having to go on first at big Panda nights out, like they were playing some benefit gig at the Brixton Academy or something.

Nonetheless, considering that the Club Fandango vibe was an entirely selfish premise based entirely on my bone-idle reluctance to trawl around the toilet circuit it went on to do astoundingly well. Razorlight, Death Cab for Cutie, the Futureheads, Fightstar, Bloc Party, Hot Chip, Go! Team, Kaiser Chiefs, the Killers, Arctic Monkeys and Keane stormed the Dublin Castle turrets, as did dozens of briefly indulged A&R favourites and many more hopeful fellows and fillies seeking to have their fill of the thrill of the chase. And I Like Trains + Holy Fuck + Cats and Cats and Cats was obviously the greatest Club Fandango poster of all time.

If the bands were rubbish, the company was great, and if the bands were great then the company became even greater. For one night only per week, we created dream pop-up indiepop events where once again sweet-faced fanzine kids could rub shoulders at the bar with shady music industry execs – like Club Spangle, Fandango became the place to play, the place to be seen, the place to be *obscene* in. In an innocent indie way, natch.

We thought it would last for ever, and for many years it did. When DCI Barnaby's sidekick Sgt Scott turned up at the Dublin Castle bar one night and endured a chat with the frankly giddy Club Fandango promoting team, it was the strongest, strangest case of art imitating life imitating more art since an unfortunate Suzi Quatro got electrocuted to death onstage at the Midsomer Rock Festival. You can take the girl out of Essex . . .

But those chewy Tuesday nights didn't last for ever and ever. In fact, I suspect that we stayed at the Dublin Castle for two years too long. In fact, I know this because we seemingly endured putting on every single raggedly pissed post-Libertines band of urchins, and then, on 4 August 2009, the Crookes played and a few things changed for ever. There were some industry faces there for the loafered New Pop pups – but only a few. Where were the rest? 'Some band called Frankie & the Heartstrings are playing some night called White Heat at some place called Madam Jojo's,' sniffed an A&R insider, and they were as well. With Artrocker already artrocking at the Buffalo Bar on the same night, Tuesday was suddenly the fruity new Friday and Wednesday simply didn't know where to look. Club Fandango was now the third coolest Tuesday night in town.

We always seemed to be on the cusp of the edge of the precipice of taking great leaps forward: there was a development deal with Live Nation, there were regional Club Fandango shows in Derby, Bristol and, most successfully, Manchester. There were the annual mini-festivals – Pandamonium kicking off January, a Fistful of Fandango in the autumn, where we took over both rooms at the 229 with British Sea Power, Camera Obscura, Friendly Fires and Electric Soft Parade. There were branded nights with *Rock Sound*, Radio 6 Music, Ben Sherman and Doc Martens. We were regular strollers on the Camden Crawl, occasional intruders into In the City, general gadabout townies never lacking in ambition and never not looking for the next amazeballs gigging opportunity.

But, as the '00s shuddered to a close, it was becoming harder and harder to run our showcase nights: there were more and more bands and more and more promoters, but not necessarily any more fans to pick up the promoting slack. In fact, it is almost impossible to over-emphasise the explosion in live music around this time: the bigger national promoters were suddenly more inclined to take chances on fresh talent and swoop down to our entry level to snap it up, as were live agents, who suddenly wanted paying for bands (often apologetically) who weren't worth any punters and had mad ideas about rocketing their bands up out of the toilet circuit as speedily as possible. We started to see bands not bring a single person to their own show. We started to see bands not bothering to turn up without telling us. Venues had to start providing backline because headline bands couldn't be bothered to bring their own drum kit or amps because they didn't have a van or a plan – the idea of gigs being a loss-leader leading towards future glory was a perturbed concept.

We put on live shows in the Buffalo Bar in Highbury, Birthdays in Dalston and the Borderline in Soho – and they are just some venues beginning with 'B' that have since been shut down. We put on bands at the Camden Caernarvon Castle, which burnt down, at the Metro, which got closed down in the same Crossrail rebuild that did for the Astoria. We injected some colour into the Red Eye in King's Cross, which became a block of flats, and almost fell through the hole in the middle of the floor of the Archway Tavern, which presumably collapsed in on itself. And, despite us promoting there for nine years or so, the Dublin Castle is still standing proud.

Luckily, myself and Andy had a Plan B. Or, in this case, a Plan B&G. We actually tried to buy the Bull & Gate at one especially optimistic point. We got a daytime guided tour of the building and I have very fond memories of casually noting that the empty venue smelled very much like the gorilla's cage at London Zoo. We couldn't balance the numerous business numbers in the end, but that didn't dent our ongoing enthusiasm for the old gaff. We got on well with the landlords, Pat and Margaret, who'd been in charge since the early '80s, and we'd still been dabbling in monthly shows there through much of the '00s – Keane played the Panda's eleventh birthday show in 2005, the Maccabees played our twelfth anniversary a year later; the Wombats' first London show took place there soon after – and we took over the booking diary in the summer of 2010 when Andy and Phil Bull & Gate retired and invited us to take over, which was exceedingly nice of them.

There were several excellent things about this venture. For the very first time ever we had complete control over a venue diary. We brought in nice people like Mybandsbetterthanyourband and Myspace to co-promote shows, while Steve Lamacq had a monthly Going Deaf for a Living gig. We mixed up the artistic sensibilities and put on quizzes, comedy nights and quirksome musical talents aplenty. We smartened up the venue, tarted up the promotion, tightened up the booking. To totally screw with the indie-promoting timeline continuum we even resurrected Club Spangle under the Club Fandango umbrella. And we finally got the chance to use our very, very excellent Pub Fandango joke, which we hung on a sign above the front door, free to creak in the cutting, cutting, cutting Kentish Town Road winds.

There were also several not so excellent things about this venture. There were some great nights, big fun to be had – we had the cheapest lager of any live venue left in town (£3.50 for a pint of Heineken) and the likes of Slaves, Coasts, Lonely the Brave, Future of the Left and Public Service Broadcasting all came to partake, but truth be told these weren't the most glorious of glory days for the venue. Still, we tried our very best. The relaxing of the licensing laws meant that venues could stay open until all hours, and so over the weekend the likes of the Dublin Castle and the Barfly raked it in by playing the Rakes at indie discos until 3 a.m. We tried it out one Friday night after much pleading with Pat and Margaret and, as expected, the Libertines' liberteenies turned up in their feral hoards and did unmentionable things in the indescribable toilets and Pat and Margaret said never again.

In a no less ghoulish way, Sundays were given over to death-metal shows, sometimes all-dayers (it was the black sabbath after all), where the bands' names were so metallic and deathly you needed subtitles to comprehend their mentally flamboyant logos on the poster. Brutal Dwarf, Bloodied Scrotum and Belligerent Necrophiliac Fuckdogs are just three names I've made up. But, then again, perhaps I haven't. Pat and Margaret – Irish Catholics to the core – put up with much of the metallic chaos with a sorry sigh and a turn of the old blind papal eye. But at one especially memorable show the headline band decided to carry a coffin in through the front door, through the crowd and right up to the stage – whereupon the lid flipped open and the singer popped out, very much alive. The land-lording religious sensibilities could take no more. That coffin was the final nail in the Sunday death metal . . . oh, hang on a minute.

Another tricky problem was the creeping gentrification that had seen musicians and artists priced out of Camden and up to Kentish Town – thanks, Britpop! There was no further for them to go with upmarket Hampstead the next stop on the line, so the artists and musicians decamped to the cheaper wildlands of Dalston and Stoke Newington and Hackney. No worries – they were only fifteen minutes away on the overground train. Big problems – those musicians and artists started creating their own east London musical communities and putting on their own free gigs in brand-new venues like the Old Blue Last and the Shacklewell Arms. They had no need of north London any more. Thanks to Myspace and Mybandsbetterthanyourband we were still able to get some of the cool bands to play, but getting their cool mates was a different struggle altogether.

As the months went by there was also the creeping shadowy sense that other potential buyers were lurking, ready to take over the venue and find a way of balancing those bullish books. Eventually the Bull & Gate closed its doors for ever to live music on Saturday 4 May 2013, pretty much exactly three years since that venue diary ended up in our paws. In the end it wasn't creeping gentrification that did for it, not directly, anyway – it was its second cousin gastrofication that fired the final bullet in the Bully head as the incoming Young's brewery brewed up takeover ideas about poncing the pub up, notably turning the lovely old live backroom into a restaurant serving gastro burgers to what I could only presume would be ghastly music haters. You can say many things about the Bull & Gate over the decades, but 'poncy' really wasn't one of them.

It got a grand send-off, a whole week of events full of friends and indie family, some of whom had been drinking there for nigh on forty years, under the tidy banner of 'Play Your Respects'. There were headline shows by Six by Seven, by Jesus Jones, and with Steve Lamacq presenting Goldheart Assembly on the penultimate night with Nadine Shah and the Hosts in support. In typically haphazard pandango fashion, I wasn't there for the very last night, when Ed Harcourt courted the weeping hordes with a pub piano plonked in the middle of the venue and 'Hey Jude' serenaded the farewell to indie twilight. I'd got too honkered the night before. It was Lammo's fault.

'I'm taking Friday afternoon off work so we can get to the pub early,' he'd announced a few days before. Fair enough. Get in a few liveners around teatime then? No sirree. 'We're meeting at the Abbey Tavern at 2 p.m.' Sweet Jesus. It was one of those days where half the audience hit the curry house *before* the gig. It was also one of those special, spicy gigs where emotion fizzed in the air, the sense that sweet, sweet music was floating around absolutely everywhere, even in the toilets. In fact, *especially* in the toilets.

Once again, I walked out of the Bull & Gate, this time as Goldheart Assembly finished playing 'Sad Sad Stage' on one of the saddest, saddest stages in old London Town.

I went out for a cry and I never went back.

No matter how often people told me the ghastly gastroburgers really were excellent.

15 MARCH 2020

*Liann was told time and time and time again by the medics and psych team-
sters and experts at the Royal Free that even out of hospital this was going to
be hard. I had no more need of that acute bed but I certainly wasn't out of the
troubled woods. I'm still alive, but I'm in a really bad place. It couldn't be
any worse. I'd definitely failed to kill myself— typical. On the other hand, I'd
certainly given it my best shot. People who make that much effort to end it all
have got serious problems, said the psych experts. Crucially, I was going to
have sessions with a psychiatrist who was going to tear me down and rebuild
an entirely new me from the double-trouble rubble.*

*None of these things actually happen. The psychiatrist is very nice and non-
challenging. He tells me that depression is an illness, an ailment, a sign of
internal damage. You break the leg, you heal the broken leg. You break the
brain, you heal the broken brain. After half an hour of chatting in his top-
secret office (BMI hospital Ipswich, near the Witches' speedway track) he
studies his copious notes and decides I am what they call a 'happy depressive', which, he says, explains why I was unable to make people aware of the
blackened seriousness of my predicament. Smile and the world won't be with
you. Right towards the end of the first session he asks me about my father. I
do a bit of explaining. I swear his eyes light up as the note-taking hits fever
pitch. Psych Gold! 'That explains everything,' he says. 'This has been lurking within you for fifty years. It had to come out at some point, it just needed
a trigger.' Wait — there's actually an underlying psychological reason for this
malarkey? That explains a lot of everything.*

*He prescribes me some drugs. He says there is every chance I will need to take
them for the rest of my surprisingly elongated life. As we leave the top-secret
BMI hospital my psychiatrist says I am the perfect patient. I still don't know
if this is a good thing.*

23

GOING TO HEAVEN
TO SEE IF IT RAINS

If forty-one is always the very, very worst chart position for a record company, then forty-one is presumably always the very, very worst age for a record-company owner. In fact, as any A&R person turns forty-one years old, when the room is quiet and the daylight almost gone, I trust that a ghostly shiver crosses their soul as they slowly topple out of the hit parade of life. It certainly did with me. The year after we peaked – in so many ways – with Chart Brut, I myself felt that spectral tremble.

For me, it seemed like in the space of twelve months I'd aged 13,000 years, if not a bit more. Like that bit in the Paddington Bear movie when Mr Brown roars up to the maternity unit with a pregnant Mrs Brown on the back of a Triumph Thunderbird motorbike, and then returns to pick her and the newborn up in a beige Volvo estate, you go from rocking leathers to rocking chairs with seemingly nothing in between.

In short, in 2006 we moved to the countryside and I tried very, very hard to grow up. The reasons for moving the family were simple enough: with a small child called Scout and a large dog called Shadow the foreign sunshine holidays were usurped by staycations in cottages in Norfolk and Suffolk, away from the moshing masses. Peace at last. After a few such praycations you start thinking, 'Perhaps we could buy one of these cottages and use it as a holiday home!' And after a couple more sunnydaycations you start thinking, 'Why, we could just move rock, stock and barrel from Holloway Road!'

So, after some serious reconnaissance of horse jockeys' play rooms in Newmarket and wise kitchen basements in Wisbech, not to mention a good hard look at fancy dan property near Eye, we landed in Stowmarket, smack bang in the middle of Suffolk. Postcode IP14, on the mainline from London Liverpool Street to Norwich, just turn left at Ipswich. The geographical location was geo-logical enough – any closer to London and it would have been too expensive, ditto if it had been any further up towards Norwich, or further east to the coast, or further west to Cambridge, or further south-south-west to Lavenham. Stowmarket was just right.

Plus Goldilocks and all of her three bears would have had a field day exploring our lovely new wonky rickety old farmhouse, with its bendy beams and comfortably scorched fireplaces and some bits from mediaeval times and other parts, like the giant old chimney, seemingly perpetually bending against the wind. An acre and a half for Shadow the dog. A 23-minute walk to Stowmarket station to catch the one-train-an-hour to London Town for paps the old hound. On 31 October 2006, we made the big move. At the age of forty-one years and thirty-six days I'd finally become a farmer's boy.

PANDAMONIUM!

To say it was a shock to the old system would be something of a blunderstatement, a wonderunderstatement. Having bowled around north-east London for four decades with Tubes and buses and urban chaos aplenty, we had been dropped into the middle of the middle of nowhere. No Tubes. No Waitrose behind the back garden. No pubs within a two-minute stroll. No live venues within any walking distance at all, at least until the John Peel Centre for Creative Arts was invented in 2010. No packing up and going back to London after a week of getting thoroughly peace-d.

Maybe it was the crushing rural sound of silence. Maybe it was the starry, starry nights. Maybe it was the fresh air. Maybe it was the lack of a decent local, but when I got to forty-one on my own farm I definitely started doing strange things, and not just on the sit-down lawn mower. Scout was turning three years old and investigating everything, so those tiny grabbing hands saw the removal of my ear rings and the nose ring. And I stopped wearing band tees. I call these the Gap Years, primarily because I made a concerted effort to wear logo-free T-shirts purchased in bulk from a certain fashion store I won't mention here. Only problem was, without a band name on the front and a sticky-out label on the neck, I couldn't work out which way on the shirt should go. A sartorial disaster when dressing in the stumbly half-light of the Suffolk dawn. It's very difficult, this grown-up hoopla, I mulled to myself on several occasions.

There was also something about our postcode that was really nagging at me. IP14 had sounded so familiar from the very first time we visited Stowmarket, but I couldn't for the life of me think why. Then one day we had a plumber round to fix the first of a million plumbing issues that plague our wonky old pipes.

He apologised for being late: 'I was just finishing off a job at Peel Acres,' he said.

Wait – did you say you'd just been finishing off a job at Peel Acres?

'Yeah, it's just over the fields out there,' he said, pointing in a south-south-westerly direction towards the nearby village of Great Finborough.

And so it was, and so everything fell into place – IP14 was the postcode on all the record envelopes sent to John Peel over the years. Indeed, the man himself had once sent a youthful Fierce Panda a postcard out of the blue apologising for the intrusion, but if we didn't have any profound aversion to sending him any of our music, might it be possible to send our records his way for his show? The postcard was in the traditional seaside style, with four small pictures giving us a summary of the wonders of Stowmarket. It was only on closer inspection that I realised those 'wonders' included some abandoned roadworks and a surly curry house. It was a message.

Sadly, the man himself had been abruptly taken from us on a South American holiday in 2004, two years before we moved. But for me, those East Anglian musical roots ran deep, and from UEA in '82 to IP14 in '06 there was a mystical radio aura shrouding our new surroundings. As well as John Peel living in some magical land called Great Finborough in Suffolk, Steve Lamacq was born in Essex, hence his previous life spent watching cool bands at the Square in Harlow and the never-ending heartbreak of supporting Colchester United. We'll even throw Alan Partridge into the megamix, if only because, far from being region-shamed by the Crimplened one's cringeworthy allegiance to the Broads and ladies of Norfolk, when the *I, Partridge* book came out Norwich train station was quite literally emblazoned with Partridge promo pizzazz. Embrace the madness, kids. Embrace all of the madness.

And lest we forget, the potent influence of the radio stations anchored off the east coast in the North Sea in the '60s, when newfangled disc jockeys would canter up on the mainline from Liverpool Street to Harwich to catch the boat to rock 'n' roll hope and glory on a bigger boat. I often take the pups to the Suffolk coastline, not to Islington-on-Sea, i.e. Aldeburgh or Southwold, but much further south to the more rough 'n' ready seaside fancies of Felixstowe. Position yourself correctly and you can see Harwich over the Stour estuary, the booze ferries heading off to the Hook of Holland dodging the giant container ships sneaking into Felixstowe Docks from Hamburg, Algiers, Colombo, Rotterdam or anywhere.

And I look across the sleet grey water and I think of all the things they would have been playing on board *Caroline* under the debonair auspices of pirate radio. Is that the ghostly nautical whisper of 'Arrrrrr You Lonesome Tonight?' being washed in with the tide? Yes, yes, I think it is, matey.

Crucially, as if Fierce Panda experienced its very own muddled-life crisis, at this very same time the label stopped releasing one-off singles. It was a way to go – between the spring of 2005 and the autumn of 2006, between NING 169 and NING 190, we released debut-or-pivotal tracks by people with names like Battle, Gledhill, Boy Kill Boy, the Revelations, the Maccabees and Dead Disco. You may well remember some of these acts, you may well never have heard of many of them. We remember them all because we released their pivotal-or-debut singles on mostly 7-inch and CD, put on some terrific launch gigs with them, drank some lovely drinks at those launch gigs, let the good times roll.

In the space of twenty-one single releases those six bands got better and bigger deals. One of these bands got £1 million because they were about to sign to Warners, but Universal caught wind of the deal and simply doubled the Warners offer. Between them these acts signed deals with Atlantic, Mercury (they nabbed two of them), 679, Polydor and Sine/Sony. One of them was even signed by Korda Marshall.

That being the case, we didn't decide to stop releasing one-off singles because they were crashing and burning and nobody cared. No, we stopped doing them because we knew the system was no longer working. To sound monumentally conceited for a moment, I felt that Fierce Panda had become a total A&R cliche. We were, in many ways, a massive success. A massively useless success, but a massive success nonetheless. We were lucky – there was still a semblance of an A&R boom time, and as far as I could ascertain we were still firing on all cylinders in terms of our contacts and the sense of community at our Club Fandango nights. And in many other ways I hated myself for playing the game.

Because the major labels wanted our bands, not our ears, they were content to pay over the odds and outbid each other rather than dig any deeper and go direct to the A&R source – us – and try to get those acts much earlier and therefore much cheaper. Buy, buy Battle, Battle bye-bye. Not that I blame the bands or their teams for a single moment – it was never their responsibility to pay for my tea bags or cover my mortgage. We even dallied with overrides – one major offered us a point on profits after their ex-Panda act achieved 100,000 album sales, another conversely offered us a point of profits capped at 100,000 album sales by their old Panda act, by which point we looked very confused and gave up. To prove our point, taking on board those advances and flurries of A&R fury, out of those six acts, who really succeeded? The Maccabees' three albums on Fiction would suggest they carried off a pretty decent career, certainly in terms of credibility and kudos, but out of the other five acts you'd struggle to pick out any notable post-Panda glories that anyone has told me about.

It was of course in one way total commercial fucking suicide. Over the previous twelve years we had built ourselves a tiny reputation as the little old label who released early singles by bands who signed to bigger labels, and we were very deliberately standing on that tiny reputation in our boots and stamping on it. Or we were cutting, cutting, cutting off our broken nose to spite our sagging face. But beneath the corporate covers there was a massive commercial shift occurring. We've already noted that downloads started qualifying for the charts in the middle of 2005, pointing towards the dizzy digital horizon. (By some frantic irony, the Revelations, who were an indie version of a '60s girl group, were put together by sometime Hoover Dam frontman Adam Howarth, who worked at some new online shindig called Napster.)

Top of the Pops popped its televisual tip-top clogs in 2006, removing the need for major labels to blag multi-formatted indie-ish bands high enough into the charts to catch the ear of the top of the poppermost bookers. There was already a drop-off in terms of decent new guitar bands at key A&R showcase shindigs like In the City as electronic duos and pop trios started to proliferate, while the Nu Rave scene had seen a generation of post-Libertines kids feel liberated enough to throw dayglo sequencers and cow bells into the mix. In fact, I distinctly remember lying under the bar of the Midland Hotel in Manchester at In the City in 2008 when I was told that Little Comets had signed to Sony. I distinctly remember that because I defiantly remember thinking, 'Well, they're the last guitar band to sneak under the A&R wire, then.' And, for several barren years, they were.

We could see which way the wind was blowing, and that wind was blowing towards major labels not signing guitar bands again for a very long time. Besides, it wasn't as though we weren't the only ones who could sense the way that indie wind was blowing: on 11 September 2006, exactly two weeks before my forty-first birthday, Leeds all-girl trio Dead Disco released the last ever bona fide one-off single on Fierce Panda, called 'Automatic'. Within two years singer Victoria Hesketh had left the Dead Disco band for dead and reappeared as pop diva Little Boots.

I don't actually have any regrets about killing the golden one-off-single goose. There'd be something sensationally creepy if we still aspired to be hanging with supercool singles labels like Speedy Wunderground or Nice Swan nowadays, something a bit grubby, a bit gruesome, a bit Peter Stringfellow about it all. Or Peter Ningfellow. It was high time for us to do some growing up, to become a serious label for serious people, or at least make an attempt to progress from the punnery and funnery that had defined us since 1994.

We'd also got some proper investment by the mid-'00s, total-ling half a million quid from enthusiastic investors Michael Burke and Steve Dickson in Canada. It was a deal that simply had to be done, we had to evolve. And evolve we did, releasing one great album by Goldheart Assembly, two nonchalantly ace albums by the Raveonettes, three tub-thumping albums by the

Crookes, and dozens more mournfully excellent projects. We upgraded the Panda office, upping sticks from Holloway Road and moving into some gaff called Aberdeen House in Highbury Grove. Yep, the very same place where Sub Pop had been based a decade earlier. Lovely office, too. It had a sink and a mezzanine level and we were right near the front of the building, near the cafe, which was handy for indulging in their house speciality of frittata while we tried to work out how people actually danced to the Fratellis.

There wasn't actually that much of an alteration in the Panda working methods – by 2006 we'd already released a riot of colourful compilations, mini-albums and long-players by the likes of I Like Trains, Winnebago Deal and Death Cab for Cutie, and even in that very year we popped out crackers by Shitdisco and Capdown, our forty-eighth and forty-ninth NONG-prefixed releases. So it wasn't that much of a gear change for Fierce Panda to 'start' releasing albums, but nobody else needed to know that. All anyone needed to know was that we weren't going to be taken for Spider-Pig singles club mugs again. Often.

And it was brilliant not releasing one-off singles. Totally refreshing. Liberating, in fact. For at least six minutes, at least. And then I started crying. And so then Andy Pointy and I went to the Big Red pub on Holloway Road one lunchtime and we drank some drinks and we invented Label Fandango, a 7-inch vinyl indie concept with generic sleeves and a Galagos squirrel as the logo, which was designed to be as DIY as they come. One thousand vinyl singles, no CDs. I wanted the colour scheme to be bright orange, like if easyJet were ever mad enough to ever set up easyRecords, but Andy crunched the numbers and said all artwork had to be monochrome if we weren't going to go bust by Galagos 003. We were going black to basics.

Consider that Label Fandango released debut singles by acts with names like Films of Colour, Daggers, Freerunner and Nadine Shah and it doesn't look like the greatest A&R launch pad of all time. But then consider those names eventually became Honne, Hurts and Little Comets, while the noirishly effervescent Nadine Shah very much stayed being Nadine Shah, and it transpires that for four minutes Label Fandango actually had a better A&R track record than Fierce Panda.

As with Fierce Panda, I hope that we provided a real learning curve for artists. Certainly, other than the bonus CD formats and four-colour sleeves with awful pictures of offal or off-kilter television personalities, the Label Fandango releases got as much love and affection as the Panda releases. For a while, it was even our own fertile A&R nursery, or at least slightly tattered allotment. The Hot Puppies, Capital, the Hosts, Albert Gold, Desperate Journalist and Ultrasound all progressed from one end of the office to the other as Fierce Panda used Label Fandango like other labels used Fierce Panda, which in many ways felt a little bit like robbing Peter to pay Paul to play with Patrick at Paypal, but it was a sorted system of sorts.

To add more layers of iced fruitiness to the irony cake, as well as Fierce Panda, Livid Meerkat, Rabid Badger and Label Fandango, Ellie Panda was running her Cool for Cats offshoot, Martyn Panda was building Giant Haystacks, and Club Fandango teamsters Tom and Adie were earning their stripes with Tigertrap Records. One hopes the good honest journalists at *NME* were suitably sickened by the number of record companies being operated out of our record-company office at that time.

12 APRIL 2020

Sometimes I feel very much like lemon jelly, all wobbly and opaque and a bit fruity. Not entirely unpleasant but not very practical either. It seems selfish and perverse to say that at least I now have no FOMO, simply because there is nothing to MO on. It would be ridiculous, verging on the absolutely obscene, to suggest that the timing of the Grand Malarkey was in any way decent. But flipping it on its head, considering the state of my mind at the end of 2019, that very same mind boggles as to what crashing, crushing damage the entire COVID closedown would have caused it.

Later on at home, the news got weirder. Looking at one of the first sets of blood tests taken locally, my GP examined the way the liver and kidney numbers were levelling out and said it was obviously down to my levels of fitness. 'It's good that you're so fit and healthy,' beams Dr Muir. 'It saved your life.' Say, what?

'It felt like a dream,' says Liann of the Grand Malarkey, struggling to get it out. 'I just felt like I'd been picked up and dropped into a situation just like that – bang! I didn't know you were depressed. It was a complete shock – I went into autopilot. I subconsciously tried to block everything out.' She says one of the most chilling moments surrounding the Grand Malarkey was realising that I hadn't taken any of my new Christmas clothes away with me to London. In fact, my new jeans and jumper still had their labels attached, like they were never going to be worn, which was pretty much the plan.

I buy some face masks from Redbubble, four of them. One is a panda face. One is a Ziggy flash. One is Stone Roses' album artwork (first one, obviously). The fourth is a Winnie-the-Pooh E. H. Shepard design. I'm tempted to ask my psychiatrist what he makes of my choices. But, then again, why ruin a beautiful relationship? Liann catches me singing a Simon & Garfunkel song. A good sign. Perhaps. 'It's not the one about hello darkness my old friend, is it?' Scout asks her, ever concerned.

24

FOXHEADS

You know that bit I nicked from the Korgis about leaving Island Records and not looking back and walking away and burning the past and living today? All total bollocks. I carried my pain and embarrassment and raging frustration like a U2-loving asthmatic carries their inhaler with their *Inhaler* album, digging it out and waving it around during times of chest-hammering stress and breathless booziness. I bored good friends to tiny tears with nocturnal tales about the daylight robbery I had endured.

Luckily, many other industry people much bigger than me were good enough to share their tales of misery, hardship and good old-fashioned stitching-up at the hands of the corporate monster. 'You think that's bad,' they'd say. 'Let me get you a pint and then let me tell you about the time I got royally screwed over by Band X getting a new manager without telling me.' Or: 'Sit down with this cider and I'll explain how I spent three years developing band Y on the live circuit and then, five minutes before they inked their major deal, the record company got me sacked.'

Or: 'Slide yourself over a chaise longue and treat yourself to a teat pipette of the finest Pernod and I'll painstakingly detail the time in an A&R meeting when my boss threw the CD of this brilliant new Band Z out of the window, raging at its uselessness, and then raged at us again six months later for not convincing him to sign Band Z before Band Z were number one for ever, having signed to a far less stupid label.'

It isn't for me to elaborate upon the intricacies of and identities behind these tales here, but rest assured those were just a cross section of some of the nicest people coming out with some of the most horrible accounts of pretty vicious behaviour at the hands of cretinous gits. Still, in spite of all that ghastliness, surely the question has to be this: After 'launching' Coldplay and Keane, why doesn't Fierce Panda have an office crafted from diamonds and pearls on the moon, if not the roof of the Universal death star?

Sadly, I bored some of those same good friends to the point of silent goodbyes with that very same question, and by bleating on and on about not being able to fit into the major label system, no matter how hard I squeezed or how loudly I whined or indeed dined. Fact is: many major label people are not like you or me. They are a different breed. Major label people can scent the indie fear, that sweaty alt-pop desperation from six floors up. In their Gucci loafers and cashmere sweaters and glasscut towers they lounge, gazing impassively across impossibly shiny desktops while I sit in my charity-shop chic, suffused with that heady morning-after-cocktail of cooking lager fumes and kebab onion vapour that I've vainly tried to mask with a flash of Febreze and a brutal splash of Eau Sauvage. Truth is: like a broken Soft Cell lyric, it was simply never going to work. Say hello, wave goodbye.

Thankfully, our search for the next next next Coldplay or Keane wouldn't last too long. Just about fifteen fretful, fateful, fanciful, fucking fruitless fucking years. We marked the moment by making our one and only televisual appearance, which I quite reasonably saw as our chance to tell the truth! I'd always avoided these talking-heads gigs like the plague, scarred by watching old *NME* colleagues of mine diligently describing the hectic delights of bouncing up and down upon a Spacehopper while right behind them they showed fruity '70s footage of people bouncing up and down on Spacehoppers, but this programme was going to be focused on the top-selling albums of the '00s, or some such media whiff whaffery, and my talking head could tell the public what really went on at last.

So they sat me on a stool in the middle of the backroom of the Dublin Castle in the middle of the afternoon and the ghosts of Birdland looked down and chirruped happily as I said how it was. 'The thing is: Fierce Panda should never have been ALLOWED to get near Keane and Coldplay,' I frothed, like a frothy pint. 'They should have been SIGNED by major labels WAY before we tripped over them. But they TOTALLY ballsed it up by dropping the BALL.' Or words to THAT effect, anyway.

Predictably, this one chance became some fat chance. Come the Saturday-night national television premiere everything remotely interesting I had said in the middle of the Dublin Castle had been puked onto the cutting, cutting, cutting room floor and stomped into silent oblivion, leaving me with my insane eyes gurgling something pathetically inane like 'The first time I saw Coldkeane I abso-fuckinglutely knew they were going to be bigger than *Gogglebox*!' I have never been on the gogglebox since.

The first problem we saw with accidentally trying to find the next melodic indie MOR sensation around 2005 was the majors starting to overcompensate for their previous general uselessness. Having ballsed up on both Coldplay and Keane – and let us also add Snow Patrol and Elbow to that short list, two other bands who had to fight tooth and nail to be given the opportunity by Jim Chancellor at Fiction to give the public the chance to fall in love with them – A&R departments the land over were having their butts spanked. This Must Never Happen Again. So, for a while, everyone completely forgot how Coldplay and Keane, and indeed Snow Patrol and Elbow, had originally struggled to gain any momentum or traction and had to make themselves generally radio-tastic to get noticed. Any bunch of mopey melodicists with a half-decent demo were suddenly in with a chance of getting a record deal after two gigs. No fanbase, no radio play, no 'Yellow', no plan . . . you know the drill.

The second problem was that most of these bands crashed, burned and crashed again because they weren't getting any cool attention from the *Evening Session* or playing Club Fandango, because most of these bands were going straight for the big time and weren't indie at all, not even pretend indie, like the Feeling (although a respectful nod is due here to Scouting for Girls, who played a good pawful of Club Fandango shows). We tried our best with some swift Label Fandango singles by good people like Air Traffic on their flight path towards a Parlophone deal, but it wasn't really working, they simply had no wind beneath their wings. If you will.

The third problem was that a lot of these bands were immediately dropped after not selling any records, spoiling it for everyone else, and the fourth problem was that the music industry didn't really much care because the cash registers were ringing off the tills. Or, in this case, the kash registers, as Keane were joined by the Killers, the Kooks, Kasabian, Kaiser Chiefs and Kings of Leon all going commercially ballistic. The majors had harnessed the power and the magick of indierock and the world was going to be like this for ever and ever and a bit more ever.

Still we skulked in the shadows, hugging the clammy walls at the dark end of the melodic indie MOR street with Gledhill, with Royworld, with Longfellow. You may have never heard of these bands, but at some point they were all seen as Genuine Contenders: Gledhill's live agent was Russell Warby, a man of men seen booking shows for the Foo Fighters, White Stripes and the Strokes. I stood next to him at a Monarch gig while Gledhill rolled out a succession of infuriatingly upbeat guitar anthems and he merrily planned all manner of festival slots for the band in the long hot summers ahead. Royworld were absolutely brilliant; they looked like a Genesis spin-off, all waistcoats and ponytails, but the songs were uniquely elegant and bendy. Their key moment was a Dublin Castle show that Steve Lamacq was invited to, because I knew he wasn't going to 'get' our Label Fandango single release without seeing the waistcoats and ponytails onstage. Except the show got pulled because the band were redirected to go record in the studio with Andy Green, the man who produced Keane. FFS.

And still we cruised on. Jeff Smith wanted some of that cool indie MOR stuff. Loved Jeff, he'd had the vision to put together Lammo and Jo Whiley under the *Evening Session* banner all those years earlier. Now he was heading up Radio 2 and Radio 6 Music and he wanted Radio 2 to develop their own new acts, using 6 Music as a launch pad and thereby diverting them from the randy tiger-heads over at Radio Wunnerful. The plan worked like a dream and for a wee while we gently rocked the airwaves, notably with Sheffield '60s dramapop throwbacks the Hosts and Brockley's broken-hearted melodicists Longfellow. Chris Evans was all over Fierce Panda releases on the school run, i.e. literally talking over them, and James Chapple-Gill was king of the plugging world and our PPL statements were sensational.

But there were problems ahoy: excepting the A&R teamsters at Decca, who feared not the middle-of-the-road reaper with Alfie Boe's bow tie and Gregory Porter's portable Kangol, and Korda Marshall at BMG, who had been getting James and the Charlatans in the top ten of the album charts on the back of keen Ken Bruce airplay, A&R people were generally genuinely petrified of Radio 2. Not cool. Not sexy. Not hip. Not Radio 1. And if you took Radio 1 out of the equation a lot of A&R people quite literally didn't know what to do. There was no Plan B or C for the BBC. Longfellow went on tour with Hall & Oates and ended up being playlisted four times by Radio 2. Every playlist success was another dagger in the heart of their major label coffin.

Longfellow got onto Steve Wright's *Sunday Love Songs*, played somewhere only we know between 'The Look of Love' by ABC and, hopefully, 'The Look of Love' by Dionne Warwick, which quite possibly counts as the greatest single achievement in the history of Fierce bloody Panda. In the end the glory run was ended by moans from certain daytime Radio 2 producers who felt that the production values of a pissy Fierce Panda release jarred somewhat when placed next to the lush sounds of, say, Dire Straits and Michael Jackson and Alfie Boe's bow tie. The irony of course was that if Longfellow had signed to a major label and had the chance to record in a swanky Surrey residential studio in between tennis rallies, they could have delivered the production quality the buffed-up Radio 2 boffins expected. But, then again, the music industry rarely seems to excel at irony. Our slow-dancing days were over.

11 MAY 2020

BBC Two starts a new series of Hospital, *about . . . life in a hospital. I normally avoid all blue-light programmes dealing with disaster and death and infection like, well, the plague. But this one is different. This one focuses on the Royal Free roughly six weeks after my skinnyfit departure. The ninth floor – the Panda floor – has been commandeered by absolute quiet COVID chaos. I recognise some of the nurses, or at least their frequently tearful eyes behind the masks, but now their scrubs are covered by piles of PPE. The camerawork is coy, unobtrusive, gliding stealthily around the wards. The music is lovely, delicate and dreamlike. It's a beautiful demonstration of humankind's elegance amid utter tragedy.*

The camera crew go out and about to talk to people whose planned transplants on the ninth Panda floor have been cancelled indefinitely because their acute beds have been given over to the pandemic. They visit the house of a man who wearily explains how he has been receiving kidney dialysis at home for five years. Now he has no idea when he will get another chance for a transplant to extend his life. For the first time, I am shocked into feeling appalled at everything I've done since last New Year's Eve eve, everything I've put people through, every day I spent in that acute bed stopping weary men from getting the life-saving transplant operation they totally deserved. Frankly, it's a baleful demonstration of one man's absolute cretinously selfish stupidity amid awful peril.

25

I TAKE BRIBES

When Fierce Panda turned ten years old in 2004, we celebrated by releasing an album called *Decade: Ten Years of Fierce Panda*, and decided to do things Very Seriously. You could tell it was Very Serious because it was called *Decade: Ten Years of Fierce Panda*, which was a nod towards Factory, which was a Very Serious label. You could also tell it was Very Serious because the artwork didn't feature shagging pandas; it was a sober picture of the sombre sea that I took at Mundesley in north Norfolk on a family holiday back when Scout was but a wee cub.

The *Decade* track listing was as serious as serious does, which can be startlingly serious indeed. Twenty tracks, all the indie hits, all compressed into one compact disc because vinyl was dead in 2004: Ash, Supergrass, the Bluetones, Placebo, Kenickie, 3 Colours Red, Embrace, Lo-Fidelity Allstars, Idlewild, Seafood, Coldplay, Hundred Reasons, Bright Eyes, Easyworld, the Music, the Polyphonic Spree, Winnebago Deal, Six by Seven, Death Cab for Cutie, Keane. Everyone was cool with being on it, apart from Interpol, who thought the recording quality of 'Song Seven' was too shonky to be used again after its *Clooney Tunes* EP showboating.

Tony Linkin did the press. We told him we wanted the world on a stick, and an album review in *Heat* magazine back when *Heat* magazine reviewed albums. The last bit was a joke, but he got the review anyway. This is a man who had worked press for the face-pummellingly thunderous Wildhearts and survived, after all. *Heat* liked pretty much all of the record, but were a bit confounded by the thunderous pummellings of Winnebago Deal. Elsewhere, Tony delivered us features in *The Times*, the *Sunday Times* and *Time Out*, but sadly not the *Radio Times* or the *New York Times* or the *Angling Times*. Or the *East Anglian Daily Times*, while we think of it.

No matter. As PR campaigns go, it was excellent fun and for seven minutes or less we were in the corner of the eye of a media hurricane: Dan Cairns from the *Sunday Times* came round our Holloway HQ and quite literally anguished over why we even bothered doing what we did; Chris Salmon took myself and Nelson the Panda from a photo session at the *Time Out* Tottenham Court Road office over the road to interview us in the Bricklayers Arms. (Weirdly, Nelson got left in the Stag's Head later that day after a liquid meeting with George Ergatoudis, the then-head of Radio 1, and I had to retrieve him (Nelson, not George) from the pub the following day. Now that *was* serious.)

Throughout the history of Fierce Panda we have come up with some pretty intense taglines. To coincide with the release of the *Decade* compilation album, we really put our backs into it and started coming up with slogans that we considered to be the kind of coquettish catchphrases that would propel our product into the marketplace marked 'marketing placed genius'. These phrases would be used on the back of record sleeves, on promo copies, on press releases, sometimes even on T-shirts and totes cool tote bags, and they looked like this:

Ten years of pop tension.
Eleven years of sonic mischief.
Twelve years of rule-detonating indie dementia.
Thirteen years of seismic melodic rumblings.
Fourteen years of underground japery.
Fifteenage kicks right through the night.
Sixteen years of bittersweet pop swoonings.
Seventeen years of tune-chewing shenanigans.
Eighteen years of ear-flossing palavers.

Then we felt a little bit tired, so we switched to using: 'The sound of a flight of stairs falling down a flight of stairs since 1994'.

Then Seabrooks celebrated their diamond anniversary and came up with: 'Seventy-five Years of Brilliant Crisps'.

Fair play, crinkled beefy kids.

The moral of the story? Don't overthink things. In fact, don't think full stop. Never was this more pertinent than when Philip Ingles left after seventeen years of trenchant label management work in the Panda trenches. This frequently involved him taking me to one side and gently suggesting that £20k I'd just promised a new band could be better redistributed across a variety of projects instead of blown in one fell swoop. Not for nothing was he known as the Voice of Reason. Now, for the first time ever, I had to take control of the Panda cheque book. What I pretty swiftly realised was there is nothing as maddening as looking after the A&R department and the accounts department at the same time, because it is basically like a pyromaniac getting a job with the fire brigade – you spend your entire time putting out raging fiscal fires you started yourself, most of the time deliberately.

And nor is this more relevant than when it comes to what we can somewhat loosely describe as Fierce Panda's approach to 'discovering' new talent. What is an A&R person? Who is an A&R person? Why is an A&R person? An A&R person scours the known musical planet, very much like skates on ice, for gleaming new talent. They listen to demos, liaise with lawyers, mingle with managers, hang with producers and co-writers and other crucial creative hangers-on and go to gigs. Actually, I can't remember the last time I saw lots of A&R people at a gig, but that could just be me. Certainly, in the so-called heyday of Fierce Panda in the '90s and the '00s, the prime time for the acts on the *Decade* compilation, A&R people were the children of the night, flitting from venue to venue, flirting with singers and drummers and managers alike, float-ing on air when their signing was singing from the top of the charts, and justifiably so.

As chief tea-maker at Fierce Panda Records, I did some of those things, often not very well, and didn't do some of those things at all. But the few great things that we did do we did with-out thinking, basing those few great things on pure and simple instinctiveness. In truth, with the best bands I have pretty much decided whether they fit the Panda within thirty-eight seconds of seeing the live set, whether that live set is by Coldplay or Cavalry or Coin-Op. It's not about writing out giant comedy cheques and throwing them onstage, the starting point is simply to be engaged by the onstage antics, be that by the shirts, by the band's bants, by the musical palaver. A very good sign is when you start in the shadows at the back of the Shacklewell Arms and find yourself compelled to step forward into the middle of the room, dragged to the front by a musical force that I'd like to describe as mystical and unseen, except it can clearly be seen making forceful music on the stage right in front of me.

Sometimes I find myself watching a new band and then thirty seconds later I am standing at the bar because my body has propelled itself out of the venue room without my brain even realising it. It's like a form of very subliminal self-defence. Sometimes I've actually rejected bands before they've even played a note – here's a tip for you kids: if you are due on at 10 p.m., don't amble onstage, check the half-full venue, half-heartedly tune up and walk off again because some idiot in the crowd might have a 10.30 p.m. train to catch out of Liverpool Street.

Sometimes the Panda mind *can* be changed for the better – we looked at a band called Apartment who did that whole black-shirted U2-nuked-by-Interpol vibe and I should have loved them, but something was always missing whenever I saw them in small venues. Then they supported the Killers at the Astoria, and on a big stage with a giant PA they made all kinds of thunderously great stadium rocking sense, so we ended up doing two ace singles and really should have tried to convince them to do more, but they got funding to do the album on their own Fleet Street Records.

Sometimes the Panda mind can also be changed for the worse: in the early '00s our A&R scout was Gareth Dobson, who was enthusing about a couple of new bands called Bloc Party and Kaiser Chiefs. It's impossible to explain why they never ended up on Fierce Panda in the face of the Fierce Panda A&R scout's enthusiasm, but let me try to explain the unexplainable: in a nutshell, Bloc Party had previously been known as Union and Angel Range, and we'd put them on under both names at Club Fandango; similarly we had put on a band called Parva, who had a touch of the Idlewilds about them, and they reappeared thoroughly reinvented as Kaiser Chiefs. This wasn't even a case of liking the music or otherwise – I just didn't trust them, didn't believe that they believed in what they were doing rather than noticing the more obvious angle, which was that both bands had finally landed on a winning musical formula. Oh, I've just explained the impossible! Need I fill in the timeline blanks and point out that I was behaving like an implausibly pompous arse at *exactly the same time* that we were enduring Keanegate with Island Records? No, of course I don't.

I successfully negotiated my way out of doing a deal with the Cribs because I didn't have the vision to see them grow beyond supporting Medium 21 in Leeds. I managed to talk myself out of signing Lonely the Brave, primarily because I didn't think any-one could love their macabre Walkmen-walking-on-The-Fens twisted dynamism as much as I did. Even recently I had a good look at Pet Needs, a bunch of woah-woahing punk rock rousta-bouts living in Essex. I saw them in Stowmarket, I saw them in Colchester, I saw them in Dalston, but I just couldn't tally them up with Fierce Panda. They've ended up on Xtra Mile, touring the universe with Frank Turner. Not a bad turn of events for all parties involved, to be honest.

And, in a warped way, I'm actually happy we didn't release all those Cribs and Lonely the Braves and Bloc Party outfits – imagine how totally insufferable Fierce Panda would have become if we'd done everyone who crossed our bamboo-strewn path. Looking back at the first ten glorious years – and bear-ing in mind *Decade: Ten Years of Fierce Panda* doesn't even feature our early-and-beyond-seminal releases by Scarfo, Tiger, Dweeb, Pecadiloes, Ultrasound or Llama Farmers – sometimes even I feel like we must have been A&Rmbulance chasing, following the herd down to Greek Street.

In retrospect, however, the process wasn't like that at all: what tended to happen was we'd either stumble across a band live or get a tip-off about them and put them on at one of our Club Spangle/Panda/Fandango shows. Then, if all parties were happy, the 7-inch release process would begin. Then, working on a minimum six-week turnaround for vinyl manufacturing (now *those* were the days), there would be a launch party, and that launch party would normally be the major label fuckfest. So no, no A&Rmbulances were hurt in the making of this label.

In fact, if it wasn't a Panda showcase or a Club Fandango show, I generally hated being in a buzz industry gig. Not out of arrogance or jealousy; I just used to get creeped out by the A&R masses. Individually or in small groups some of these people were a delight to be with, but I'd walk into a neutral gig and walk straight out again if it was packed to the gills with talent spotters. Maybe it was because, as James Endeacott once said, there was no point in being there because everyone else in the room had more money than me. Maybe I felt as though I wasn't worthy, not a real A&R person. The imposter boy for the broken generation.

Perversely, in those first ten years of Fierce Panda, when we were totally independent and completely ignorant of the hows and whys of the corporate side of the industry and the one-off singles were going steady, we actually had quite a jolly relationship with an entire youthful generation of enthusiastic A&R people. They would come to our shows at Club Spangle, Club Panda and Club Fandango. They would come around the Panda HQ in Holloway Road and Highbury, especially when they could still afford to live in Stoke Newington and Dalston, and pop in for a cuppa and a catch-up on the way to their shiny desks in Kensington. I even heard stories of major label A&R meetings where the question 'What have Fierce Panda released this week?' was not unusual, and in a very good way.

But there was a weird passive-aggressive-aggressive edge to some A&R people. Even some of the nice ones. One A&R person blithely said to me, 'Yeah, I could have done a Keane single.' Yeah, but you didn't. There is also a degree of cunning and skill to proper A&Ring, which I could never aspire to. I have stood next to an A&R man at a show and listened to him list all the band's deficiencies before inviting me to join him at the bar next door after three songs. Then at the end of the night he is out front on the pavement, chatting up the lead singer of the same band, falling and laughing and presumably not pointing out his many deficiencies. Clever A&R man. I couldn't do that. I simply couldn't raise myself to that dazzling level of bullshittery.

Then again, so much has changed in the world of A&R. It's a lot more about the numbers, the streaming figures, rather than any amazing musical talent. And the modern-day A&R approach reflects that, as music industry stalwarts tell me, in hushed, amazed tones, that major labels now employ people specifically to scour the streaming services in search of unknown acts with a billion streams. I'm not sure if anyone has christened these cats ScoutBots but we will do so here.

Back in the *Decade* decade meanwhile, the plot was a lot more organic: band forms, thinks of name, writes songs, starts playing gigs, starts dreaming. Then they decide the first name is rubbish, so they think of a better one. Then they decide their first songs are bobbins, so they write some new ones. Then they decide they should make a demo to send to the music business. So they book a studio, record the tracks, get them mixed. Then they need to make up cassettes, which means they need to come up with some artwork. Then they need to find someone who makes cassettes. Then they need to go to the post office to buy some jiffy bags to post them in. Then they need some record-company addresses to send them to, but they can't find them online because Google hasn't yet been invented, so they have to look at the cool records in their record collection and collect all the addresses on the backs of the sleeves. Then they need stamps. So then they need to go back to the post office, then the cassette is posted off to a record-company PO Box number, where it sits for a few weeks. Then it gets picked up and taken to the record-company HQ, where it sits in another box for a few more weeks. Then it gets played and if it shows any promise you'll get a call; if you're in you might be able to answer the phone.

All if which takes somewhere between six months to a year, by which point the useless bands will have split up and the potentially good ones have carried on gigging and defining their sound and perhaps developed a fanbase and written a 'Bruise Pristine' or a 'Shiver' or a 'Latchmere'. Nowadays, thanks to all this breakneck techno acceleration, little Jimmy or Ginny boshes out a tune on Bandcamp at breakfast and whangs it out to the entire music industry by the time the drippy yolk has dried on their Paddington Bear egg cup, and a trillion billion streams later – and perhaps without even ever playing one live show – they can get themselves a sparkly record deal.

The problem is, then, that the demo process has basically become too easy. I'm not advocating a return to square wheels, leprosy and actually playing good gigs here, but with the cassette and the jiffy bag and the stamps and the end-less commutes to the post office you needed to put in a certain amount of effort. And because you wanted to make sure you weren't wasting your time or your post office pennies you would really focus on a core of suitable labels who you thought would actually fit your music. Oh, and you would make an extra effort and pop in a nice note to the record company, sometimes written in handsome purple ink.

Nowadays, most times we aren't even sent unreleased 'demos' per se, we get Spotify links to the tracks they've thrown out to the screaming, streaming lions. And, instead of considered purple prose, we get a woefully inadequate tossed-off impersonal email saying, 'Have a listen to this' or some such abrupt suchness. Sometimes we get sent entire concept albums. Sometimes we get sent entire concept albums from Russia, or Italy, or Turkey. We play bits of everything we get sent. This much we know, because we know that most of it is either a) rubbish, b) quite nice jazz-pop but entirely unsuitable for the label, c) completely insane, d) from Russia or Italy or Turkey, or e) a hyperspeeding combo of a) and c) with a little bit of b) and a touch of d).

So what have we learnt here? Don't send us entire albums to listen to, it's like discussing your suicidal tendencies on a first date – waaaaay too much information. Two or three tracks of your very bestest chosen songs will suffice as a starting point, always on SoundCloud, never sent as individual bloody files. Don't cc us in with another 100 record companies, because that makes us feel very unwanted. Don't email us asking if we accept demos – if you can't be arsed to type 'Fierce Panda demos' into your google-o-meter then you're not my kinda musician. Don't send us tracks to review – Fierce Panda isn't a blog. And, for Chris Martin's sake, don't cc us in with another 100 record labels when you send us your Moscovite jazz-rock double album with a giant essay explaining how you've been bullied all your life and you're fifty-nine years old and you haven't actually got a band to play your songs with in the live galaxy, because, quite frankly, you sound like a fucking mentalist.

3 JULY 2020

The numbers are looking good. Oh no – they're not. Hang on, let me look again. Nope, those iron numbers aren't looking good at all. Time for some more tests, some more poking and prodding and plodding along to meet medical experts. The suspicions of Dr Muir are proved correct – my iron levels are alarmingly high because I am afflicted by something called haemochromatosis. According to another passing medical procedural: 'Haemochromatosis is an inherited condition where iron levels in the body slowly build up over many years. This build-up of iron, known as iron overload, can cause unpleasant symptoms. If it is not treated, this can damage parts of the body such as the liver, joints, pancreas and heart.' More to the point, Dr Muir says that if left to its own devices the patient rocks up to A&E feeling very sickly and looking very yellow and suspiciously like an alcoholic, no matter their drinking routine, primarily because the liver is being fried. It appears in men of all drinking routines around fifty-five years old. More to the other point, haemochromatosis causes extreme fatigue. 'This has been lurking within you for fifty years,' says the GP. 'It had to come out at some point, it just needed a trigger.' Wait – there's actually an underlying physical reason for this malarkey? That explains the rest of the everything!

Dr Muir does not prescribe me any drugs. There is no cure, so there is no point. She tells me all they can do is syphon off a pint of blood every now and then to balance the numbers out. Off I go to another hospital, this time the West Suffolk in Bury St Edmunds. Tea, biscuits and patient nurses overjoyed at the velocity of the flow of the patient's blood gliding along the tube beneath the cool white lights. Rather excitingly for all fans of the family Mustelidae for haemochromatosis, the blood count appears to be in ferritins.

On Tuesday 14 July, I have my first haircut of the year in Stowmarket Town. I silently show my masked Turkish barber a picture of an unmasked

PANDAMONIUM!

Bernard Sumner on my phone. In the space of seventeen minutes, I am transformed from peak-time Günter Netzer into a Nitzer Ebb roadie. In fact, I feel like a New Order man. Pitchfork announces that Q magazine is closing down. I fleetingly feel very glad I clawed those two extra years out of the NME.

26

NATURE THING

One day in 2016, I was interviewed for the *Evening Standard* business section, like a proper businessman. Perhaps rather less like
a proper businessman we did the photo session in the Lexington
bar, near the antlers. I dressed in my finest black. The photographer tutted and told me they like to have some colour in their
photos. Hang onto your beagle. The day the feature came out
I joined the crushing rush hour. In 1974, the bus would have
been full of pipe-smoking Smithers-Jonesy chaps with bowlers
and briefcases perusing the evening newspapers. Nowadays,
alas, everyone is supaglued to their super smartphones and there
is just one person on the 141 reading the *Evening Standard*. He is
on the business pages. He has no idea the man sitting beneath
the antlers on the page in front of him is now standing a foot
behind him, breathing ever-so-slightly too heavily. He turns over
to something more enticing, like adverts for new teeth. I get off
at the junction of Balls Pond Road. It is the most exciting bus
ride I have ever been on.

PANDAMONIUM!

In the interview, I decided for the one and only time in my life to be provocative, and so, working on the basis that I run Fierce Panda and we had a wedding with Steve Lamacq as Best Man and Ian from Damaged Goods as the punchline to the Best Man's speech and Clint Boon as DJ and the Seafood band getting drunk on table six, I breezily claimed to be the Most Indie Person Alive. I think I was trying to elicit some kind of peeved response from the independent music community, maybe even attempting to instigate some kind of tremendously fierce pancultural conversation, but perhaps the independent music community does not fixate upon the business section of the *Evening Standard* on the 141 bus, because no indie people who are actually way more indie than I wrote into the editor or sent me an aggrieved email or posted an angry social nutworking post. Mind you, I suppose that wouldn't be a tremendously indie thing to do, would it?

Anyway, what is indie? Who is indie?? Where is indie??? Why is indie???? It's a maddeningly excellent and indeed excellently maddening question. I do know that Fierce Panda is an indie label. This much I know because we have always been distributed by independent distribution companies. We've done 'em all, from SRD to Shellshock to 3MV/Vital to Pinnacle to ADA to Essential to the Orchard.

I most assuredly know we're indie because in November 2021 Radio X told the world that Fierce Panda was the eighteenth most significant indie label on the planet. They did this in a post saying: 'We take a look at the fiercely independent record labels that have meant the most over the years.' Wait! They said fiercely! Anyhooo, Radio X counted down the top nineteen, possibly because they are perverse or weird or they can't count, and that countdown went like this: Creation, Factory, Rough

243

Trade, XL, Mute, Domino, Sub Pop, Transgressive, Silvertone, Modular, Warp, Nude, Independiente, DFA, Heavenly, 4AD, Matador and little old us. Number nineteen was Communion. Not that anyone's counting. What was especially exciting about all this hullabaloo is that, to be honest, if you look at Fat Possum, Fantastic Plastic and Fortuna Pop!, I'd actually wager Fierce Panda is barely the fourth best indie label alone in the universe with the initials FP.

To me, indie is a state of mind. A scruffy, ruffled, scuffed-up state of mind, but a state of mind nonetheless. Indie should be tetchy, edgy, *tedgy*; charming, intelligent, hectic; a bit generous, a bit stubborn, a bit melodic, a little bit bitter; sensitive, sometimes over-so, but maybe that's just me before breakfast. Crucially, indie is all about being suspended in a state of perpetual puppyhood where the next band is always going to be better than the last, the next gig even more of a giggle than last night's, and you can go to those gigs wearing DMs and rolled-up Levi's and Paddington Bear socks even as you muddle through your fiddly mid-fifties.

The indiest act we've had – and, by Peter Hook's beard, we've had a few – is quite probably Hatcham Social. If indie is about rough 'n' tumbling melodies and jangly, spangly, angular guitars, then they tick all the charity boxes. The first time I saw them was at In the City in Manchester. I was taken by the floppy fringes, and indeed the rough 'n' tumbling melodies, but what really hooked me in were the cardigans. Hatcham Social are the most *C86*-savvy band we've done, and it's telling they are the only band we've really fought for, outbidding an indie label rival by a whole crispy fiver. It's telling that they got *Artrocker* Single of the Year for 'Crocodile' and a ten out of ten review in *Vice* for their Tim Burgess-produced *You Dig the Tunnel, I'll Hide the Soil* album.

It's also telling they made the most indie video in Fierce Panda's history, in our first Aberdeen House office, for fifty whole quid. You don't need telling it was great.

Sometimes indie has got too twee, even for me – as much as we have filched heartily from the spirit of Sarah Records, I always struggled with their more radical indiepop factions who chose to drink orange juice and sit cross-legged on the floor at their live shows. For those of us who liked lager and long trousers, our indie was imbued with a certain toughness, a rugged, ragged, roughness. It was never all about sandles and sandcastles, it was frequently going to the darkest depths of the toilet circuit in the dingiest corners of the universe stalking the next plausible musical sensation.

One thing indie does not do is legitimise bullshit. We won't promise you the world if we can barely deliver a broken Curly Wurly and a crushed packet of Frazzles. One other thing indie does not do is legitimise failure: it has its confines, its restraints, its fiscal glass ceilings. It has enormous frustrations and furious injustices and wildly unpredictable ups, downs and more downs, but that does not mean you ever just shrug and give up. Every time we have really, really, really wanted to keep a band – see Coldplay, Keane, Art Brut, the Walkmen – we have been in a position to compete financially, if not spiritually. Every time those bands have moved on, we have dusted ourselves down and managed to replace them all in some small way. 'Tis but an emotional flesh wound.

We have fought with bands about their future. There have been times when we have argued with acts and their live agents when we have sensed that they have developed *the fear* of moving up the live ladder, where conception is everything and promoting bullshittery is absolutely top whack because you have to be seen to be getting bigger and bigger. It's no coincidence that, for the likes of the Crookes and Goldheart Assembly, among the very biggest gigs they ever played were headlining our Fierce Panda birthday parties at the Scala, where quite frankly we used the bullshitting art of promotery to its maximum impactitude to make the shows succeed.

We will never fight any artist's ambition, though. We will scowl over paying a PR company £900 to get one video premier, and there have been times when we have quietly raised an eyebrow when a band we know to be worth no more than thirty paying punters has been booked into headlining a 300-capacity venue, but it's not our place to tell them it's too big a step up. Many indie labels are run by chancers taking chances who perceive ambitiousness to be absolutely excellent. Always use your delusion. This is ultimately why we let bands go, to let them try to fulfil their dreams.

Some artists happily go through a distribution system called AWAL, aka Artists Without A Label. Rather less happily, some acts get really quite grumpy with their indie record company and its enormous frustrations and furious injustices and ultimately decide to sod off and leave you. These are the Artists Who Had A Really Good Label But Fucked It Up, aka AWHARGLBFIU. Sometimes they even tell you they are off. Quite often they don't bother.

Those frustrations and injustices show no signs of abating for indie bands or labels alike any time soon. In this faceless, baseless streaming world, it's not that people don't know that indie labels like Fierce Panda exist nowadays, they don't know what *any* record labels are any more. Half a lifetime ago we had a long conversation with the techsperts at the Orchard about our haplessly streamlined streaming numbers. 'The problem is,' they explained, 'the Fierce Panda releases don't fit the streaming model, and therefore don't fit the algorithm of the night, because they are too good.'

By 'too good', I believe they meant that our releases were too tetchy, edgy, tedgy; we stand glowering at the other end of the Spotify spectrum from Ed Sheeran, and that is one mighty long spectrum. In fact, it's such a mightily long spectrum that in the digital world 'indie' has evolved into a whole non-indie entity unto itself. This much we know because one day Andy Pointy came to the Famous Cock in Highbury Corner waving around his outraged headphones, having weaved across north Londonshire listening to a so-called indie Spotify playlist that didn't feature a single track from an independent label. We should be so lucky.

Having wisely decided the majors had no more need of Fierce Panda's intrepid ears we next met with some modern energy drink people called Craig and Nick. Really nice guys. We played them some epic indie rock thinking that they liked indie rock that soundtracked bold skateboarding tykes throwing themselves off mountaintops using handkerchiefs as parachutes. They didn't want that. They wanted Albert Gold's soulpop suppleness because they wanted to get some Radio 1 action. This was a surprise. We met with some futuristic vacuum cleaner people as well. Their WeWork work space had free beer in reception, but only after a set time in the afternoon, like the free milk you'd get at junior school before Thatcher the baby-milk-snatcher came on board, only this milk would get you pissed. And you poured the pints yourself. Amazing. Another surprise.

Rather less surprising was the fact that in spite of some fine endeavours on both sides and a clutch of hopeful-looking meetings no deals were ever signed. The fundamental problem seemed to be this: for all the lovely chattings and free energy drinks from the fridge in one reception, and the even lovelier free lager in the other, some of these people didn't want to work with Fierce Panda – they wanted to *be* Fierce Panda. 'We want all the glamour and the glory of finding a band and building them all the way up from the grassroots,' said one of them, by way of apology. 'You want the what and the what of finding a what and building them from the what up?' said we.

You don't know how to build bands from the grassroots up. You really don't want to. The glamour and the glory is getting pissed backstage at Reading Festival with your free AAA pass. The glamour and the glory is sitting pissed at the Dorchester Hotel at some swanky awards ceremony. The glamour and the glory is sitting getting pissed in business class on a flight to Midem or SXSW or some other international rescue powwow. The glamour and the glory is not whoring around in our world, hanging with the boys of slummer.

Yeah, they may be able to rock it by the bar at the Scala on a sweaty night when their hot new band has pulled in 500 punters. And they may well be in their element running up some elephantine drinks tab in a nice nightclub. But what about the sweat-stained perils of the toilet circuit in the Shacklewell Arms loos? How much time are they willing to waste hanging around the Waiting Room waiting for some incredible rock action? In a nutshell, can they hack it on a wet Wednesday night in Stoke Newington?

A bog-standard soggy evening in 2019: I am commuting between gigs at the Sebright Arms in Hackney and the Victoria in Dalston. It's pitch-black midweek in the middle of winter, throwing down cold, black sheets of rain. I know the route and the routine like the scars on the back of my hand: take a 48 Routemaster from Cambridge Heath to Old Street, change to a 149 Routemaster to Dalston opposite Jaguarshoes, seeking temporary reprieve from the black sheets of rain under the dark duvet of the rattling railway bridge.

I can't remember any of the bands I've seen. I hadn't spoken to a single soul throughout the evening apart from the bar person at the Sebright. I do remember thinking, 'This then is the glory, the glamour, growing the musical grass up, up, up from the roots. A wet fucking midweek night spent splashing through the piss-stained neon-lit London puddles visiting half-empty venues to witness some half-arsed bands ploughing half-heartedly through their half-finished melodies.'

Frankly, I was in my element. It takes a very special kind of perversion to endure what people like us go through. Problem is you can end up pushing yourself so hard you simply end up punishing yourself. The Greatest Song Ever Made is obviously the Philadelphian fury of 'The Rat', particularly when it laments: *'When I used to go out, I'd know everyone I saw / Now I go out alone, if I go out at all.'* Problem was I'd become a walking, talking sad-faced lyric, listening to the Walkmen on the Walkman. 'The Rat' had become an anthem, my anthem, my only lonely-boy anthem.

And, from my lonely-boy perspective, for the classic shy, awkward indie kid, social networking is a total anathema, if not downright torture. We are the old-school ghosts who like to hide in the shadows; the faceless, traceless unknowns slipping in and out of gig-goers' consciousness. My Facebook picture for several years was a headshot of DCI Barnaby from *Midsomer Murders*, until it was replaced with an entirely up-to-date snap taken in Jayne Houghton's back garden in 1989 of me with peroxide blond hair, a Naxos sun tan and a box-fresh Stone Roses tee. Curiously, I now look more like John Nettles than I do myself, which is pretty indie behaviour.

But do you want to know the definitive definition of the word? Writing a book where all the chapters are named after Close Lobsters releases – that's really, *really* indie.

30 NOVEMBER 2020

'A pub with no alcohol is not a pub any more,' says a very sad Welsh publican on BBC News as the lockdown cracks back down in Cardiff and Carmarthen and Caerphilly. Well said, very sad Welsh publican. Similarly, a record company with no releases is scarcely a record company. But we plough on, turning out a Ning Standard newsletter every month and coming up with A Pretty Good Idea, which is The COVID Version Sessions EP. *It's a return to the six-track compilations and it is mostly featuring Moon Panda caressing the Strokes, Desperate Journalist covering Pulp, China Bears reworking Fountains of Wayne (especially poignant as their songwriter, Adam Schlesinger, died from COVID back in the spring), Ghost Suns tweaking Nine Inch Nails, Jekyll doing Japan, and National Service stripping back the Twilight Sad in the weeping sadness of the evening.*

But it's a struggle. A massively, giantly, enormously large battle for our sanity. Frankly, we're only just about clinging on as a label, so how are the musicians coping? A band with no gigs is barely a band any more, surely? What's the point of songwriting when you can't record any of those songs? We lose some acts as they lose hope. Some of the key ones who manage to keep going are linked in some internally sweet way – Moon Panda are a couple, Desperate Journalist are two couples, China Bears have twins Ivan and Fraser. But they aren't invincible: band members get COVID and are floored by it; band members' families get COVID and die from it. Tours are arranged, announced, postponed, post-postponed and post-post-postponed again. Outside, it's hospitals versus hospitality, real lives versus live shows, indie hogwash against incessant handwashing.

I go to West Suffolk hospital for my tenth venesection. They have now taken an entire body's worth of blood from me. It's amazing I'm still standing, frankly.

251

27

GODLESS

Can you ever be *too* indie for yours and everyone else's own good? My life story is not one that is festooned with showbiz streamers or soundtracked by the clink of empty champagne bottles the morning after the lost weekend following the night before. There have been times when I have actually tutted at myself for my indie stubbornness. I distinctly remember two times at the Caernarvon Castle – before it burned down – when I turned down an invite from Caroline Elleray to go to the Ivor Novello Awards and then declined the opportunity to see our Gledhill band support Tears for Fears at Hammersmith Apollo because I had promised various new combos I'd be on hand in Camden to witness their indie shenanigans.

I can still distinctly remember the pain of missing out on that awards ceremony and that night out listening to *Songs from the Big Chair*. I have absolutely no recollection of the indie shenanigans I missed those events for. Did it make me feel proud and self-righteous? No, it just made me feel stupid and very sad. Nobody said running a label was sensible or fun. To wit, one day down the Bull & Gate Steve Lamacq said, 'I tried to nominate Fierce Panda for the AIM awards, but you can't be nominated for the AIM awards because you're not a member of AIM.'

Oh well. AIM is the acronym for the Association of Independent Music. We've never been a member since it launched in 1998, partly because I always thought it was weird being an independent label and joining up with loads of other independent labels, like some mighty *Life of Brian*-esque paradox. I realise I am in the minority here, and lots of other independent people really do love independing on other independent people, but nobody said being an outlier was supposed to be sensible or fun either.

A few years later, they opened the AIM awards voting to non-member muggles. You paid sixty quid and you nominated, well, yourself. So I nominated Fierce Panda for Best Small Label, working on their criteria that I employed fewer than 300 people and had a turnover of less than 30 squillion pounds. I wrote something bashful about us turning twenty years old and flagged up the fact that the previous year Alcopop! Records had won Best Small Label and it had made Jack Alcopop! very happy, which made us happy as well, and we wanted to experience some more of Jack Alcopop!'s Alcopopping happiness.

Our nomination didn't make it past stage one. A source told me the judges immediately decided that 'Fierce Panda was too old to count as a small label' and disqualified us.

TOO OLD!! INDIE!!! LABEL!!! SMALL!!! DISQUALIFY??!!!

We didn't even get our sixty quid back. We're still not members of AIM.

In other words, I now know Fierce Panda will never win any awards, apart from those sympathy trophies pertaining to stamina, persistence and incessant stupidity that get given out in the toilets before the ceremony has actually started. But I have prepared a speech, and it sounds like this: 'This is for everyone who has spent their school dinner money on that vital shiny 7-inch single. This is for anyone who has unwittingly spent their rent money on printing 1,000 fun-packed fanzines. This is for everyone and anyone who accidentally spent their mortgage money on signing that elusive American band who really, really *could* have cracked the market wide open. Thanks – and goodnight for ever.'

Continuing the no-show showbiz theme, after years of reviewing other people's records, what's it like reading other people's reviews of the records you release yourself? Quite interesting, actually. Like a band, you rarely remember your good reviews, you fleetingly notice the ones like the one in 'The Guide' where they said of the Beaker single something along the lines of 'holding a Fierce Panda single is a bit like being covered in piss'. I can't remember the exact words, but I could tell it didn't bother me because I only refused to buy the Saturday *Guardian* for the next ten years or so.

The modern penchant for album reviews that are briefer than the first paragraph of our press release is also a tad irksome. Some blogs just reprint that press release, which is either monumentally lazy or a backhanded tribute to my effervescent scribbling skills because they don't think they can do any better. But over the years Fierce Panda has had meaty spreads in *Music Week*, *NME*, *Record Collector*, *The Guardian* (the irony!) and many more magazines of varying quality of taste and glossiness of paper. Does the ex-hack like being hacked? I don't mind the interview process if it takes place in a ghostly public house, and I definitely don't mind any interview where I don't have to go back to the pub to transcribe any witterings.

In fact, in an ideal world, I meet the journalist in the ghostly public house for a chat and a natter, aka a chatter, so they get a hint of my public so-called personality, and then they send me the actual questions by email and I diligently answer them to the best of my berserk abilities, so that nobody has to transcribe anything and I don't get misquoted, aka make a totally slanderous arse of myself by talking about exactly what happened in Room 245 of the mid-price hotel room in Sheffield, which means I am very, very boring. The wordy dullinghood is compounded by the irritating fact that I look like an absolute tit in any photograph that has ever been taken of me. In the otherwise delightful *Music Week* Panda twenty-fifth anniversary spread, I got snapper Andy Willsher to do a session with Nelson the Panda and myself. I looked gnarly and growly because I wanted to resemble a psychotic Christopher Robin. In the end I just looked like I was failing a really poor audition for Ricky Gervais's *Derek*. Truly, one man's media binge is another man's literary cringe.

Other showbiz things it turned out I wasn't very good at: we once tried to get Panda people to pledge on a PledgeMusic campaign to make a whole Fierce Panda film with some very expert film-making people. We got as far as making a trailer – in the Bull & Gate, with wearying predictability – with the likes of Roddy Woomble from Idlewild and Will Champion from Coldplay enthusing about indie labelness. But in spite of all that enthusiasm and expertise and planning and teasering fun we couldn't raise the necessary funds. The film was going to be called *Endangered: the story of Fierce Panda* and the plot kinda focused on whether or not the world still needed indie schmindie windy cindy labels like Fierce Panda any more, so we kinda answered a question we should never have asked in the first place, which is meta Panda behaviour, obviously.

There has also been sporadic talk about some fly-on-the-wall Panda documentary action. This has never happened because a Fierce Panda documentary would be the most boring documentary known to indie kind, unless you've got a real taste for overhearing an indie bloke talking indiebloke talk in an old man's boozer in the middle of the afternoon, or a passion for watching a man glaring at live bands in fairly dark venues, or some perverse fancy for staring at footage of a man staring at a computer screen piling woefully through emails, hemails and shemails and generally appearing to achieve absolutely cock all in any working day.

Luckily, all is not entirely lost on the showbiz front, as you come across some absolute journalistic punnery gold. The caption on the *Record Collector* front cover was, after all, 'Fierce Panda: Top Grrr.'

25 DECEMBER 2020

Come Christmastime, I am making up for many lost times. I hand in my presents list earlier than ever before in my life – so early in fact that I eventually forget what I've asked for, which only adds to the surprise on the big day. The Gap Years are long gone. I get an ELO T-shirt from the 2018 tour. There's a New Order Technique crew tee – the money goes to roadies kicking their heels at home. An old-fashioned battery powered AM/FM radio from B&M for the garden. A Muji peasant shirt going cheap in the Muji sale. A pair of adidas VS Pace trainers (black with blue stripes) going cheap in the USC sale.

Continuing the sporting theme, there's a Spurs woolly sweater, a Spurs woolly hat, a Spurs backpack, a pair of Spurs third kit shorts (the lovely old-school yellow ones that reference the early '80s glory days) and a Spurs striped scarf like the one I had in 1974. Throw in a man-sized blue jumper from M&S, an XL-sized black linen jacket from All Saints, a sensationally large chicken and ham pie from Waitrose.

I very, very diligently remove all the labels from the new clothes and wear them and eat and read everything as quickly as possible. Not that there is any tremendous rush – Nigel Ugly Child was going to come up to mark the anniversary of the grand malarkey with a vaguely celebratory trip to the Pickerel, the celebratory bit being me still being around to celebrate still being alive. Lockdown kills it. The sickly folk of Suffolk are hurled into Tier 4 on Boxing Day. Typical.

28

SEWER PIPE DREAM

People always ask me this: how many acts do you currently have on the Fierce Panda label roster? I always say twelve and a half. This is patently far too many acts for a company our size, but it's testament to our sickeningly nice niceness and our lovingly lovely love of new bands, so it's a good thing, because we'd like to think that if Felicity Kendal ever ran a record company it would be like Fierce Panda. Truth is: like a poverty-stricken Victorian family we always have to have loads of bands on our roster in case they are too frail and sickly to make it into their second year, or the gin-addled manager drops them in the effluent-ravaged river, or we have to sell the wee mite-ridden mites off to the workhouse, or the little scallywags run away to sea and we have to find someone else to make music for us in our dotage.

Here's an example of the madness inherent in ruminating over the whys and wherefores of the music industry: we call it 'The Case of 485C v. Fontaines DC' (to be read out loud, verrrry slowly, as 'The Case of Four-Eight-Five-cee Versus Fontaines

Dee-Cee'). One of these bands got a lot of early Fierce Panda love. They were five young men who looked super cool and made angsty, zingy, zeitgeisty guitar-driven alt-rock. The songs were intelligent, instinctive and poetic, with a heartfelt anthemic overtone and immense commercial potential. They played early Club Fandango shows under the guidance of Chrisorder at the Finsbury, the Shacklewell Arms and the Victoria, accruing cool radio play, blog coverage and industry love along the way.

The other band was Fontaines DC. Or was it 485C? Actually, it was both.

In essence, for a while Fontaines DC and 485C were running neck and neck and neck in terms of credibility and creativity in their early career rise. In fact, in some ways 485C were slightly ahead at one point, primarily because their manager Andy Ross decided that to break clear of the alt-pop pack their album should be speedily released, which it duly was in April 2018, a whole year before Fontaines DC hit paydirt with their *Dogrel* debut.

So far, so many terrific songs and so much in common. But as history has proved, their journeys have been drastically different since then. In fact, while Fontaines DC powered their way from showcasing at the Victoria in the spring of 2018 to headlining Brixton Academy within two years, 485C didn't have much of a journey at all, slouching their way from the Sebright Arms back to the suburban garden of delight known as Woodford.

In many ways, fewer lessons are as salient as this one. In another way, the key thing to remember is that in this instance Fontaines DC are the woodwork-squeaking freaks: don't look at their rise from the Victoria to Brixton Academy within the blink of a Friesian's eye and think that's a model you can follow, because that's not normal. Their timing just happened to be impeccable; from browsing the bars of Dublin to sliding into

Idles' slippery slipstream on a brilliantly emboldened Partisan Records, Fontaines DC were the right right-on band with the right post-punk palpitations on the right supercool label at the right time.

But bands can't stop themselves. These glory stories inspire them, empower them. They make them want to be bigger, stronger, drive a faster car. Frankly, a lot of bands want their debut album to be their *OK Computer*. As ever, you can't fault their ambition, but a lot of these bands are blithely ignoring the fact that even Radiohead's debut wasn't *OK Computer*, it was *Pablo Honey*, which not a lot of people liked very much, and then they had to bend everyone's ears with the brilliant *The Bends* after that to get anyone to truly care.

I loved Andy Ross's attitude towards the 485C debut, which was 'We have a corking band with thirteen cracking songs, let's make an album.' I loved it because I talk to bands who have thirteen of their own cracking single and EP tracks up on Spotify but somehow they don't think they are ready to make that leap of faith towards their debut album. And, when it does come to the time when they should release that debut album, they have abandoned all those great Spotify tracks because they think they're too old, or they have split up, or the world has lost interest, or all of the above has occurred in one giant furball of failure.

In short, while a lot of things can go very right for a very select band of bands, there are dozens of problems waiting to pounce on another 485 bands out there facing the same pitfalls as 485C. Late one morning during the pre-post-COVID fifteen-band carnage of our Pandamonium '22 mini-festival event I woke up and found that at some hazy point the night before I had scrawled 'The Wobbles' on my left hand. The memory banks charge themselves up, back to the Victoria the evening before. Back a bit, back a bit . . . piles of bands, pints of Milk lager, chats with Kelly from End of the Trail . . . who came up with the term 'The Wobbles' to describe the moment when bands start to think for themselves, when they start to grow up, when they hit the first major junction in their little musical journeys. Robert Johnson might have sold his soul at the crossroads, but a lot of modern bands just bumble around in the middle of the nearest mini-roundabout walking into each other and looking confused. Which way should they bump?

The reason I enjoy the first six months to a year of a band's rise, why I cherished doing the classic one-off singles, is because they are the sweetest times because you feel as though your efforts are appreciated, or at least acknowledged with a thank you on the sleeve of the major label album release. There is an air of excitement, of anticipation, and it's a fragrant air that can mask various inter-band horrors lurking beneath the sweet facade, but this is before the egos have expanded, before the internal squabbles have started, before 'The Wobbles' have wobbled.

What very often happens for many a band is that everything generally goes tits up during the first lull, which occurs after the band has fizzed around the circuit and had four or five tracks played on the radio. When they sell out 200-capacity venues like the Lexington they have to change their live strategy to progress, they have to start spacing out the shows to climb up the live ladder: three months before they can play the Moth Club or Bush Hall; six months before they can headline Dingwalls or the Scala. The bigger the next venue, the bigger the next gap to promote the show, to sell more tickets, to spread that word. It's a lot easier and faster to clamber up the live ladder when you are on a label with money, but it's tougher than overcooked mutton chops when you're on the indiest of indie labels.

It's here where the hard work starts, especially psychologically. Because for the first time since those excitable early rehearsals, bands start getting time to think, and when that happens bad things happen because a lot of bands are very, very bad thinkers. Once you are up over the Lexington hurdle things should be easier for the whole team around the band: it means you have a fanbase you can build on, a crowd you can call your own, an audience that legitimises your work, your art, your songcrafting. If you hit that next target of 300, 400, 500 real punters, you continue that momentum onwards and start making money – the glue that holds an extraordinary number of cracked bands together.

But so many bands on our bunker-high level don't even make it that far. Some of 'The Wobbles' are entirely logical: band members might need to get proper jobs because they have London rents to pay, which restricts their touring potential. Conversely, some bands consist entirely of nineteen-year-olds fresh out of sixth form living at family homes, but they are too young to drive tour vans because, I presume, their little legs don't reach the pedals. I know of one band who held it together for just long enough to release an album on the Panda, and I know of another band who had an excellently successful Panda album launch at the Lexington – and promptly split up the following day.

We do actually do due diligence on all potential signings – ironically enough considering how fast you can get music out to the marketplace, often nowadays it will take a year or more from getting that first demo to getting out that first release on Fierce Panda. We will sit down with the artist and the manager and explain in precise detail how we don't give a toss about streaming numbers and everything we love about live shows and radio play, and they nod knowingly and then three months later they are moaning like crazy about their streaming figures and fucking off to do a much better job themselves.

So there they go, underground, overground, wobbling free. The bassist wants to go to art school. The singer wants to get rid of the drummer. The lead guitarist wants to stay home with his partner. The singer wants to get rid of the keyboard player. The rhythm guitarist wants to join another band. The singer wants to rule the world. One thing that always perplexed me is why it seemed like it was always my favourite band member who left first. Maybe that was because they didn't hang around long enough to have a moan-up, so I have fond memories of them. Maybe it's because they didn't have enough time to become poisoned by their surroundings. Actually, most bands don't really moan to us – they moan to their manager or their agent or their partners, but not us. Then they just leave or split up to go spit into the eternal darkness. So the pain of dealing with pissed-off bands on the label is fairly ephemeral – you rarely get the full extent of any aggrieved band's moanings because there is a manager in the way taking the brunt of it. But when you *are* the manager of the band . . . oh boy, oh boy, that's taking 'The Wobbles' to another level of absolute wobblitude.

The worst bit is when you manage a band that simply stops listening. After the glory days of the early radio play, the bloggy compliments and the A&R interest this is when the hangover strikes, the party's over. All of a sudden, apropos of absolutely sod all – apart from a severe attack of The Wobbles – they suddenly think they can do better themselves. The once-jovial bants and innocent plannings are usurped by mutterings and mumblings and grumpy grumblings. Worse still, that fresh-faced manager who was once seen as a visionary, pushing that band forward, plotting out a career path, sorting a great plugger and a top live agent and a tidy publishing deal and meetings with half a dozen major labels, now sounds like Miss Othmar, Charlie Brown's school teacher from *Peanuts*, droning on and on: 'Wah wah wah wah wah wah!' Heat indeed.

Of course, when bands keep leaving because they've stopped believing in the Panda's lo-fi, no-finances philosophy it's easy to blame a succession of musicians and managers for their short termism and their hi-falutin impossible-to-achieve ambitiousness. But, then again, it's just as easy to consider that possibly, just possibly, being on Fierce Panda Records is not quite a bed of roses (apart from the little pricks, natch), and maybe, just maybe, as a label we're a woeful disappointment to the indie disco kids, stupefied as we are by our own thick stupendousness. It's a valid point.

In other words, even as I write this I can absolutely guarantee that one of our acts will be talking to Another Label With Big Budgets; another will be being romanced by a New Manager With Big Plans (which will almost certainly involve talking to Another Label as well); another will be talking to a groovy PR company or cool blog who've decided to launch a new label much groovier and cooler than Fierce Panda; and another will be planning to self-release their next single to keep all those Spotify 'millions' to themselves. Oh, and another will be looking at the entire streaming income from those Spotify 'millions' and thinking, 'Just what is the fucktwatting point?' before they spend that entire streaming income on one last round in the Give It Up Arms.

PANDAMONIUM!

This is why we never, ever say we are too full to sign just one more wafer-thin act to Fierce Panda Records. This is quite possibly why I was still going to so many futile gigs watching so many bands with absolutely no future towards the finale of my previous so-called life.

WINTER 2020–21

I am becoming alarmingly domesticated, to the point where I have taken over the family washing and ironing. As a man who can make a Desperate Journalist Grow Up T-shirt last for four days, there is one thing I immediately notice – why do girls wear SO MANY CLOTHES?

This year there will be times when there are live shows, and there will be times with no live shows. SXSW is once again shunted online, which kinda sets the unsettling agenda for the muddled months ahead. In lieu of any Austin action I pop out for a haircut and accidentally come home with some tattoos. Well, first I decide to get a tattoo of Scout's name in Japanese, and that goes so well I go back to the top-secret tattoo parlour (Inked Tattoos, just around the corner from the Pickerel pub near the train station) and get two more. One is 'NING 500', the other is 'It's a doggie dog world', which is one of the funniest malapropisms known to proper jokers with slightly poor hearing. It's in Indie Flower font to make it look really amateur and, indeed, indie. 'It's a Doggie Dog World' was also going to be the name of this book until someone sensible stepped in. But it captures the essence of the story – this isn't 'kill your friends', it's thrill your friends. Or maybe kiss your friends. Either works for me.

29

VIOLENTLY PRETTY FACE

I've always been a maudlin fucker. One day I asked Nigel Ugly Child what he listens to before he leaves the house to meet me in the pub or heads off to a live show: 'Oh, something like the Ramones or Motörhead,' he breezed, 'something to vibe me up.' I, on the other hand, listen to serene, sincerely sad songs by Mercury Rev and the Flaming Lips. Maybe I'm convincing myself things can only get better.

Even as an unknowing nipper my favourite Simon & Garfunkel songs were the weepies – 'So Long, Frank Lloyd Wright', 'The Only Living Boy in New York', 'April, Come She Will'. Armed with my transistor radio I fixated on Nilsson's 'Without You', Bobby Goldsboro's 'Summer (The First Time)', 'I'm Not in Love' by 10cc. Even with the Wombles it was the lachrymose 'Orinoco's Song' which took the battered biscuit. And, even amid the kaleidoscopic space-age charms of *Out of the Blue* by the mighty ELO, it's 'It's Over', 'Big Wheels' and 'Wild West Hero' that always seemed to tinkle the melancholic music box. In my world, as in so many others, the musical weather channel is always tuned to 'Grey Day', never 'Mr Blue Sky'.

I never considered that indie music was ever really noted for its raw emotion. Leastways, not until 'Wonderwall' invented indie MOR wedding songs and then 'Fix You' by Coldplay, 'Bad Day' by Keane, 'Run' by Snow Patrol, and the-one-about-pulling-the-curtains-wide by Elbow filled dewy-eyed Father's Day Dad Rock Anthem Albums from here to infinity and Beyoncé.

When I were a lad, any self-respecting indie outfit writing an overt love song would be seen as terribly uncool and quite probably mocked down Bay 63, with the possible exception of 'Lovesong' by the Cure because everyone secretly wanted to be Robert Smith in their maddest, cat-huggingly hair-sprayed nightmares. But that doesn't mean to say that some of those gently adored leftfield records didn't lack emotion to go with all the rumbling, tumbling motion: 'I'll Be Your Surprise' by Hurrah! and 'Therese' by the Bodines and 'Frans Hals' by McCarthy all encapsulated that giddy rush of falling and laughing in and out and in and out of love.

There's an intelligence that links those favourite tunes, bonded by an artistry and sensitivity that somehow contrives to create its own instant nostalgia – just add waterworks. Some expressions take me back, back to a time of earning your tiger-cub stripes and listening to artists yearning for the unknown: in the Red Guitars' 'Sunday Afternoon (National Avenue)', a glum groove gently comforts a tale of fragrant regret as the lyrics create their own crushing narrative. In the sensationally minimalist 'Tiny Children' by The Teardrop Explodes, Julian Cope's hope is gone as he croons, *'Oh I could make a meal of that wonderful despair I feel / But waking up I turn and face the wall.'* Amid the dusty glamour of 'She Gets Out the Scrapbook', Furniture ask, *'Did we really live like this?'*

Did we really, really live like this? And when words are never enough just dive into the ecstatic musical pools of 'Those Eyes, That Mouth' by Cocteau Twins, because there's an imperfect elegance to these songs, a poignancy that warrants the crackling vinyl and stuttering CD re-re-replays even these days.

Perhaps I'm being too sensitive, too susceptible, just too bloody stupid. But listen to the Bodines on 'Heard It All' sighing, *'When you think she's lonely / You phone just to make sure.'* Then try to stop listening to 'Don't Look Back' by Teenage Fanclub, 'Don't Look Back' by the Korgis, 'Don't Look Back in Anger' by Oasis, 'Don't Talk. . .' by the Beach Boys, 'Don't Sing' by Prefab Sprout. In so many ways, you were always leaving me now.

It is often said that life imitates art. But at what point does death imitate art? I spent seven years itching to set up a website called itsyourindiefuneral.com – I especially liked the way you could pull out the words 'die' and 'funeral'. This was partly triggered by a series of deaths of everyone close to me, like Auntie Norma, Shadowfax, Uncle Jimmy, 'Uncle' John – another year, another passing – and the intense conversations I had with cousins Linsey and Jonny about the funeral tunes that should be played (their grandparents Jimmy and Norma's celebrations were both soundtracked by Paul Simon). It also stemmed from some time spent sitting in the Hoe Street Co-op funeral directors in 2012 sorting the final points for my mother's farewell, being threatened by hulking West Ham United-themed coffins and perusing the frankly giant funeral song catalogue.

Amid the hundreds and hundreds of tearful tunes – little wonder the pages were laminated – I found Coldplay, Snow Patrol, Keane and 'Wake Me Up When September Ends' by Green Day. And that was it. The world, I quite rightly decided right there and then in the back room of the Hoe Street Co-op, needed a new source of mournful material: a fresh angle on 'Angels'; an alternative path to 'My Way'; a wind of change to blow out 'Candle in the Wind'; a new sound to steer you away from the classic last knocking rockings of 'Stairway to Heaven' or 'Highway to Hell' or 'Spirit in the Sky'.

Plus, as my mother's demise came as more of a surprise to her than anyone else, she had left no funeral requests and, as an only child, the onus was on me to organise the whole shebang, from the bamboo coffin set for a-smoulderin' in Wanstead Crematorium to the wake at the Sir Alfred Hitchcock in Leyton, including, but of course, the music. Something classy and classical to kick off with, I thought, like Mozart. Something folkie and fun to close with, like Steeleye Span's 'All Around My [Bloody] Hat', thought I. And something groovy and emotional right in the middle, like 'Bridge over Troubled Water'. Sorted for tears and fizz.

Oh, hang on. 'Ooooh no, she hated that song!' her friend Roger exclaimed when I told him of my playlist plans. Did she?? Blimey. So I chose 'The Boxer' by Simon & Garfunkel instead, which gave the entire congregation the opportunity to be comforted by the fury of twenty-one increasingly raging cries of 'lie-la-lie' over a hurricane of strings. It really is quite the angry tune.

When it comes to funerals, you have to be strangely careful, if not downright carefully strange. There is a certain caustic pithiness to song titles like 'Going Underground' by the Jam, 'Miles Apart' by Mega City 4, 'Monkey Gone to Heaven' by the Pixies, and 'Whenever I'm Gone' by the Prisoners. And, if there is a cheery insouciance to choosing 'Bye Bye Baby' by the Bay City Rollers, you get added bonus indie points if you go for the Pop Guns' version, putting the 'fun' into 'funereal' for sure. Forty-one years after my holiday in Whipps Cross Hospital,

I heard 'Seasons in the Sun' played by Ken Bruce on Radio 2 while sitting in the Knutsford Services car park on the M6 way up to the north and finally twigged the whole bally Terry Jacks song was about suicide. This was shortly before I almost choked to death on a chunk of chicken zinger burger. The irony. It's finger-kickin' good.

There was to be no mirthful musicality at my farewell. I left very specific instructions back in my Tavistock Hotel shrine, a definitive list of funeral songs. Or, in this case, a deathfinitive list. What is on the sad-faced shortlist? The lovely, lovely 'Sad Sad Stage' by Goldheart Assembly is knocking about searching for a final curtain call. 'Love Her' by the Walker Brothers almost makes it as a proper '60s epic message from the Other Side. 'Be Kind' by Desperate Journalist is closer still, all apologies and raging melodies from the edge: '*I hope you don't mind all the stupid things I put you through.*' The hypnotic 'Feeling Yourself Disintegrate' by the Flaming Lips is also close, but once again perhaps the line '*Life without death / Is just impossible*' might cut a touch too much to the raw emotional core.

In fact, it is typically, classically, fringe-flappingly, navel-gazingly indie behaviour to think about these things so much you end up jettisoning potential funeral songs because they would be too much for the congregation to take. I mean, it's like you're even going to be there to see their reaction, is it? Anyway, me and my old Club Fandango mucker Adie, who knows a bit about building a website from scratchy conversations in the Enterprise, wisely decided that itsyourindiefuneral.co.uk was a rubbish name for a site about sad songs, so we rebranded it mourningglories.co.uk because that's both funnier and sadder at the same time, which is a very difficult trick to pull off when it comes to the world of maudlin fuckering about.

Somewhat handily, the first three tracks we uploaded were nailed down for my last dance. The first is the stark tumult of 'Bloodrush' by Bark Psychosis; the second is the song for all rages, 'The Rat' by the Walkmen; and the third is Richard Hawley's 'Open Up Your Door', which as a starting point for funereal farewells goes is possibly not the most obvious seeing as how it has soundtracked commercial jollities such as advertorials for Renault Meganes and Häagen-Dazs ice creameries, but in fact, 'Open Up Your Door' works perfectly because it is epic, emotional, immaculately constructed and very, very classy.

The picture on the Mourning Glories home page is of London's Malet Street in the drizzle, caught in the haziest shade of winter, with University of London Union in the left-hand-side corner. This I know to be true because I took that very picture on the night of 31 December 2019. You could call it the last picture of ULU to fit alongside 'The First Picture of You', but that would be a wee bit clumsy. You could also call this insufferable self-indulgence, which is also fairly clumsy, but after you've seen the things I've been through you might just call it sensible forward planning. My psychiatrist says obsessing over funeral songs is not a healthy thing. I wonder what he thinks about me devoting a whole wide world-wide website to them.

Beyond the admittedly limiting parameters of my own insuf-ferable self-indulgence the ultimate ambition for the Mourning Glories site is to have it sitting as a portal of comfort for those feeling a little bit mortal; a central hub for the remembrance of lost loved ones, whose families might want to contribute their own choices to the list, so it becomes a source of celebration amid the grief; a living librarium of farewell songs for people holding on and looking for that ideal song to soundtrack a far from ideal situation. And, if you have any doubt about the need of such a website for bloodshot eyes, just go and take a look at any of those songs lurking above 'swooning' on that there YouTube and read the comments flowing below from people pouring out their shattered, tattered little hearts.

Back in 2014, the day before Shadow was going to be put down by the vet after a long battle with illness – she was on the cusp of her fourteenth birthday, a proper big old achievement for a big old Weimaraner – I don't mind admitting that before the rest of the house was awake I was giving her a big old snuggle lying on her bed on the kitchen floor during Steve Wright's *Sunday Love Songs*.

And I certainly don't mind admitting that halfway through 'Love Me for a Reason' by the Osmonds, Panda tears were gently trickling down onto Shadow's lovely silky, flappy, tired old ears.

'*Love me for a reason / Let the reason be love.*'

Key change.

It's a doggie dog world.

SPRING 2021

On 20 May, I go to my first gig since for ever, Gladboy at Norwich Arts Centre. I work out that while I very much love table service, this is counterbalanced by the sitting trapped by those tables during rock 'n' roll antics. The indie tiger is somewhat tamed. Not as tamed, mind you, as when China Bears play a Sofar Sounds show on 30 June, one of those funny little communal things where nice people pay good money to sit down and shut up and pay attention to a selection of live acts playing stripped-back sets. Intriguingly, these people pay their money without knowing who is playing or exactly where whoever may be playing might actually be playing. What we do know is that – thrill of all thrills – China Bears are playing somewhere in Walthamstow, which gives me a ripe opportunity to wallow in various old alleyways.

The old top-secret Damaged Panda office next door to the Labour Party HQ is now an indie flower shop. I sup some old-time lager in the Nag's Head pub with a handful of salted nuts and a headful of salty memories before meeting Chrisorder in the Goose at Walthamstow Central station. At some point this evening I will go online and treat myself by purchasing an utterly lovely Finland national team shirt, as advertised in the Euros. At another point I will lose my Stone Roses facemask on the lengthy journey from Walthamstow Central to Blackhorse Road, because China Bears aren't playing WAH 17 or even the Royal Standard, and this we know because they are playing one of the new-fangled breweries by the reservoirs, and on the way to it we go past the Royal Standard, which is very much XXXXing shut down. At the end of the evening, I walk the length of the longest market in Britain and whistle down the Waltham Forest wind, past the old Sainsbury's and back to lodge at a Travelodge that didn't exist when I last lived and loved in E17.

30

NEVER SEEN BEFORE

It seems a bit harsh to keep blaming my mother for missing out on seminal gigging events four decades after the actual gigging event, especially over her dead body. But rest assured she still had a tiny ghostly hand in me swerving an encounter with ELO when they hit the comeback trail even after she'd been laid to rest, if having your ashes tossed over the Mousehole harbour wall into the churning Atlantic Ocean in the middle of a Cornish gale can be considered in any way 'restful'. The one good thing about the single parent/only lonely child interface is that when she died, far too young, far too far gone, there wasn't a tremendous amount of debate about the will or ownership of the family home sitting empty in Forest View Road.

The inheritance money we didn't spend on fixing up the farm or burn through keeping Fierce Panda and Club Fandango alive for another six minutes went on a dream family holiday, a week on Sentosa Island in Singapore followed by a week in a villa on Koh Samui in Thailand. All went fabulously, swimmingly well until the penultimate evening of the fortnight when, leaving the villa to go to dinner, the somewhat erratic outside security light decided to turn itself off and I decided to miss a big step in the sudden pitch-black tropical darkness and crashed down onto my left ankle. In the olden days of the '70s no doubt we'd have shrugged it off as a sprain and crawled to the bar for a cocktail and a kickabout, but this being the modern world, and this being me rolling around the pitch-black tropical garden spitting out miraculous expletives before going into shock, instead there was a trip to the local (very nice) hospital. Gliding beneath bright white lights through eerily deserted corridors, the X-ray revealed a broken metatarsal and heaps of ligament damage. The doctor was friendly and very much to the point. 'As soon as you get home,' he said beaming, 'you will need an operation to fix this.'

Luckily our holiday was coming to an end anyway, so after a bit of calculating to ensure British Airways wouldn't refuse to carry us lest I died mid-flight, we flew back home, out of the delightful Koh Samui airport – it really is lovely, if Sylvanian Families made departure lounges, etcetera – transferring via a blood-thinning injection at Bangkok, just to make doubly sure I didn't pass away 30,000 feet above Belarus.

After a couple of days back in Blighty I headed to the BMI hospital in Bury St Edmunds to be fixed. From here on in the break wasn't the problem, per se – once the metatarsal was back in place and the sprain damage started to recede, it was the meds from the operation that were causing a mess. I wasn't going to be leaving Suffolk for weeks. To make no attempt whatsoever to cut a long story short, this meant that I missed ELO's great comeback at Hyde Park for the Radio 2 Live show in 2014. Chris Evans had convinced Jeff Lynne that his time was now. Sadly, mine was not.

So, if my mother hadn't died when she did, I wouldn't have gone to Koh Samui and I wouldn't have savaged my ankle and I would have got to see ELO. Butterflies in Singapore. Broken metatarsals in Thailand. Etcetera bloody etcetera.

Having also successfully avoided the subsequent Electric Light Orchestra shows at Glastonbury and Wembley Stadium owing to reasons beyond my dead mother's control, in 2018 they announced a UK tour, with four nights at the O2 in London. What to do, what to do, what to do? Got my arse into organisational gear. Got a pair of free tickets from my man at Live Nation, who happened to manage one of our Panda acts. Who to take, who to take, who to take?? Scout. She was fifteen, just three years older than her old paps was when ELO played Wembley Empire. History would not be repeating itself.

On Sunday 21 October 2018, we take the big train to London Village and the Jubilee line to the east. On the guest list, so get there nice and early in case of queue madness, but there's hardly any mad queue at all. The guest tickets are worth somewhere north of 100 quid. Each. Time for a tipple in the All Bar One. Pint for the paps, a J2O at the jolly O2 for Scout. There's a lovely chilled vibe, no shouting, no madness, just loads of fifty-something couples and groups of friends smiling and nodding knowingly at the ELO tunes being piped through the bar. Excited.

Northampton singing roustabout Billy Lockett is supporting. Last time I saw him he was exhausting twenty-three people at Norwich Open. This time around it's slightly different and he's very grateful to be playing to a good few thousand people more here, but I still feel very sad that the venue hasn't been rebranded the ELO2 for the four-night stint. Seven quid for a pint inside the arena? Why, that just means the bars are empty because nobody else is insane enough to pay those lunatic prices. In fact, the last time it was this easy to get a drink at a gig was Jason Donovan at Hammersmith Odeon, primarily because 86 per cent of his crowd was nine years old and would struggle to see over the bar, let alone be able to afford to actually buy anything.

ELO start. Scout knows a few of their songs from some things called 'memes'. 'Concerto for a Rainy Day', 'Sweet Talkin' Woman', 'Turn to Stone', 'Wild West Hero', something called 'Mr Blue Sky' . . . Amid the blazing green lasers, the thought occurs they could actually just play their way right through *Out of the Blue* and everyone in here would be over the moon. But there is more: 'Livin' Thing' and 'Telephone Line' from *A New World Record*; 'Shine a Little Love' and 'Last Train to London' from *Discovery*; 'Showdown' and 'Do Ya' and 'All Over the World', all performed with a fizz and a muscular panache by Take That's backing band with Jeff Lynne standing in the middle of all the luminous lights, perplexed by the acclaim, the most normal rock star in the arena full of utterly normal Normans like me.

We know many of these songs from our long-lost childhoods, although things have changed since the Wembley Empire shows of 1978: there is no Bev Bevan on the beefy drums; there is no Mik Kaminski on the violinski; there is no spaceship descending from the open skies. And in my head I mentally scribble an entire setlist of songs that they didn't play – 'Twilight' and 'Calling America' for starters, 'Mission' and 'It's Over' for enders.

But Richard Tandy is still there on keyboards, vocodering his way through the ending of 'Mr Blue Sky' with the infamous vinyl-era spoken word line of 'Please turn me over'. And for a few serene soft-rocking moments, with Scout and 16,000 gently rocking middle-aged musicateers by my side, I don't actually feel entirely alone in this universe. In fact, I think it might have been the last time I was truly happy in My Other Life. Sweet, sweet is the night.

SUMMER 2021

A new kind of gigging semi-normality is settling upon us, a semi-normality where you basically cross your fingers and hope that what you've planned to happen actually takes place. So Scout and I go to Newcastle to check out Pit Pony at the Cluny and aim to see the relatives, but the mother-in-law is still shielding so we can't pay her a visit. Then we go to Bristol to see some old family friends called Mike and Jan near Bath and on to see China Bears at the Bristol Thekla to find that one of the Bears have been pinged, so we end up going to see Lovely Eggs at the Fleece instead. Any port in a storm.

In the middle of it all there is the return of Latitude Festival, which I believe is cleared to go as a COVID test event, i.e. a mask-free hoedown. It's certainly a shock to burst out of the woods and be suddenly confronted by thousands upon thousands of muddled-class revellers going gently batshit in a Suffolk dustbowl trying to work out which acts have been pinged and therefore replaced by entirely different acts. It certainly keeps us on our dusty toes.

31

FIRESTATION TOWERS

The second time I walked out on Coldplay was on 14 November 2018. Out of the Curzon Cinema, right opposite the fire station on Shaftesbury Avenue. The premiere for the *A Head Full of Dreams* film. Exciting! Andy Pointy and myself had been invited along. Be churlish not to.

The evening had started very well: a stroll along Wardour Street; a couple of snifters with Andy around the corner in the Spice of Life, then the two of us going excitedly into the cinema, like '60s kids going to see *The Jungle Book* at the Walthamstow Granada. Except instead of choc ice and Revels here we were served classy free drinks and canny gratis canapés.

There's Gavin Maude the lawyerman, there's Caroline Elleray their publisher, there's Debs Wild, the optimum discoverer . . . the original gang's all here. In fact, one reason I was feeling especially relaxed was that a few weeks before I'd been riffing with Debs. She'd just written the Coldplay book, *Life in Technicolor*, which told the full story of the band's authentic rise and rise, including quotes from Andy Pointy and myself. She'd also had a massively helpful hand in the plotting of our reissue of the *Brothers & Sisters* EP on a pair of coloured vinyl 7-inch singles in the pub. We always go to the Wetherspoons on Highbury Corner and laugh heartily about the irony of the two of us boozing in a cosy booth of a midweek afternoon, raising the cheapest of glasses to the biggest band in the world.

'Seeing as how I don't remember anybody interviewing me with a camera recently, I presume I don't make an appearance in the film?' I joked.

'Oh, none of us do,' she replied cheerfully, referring to the original gang with the canapés and the can-do spirit. 'It's not *that kind* of film.'

Hurray! So I didn't have to sit there waiting for my fat sweaty face to appear bursting out of the giant screen with inane platitudes and insane eyes. Apparently, it was supposed to be an arty state of intent. And it started amazingly, with some live footage from some South American supergig. An explosive entrance, followed by some no less sensational rare footage of the Coldplay (as they were) from the Camden Laurel Tree (as it was). And then, very slowly, it started. The story. The routine. The blah blah blah. This happened, and then this happened, and then this happened. Basically, they did a couple of toilet-circuit gigs and they had a big plan and then Steve Lamacq saw them at the Falcon, and then they signed to Parlophone and then they became the most enormously large band in the known universe. No Panda, no point. Alternatively, no FP, no comment.

Actually, it wasn't all sweetness and sugar-coated light – there was some pithy work on the ill-advised sacking and reinstating of drummer Will Champion, for starters – but in so many ways I'd seen this film before. So halfway through I stormed out. Well, actually I scurried out, hunched over so as not to ruin anyone's view, but out I went into the grizzly West End drizzle, back down Wardour Street, through the wary dark shadows.

Andy Pointy didn't get off so lightly. He stayed until the end when there was a Q&A with the director, who had to apologise to a lot of people pissed off about a lot of people who hadn't got a mention in his film, so it wasn't just me. But still, petty and petulant behaviour? Of course. Trust me when I say I hated myself for doing what I did far more than you ever could. Which, in many ways, is the theme of this book. Is this the start of the breakdown? I can't understand me.

One day in the *NME* office at the start of my '90s, waggish West Country correspondent Stephen Dalton said, 'You've got a hole in your head!' Or was it an ever-sympathetic Swells? A what in my what now?? Oh, I see. Sadly, it wasn't the kind of hole that meant you could look through a bionic eye, like on the Six Million Dollar Man man-doll from the '70s. This was a hole in the back of my hair, and it was the start of an off-off relationship with alopecia that carried on for the next couple of decades.

At its very worst, I thought it would be an entirely good idea to get all of my (remaining) hair cut off in a Turkish barber shop on the Lea Bridge Road. This in fact was an entirely bad idea as my head then looked like a very shaggy map of the world reimagined by, well, a drunk barber on the Lea Bridge Road. At its best, it was a patchy situation cunningly disguised by a Greek fisherman's cap, and illuminated by the weird fact that the fallen follicles eventually grew back in shocking white patches.

Either way, it was a clear manifestation of stress. As a freelance music journalist you literally can't afford to be ill, so you gig and you write and you drink and you drink and you write and you gig and you push and gig and write and drink and push yourself until eventually the relentlessly unhealthy, recklessly fantastic lifestyle takes its toll and the physical system either starts shutting itself down or, in my case, causes my barnet to start committing some kind of hairy hara-kiri. Eventually, it simply has to come out somewhere.

So there was never any massive breakdown on a Jumbo Jet – just a gentle decline, a serene glide towards insanity. Although one day in my early thirties I thought it would be quite interesting to try flying sober for once. As ideas go, this one was on a par with getting my hair shaved off by Sweeney Timur. You could say I was flying without nings. I was certainly 30,000 feet up with my unusually clear head in spin. My God! How does this thing stay up? What am I doing here?? Is this food??? The take-off was torture, the landing even worse, the knock-on effects ghastly.

From that day on it seemed like I'd crossed some mad divide. I'd triggered something lurking deep inside, or perhaps the workaholic lifestyle had finally caught up with me. After all, if just scribbling some words for the *NME* caused my hair to fall out, imagine the inner chaos caused by releasing records, DJing and putting, putting, putting on live shows on the side? Either way, having been fearless and rarely beer-less since 1986, all of a sudden everything on the outside world was an unnerving challenge, epitomised by public transport.

I'd always loved going underground. In fact, I loved going underground as much as I loved 'Going Underground' by the Jam. But at one point, at the so-called peak of Fierce Panda's so-called underground credibility around the millennium, ironically enough I was too scared to get on the Tube. Even the fastest five-minute journey seemed to go on for fifteen days. It wasn't so much fight or flight – neither would be entirely recommended when squeezed onto a stationary crush-hour carriage stuck in the long, long tunnel between Seven Sisters and Finsbury Park – as the relentless, churning hot sweat of claustrophobia mixed with the cold fear of agoraphobia. Next stop on the Mental Central line: Panic Station.

So one day I just stopped getting the Tube and either got buses or walked everywhere. Living in Holloway Road meant that I wasn't lacking in local gigging entertainment, after all – at one point I had the Garage, Hope & Anchor, Buffalo Bar, Archway Tavern and Nambucca all within slouching distance of the front door. But that brought its own problems as every one of those gigs seemed to be packed out. It wasn't so bad if I was on a solo mission and could make a swift getaway, but not so handy when it was our own gig where I had to perform, to engage, for the entire evening – as outlined in big nights out previously we weren't lacking in live soirées. I could stop the tubing, but I felt that there was no way I could stop the gigging.

Liann was a great help: at some especially stressful gigs I would simply hide in the shadows while she made her apologies for me and generally entertained bands and friends at the bar to divert them from any puzzlement as to my mysterious whereabouts. I think some people could see I was troubled, but I never discussed it with anyone. They looked concerned and asked, 'Are you okay?' but I never said, 'No'. What could I say? 'Oooh, I'm a bit scared of the tubey-wubey?' What next, 'The Endless Terrors of Thomas the Cantankerous Cunty Tank Engine'? Well, yes, but that's for another book. Just get on with it. Don't want to be a bother. There's work to be done, more bands to be signed, more records to be released, more gigs to be promoted, a morose business to be run right into the ground. Two medium glasses of house white will calm me down anyway. Be fine in the morning.

One day I was an hour late for a meeting with John Kennedy, Lucian Grainge's predecessor in the Universal hot seat. He was splendidly polite about it but I realised I had to get over myself. Sort yourself out, son. I eventually came out the other side, but the damage was done. Actually, I'm not sure I ever came out of the other side of anything, because in truth the relentless, restlessly distressed stress levels never really went away.

Earlier in 2018, not long before the Coldplay premiere, we did an album with molten Milton Keynes alt-rocksters Sean Grant & the Wolfgang. It was dark, riffy stuff that reminded me quite a little bit of Afghan Whigs and was called *The Shadows Are Lengthening*. As is traditional, I asked frontman Sean himself for a few insider thoughts on the album to spice up the press release. Those thoughts were so open and frank we had to double-check he was okay with us using them on that spicy press release. He said yes, so we sent out this:

During the writing of the album, I was in a very dark place personally, dealing with a lot of inner conflicts within my own life, battling with a depression that I'd struggled with and hidden my whole life . . . even from myself. The whole album is a box of inner demons, a diary of my internal voices. 'Souls Out' in particular is when everything has been stripped back to the bone, but even further than that, to your soul. You're standing naked, but more than naked there is no body, there is just your consciousness left floating like a tiny cosmos with no material things to

cling onto any more. 'Souls Out' is the end of the rope, the end of the line
when you've exhausted all other avenues.

To be fair, it gave me the chance to sign off the press release
with the line 'Never a Dulli moment indeed' in tribute to Afghan
Whigs' frontman Greg, which made me momentarily happy.
But it was a very brief moment. We ended up partnering with
CALM, aka the Campaign Against Living Miserably, for the
promotion of the *The Shadows Are Lengthening* album, so I know
where the very becalmed CALM staffers work (on the South
Bank, pretty much opposite the Tattershall Castle boaty pub). I
also know exactly where the Samaritans helpline number on the
bridge across the lines at Stowmarket train station lurks.

I have also read books about suicidal German goalkeepers – *A
Life Too Short: The Tragedy of Robert Enke*, which I first heard about on
a harrowing Radio 5 Live documentary in the bath; it does exactly
what it says on the cover. And I read *Quiet: The Power of Introverts in
a World That Can't Stop Talking* by Susan Cain to get to the source of
blushing indie shy boys battling against extrovert-factor corporate
sociopaths, only to be befuddled by an ending that decided that,
actually, you know, after all that, you could actually be an ambivert.
As an embattled fake messiah, aka Graham Chapman, once said,
'What sort of chance does that give me?'

Did it help? Well, by the summer of 2019 I'd say I'd pretty
much diagnosed myself as being catatonically depressed. I was
travelling into London after a long weekend at home feeling
more tired than I had been travelling home to Suffolk after a
slew of meetings and gigs. I was disappointed by those meetings,
disturbed by those gigs, increasingly disillusioned by bands and,
inevitably, dismissive of my own ailing talents. From being fully
supportive of the fragrantly chaotic Fierce Panda ethos and

fretting about our streaming numbers, the Orchard teamsters rather dramatically switched tack and decided that it was all my fault because I was old-fashioned and I should just sign things that sounded like everyone else and told me we were free to leave for another distribution company. I was exhausted, exasperated . . . *exhausperated*, in fact.

I presumed I couldn't afford therapy, even if I thought any treatment would help, which I presumed it wouldn't, so I followed what I presumed was classic therapy advice and kept a diary, giving myself marks out of ten, and I only stopped when one day I gave myself minus ten out of ten, because I thought that wasn't a very good sign. In November 2019, I had a meeting with Andy Pointy in the Famous Cock one chilly lunchtime to throw some ideas around, to try to come up with one more wafer-thin concept for a new Arts Council funding application to follow on from the two Fierce Panda Singles Clubs and the two Fierce Panda EP Clubs we'd run previously, some ace new idea to capture the imagination of the ACE overlords and get the cash flow flowing. We managed to flam up some half-arsed live touring concept, but the fruitiest of house rose-tinted inspiration was undermined, if not underwined, by my ceaseless exhausperation.

By this point I was not even making any attempt to hide my plight under a bushel: when asked how the label was going – which was not an infrequent occurence – I would always respond with, 'Oh, it's fucking terrible – never run a record company when nobody wants to buy records.' Of course, that isn't true – for me the truth was closer to 'Never run a record company when nobody wants to buy *your* records,' but by this grim point the semantics were starting to elude me.

Even traditional Christmas music business shenanigans brought little relief. At parties, where the free drinks would flow, I would bump into people from distribution, from other labels, from press, great people who'd been nudged out of their employment comfort zones by company cuts, by internal reshufflings, by infernal industry injustices, and who were now forced to do three jobs to pay the mortgage. Even as Noddy Holder was holding onto the stereo system, I was sucking up other people's pain like a totally sucky SpongeBob SquarePants. Merry cocking Xmas, everybody. You'll miss me when I'm gone. Perhaps.

AUTUMN 2021

On 31 September, furlough comes to a grinding halt. So we're officially back in the groove, if anyone can actually remember where they left their groove eighteen months ago. The very week the furloughing ends we host Pandemica-monium at the Victoria, a gentle six-night celebration of the return to gigging with the likes of Prima Queen and Gardening and Memes and Hatcham Social all appearing. And then everything appears to go slightly gig-tastic, if not entirely concert-mungous.

We live our wilder days in Norwich on 10 September when the Wildhearts go wild at Norwich Waterfront. On 17 October, we're back for Wild Paths and flowery sets by China Bears, Aphra, Feet, Bull, Grandma's House, Odd Morris and Hamburger Momma, who sound so unlike what you'd expect a band called Hamburger Momma to sound like (ethereal shoe-gaze whispered by waif-like girls), Hamburger Momma almost becomes a genius name. Almost. On 28 October, our very own Moon Panda headline the Lexington and you can virtually feel the crowd breathing a long sigh of relief at being back at the back of a tidily proportioned venue listening to a band deliver a set that itself sounds like a long, chilled, elegant sigh of musical relief.

On 12 October, we are invited along to see Coldplay play Shepherd's Bush Empire. It's quite the underplay, just the 2,000 souls. Ed Sheeran is invited along as well, but he gets onstage and plays some song called 'Shape of You'. There is an aftershow party, upstairs behind the Muppets seats. There is a very large queue to get into what appears to be a fairly small room. What do to, what to do, what to do? 'Dad,' says Scout, tugging on my sleeve, 'I'd quite like to get some noodles.' Showbiz be damned! We leave the Coldplay band – again – and their aftershow queue to get some warming Oriental sustenance way out east. Clever dad.

PANDAMONIUM!

On 13 November, the fantastical Finland footballering shirt I bought in the Walthamstow Goose on 30 June finally arrives. A great day. The 17th is another great day because it's the Great Escape's First Fifty party at Oslo and I see at least forty-eight of the shiniest happiest faces known to indiekind drinking free drinks like they thought they'd never see another free drink again. On 18 November, I face Facelift playing at Kelly End of the Trail's night at the Good Mixer, which makes me very happy because for at least four songs they sound mightily like the Higsons. These things matter. In fact, they matter more and more and a little bit more with each passing gig.

32

WHAT IS THERE
TO SMILE ABOUT?

I apologise. I really don't want to give the impression that I was a totally morose boredog through the final year of my previous life – in actual fact, I had just about mastered the dubious art of being a fully functioning anhedonic, and there were some really good times to be had, by other people at least.

There were significant family matters in the north-east-east of Englandshire, with cousin Linsey's lovely wedding to Daniel at Woodhorn Museum in Ashington NE63, and mother-in-law Jeane's significant birthday at North Biddick Social Club in Washington NE38, where it was two quid for a pint, which, if nothing else, gave me a fighting chance of redressing the fiscal imbalance triggered by those uber-pricey ELO2 pints a year earlier.

There were the Spurs' European glory glory nights with Russell and Martin in the pubs – Manchester City versus the Hotspurs in the Champions League quarters in the Three Compasses in Hackney, Ajax versus the Totteringtons in the legendarily seminal semi-final second leg in the Shacklewell Arms with a Dutch band headlining in the backroom. Divided loyalties? Not really – they were from Rotterdam and wanted the Hotspurs to win even more than we did.

This footballing extravaganza was only slightly undermined by bumping into Karen from Key Production the following lunchtime on the train from St Pancras to Brighton for the Great Escape, because she was at the Johan Cruyff Arena itself and so she saw the Poch fist-pumping frenzy in the flesh. Which reminds me, we had a smashing official showcase at the Great Escape with VC Pines, China Bears, Peeping Drexels and Skint & Demoralised playing Three Wise Cats between midday and 4 p.m. on the Friday. You poked your head out of the venue door and you could see the sea. If you timed everything swimmingly, you could check out a whole bill of bands and be totally rat-arsed and asleep on the beach by the middle of the afternoon.

There were stag dos for Steve Lamacq – one in a private box at Colchester United versus Leyton Orient, aka the A12 derby, with twelve angry indie men, the second a top-secret gig at Brixton Windmill with Idles and Goldheart Assembly. Then came Lammo's wedding to Jen in south London, a personal highlight being in the porta-queue for the Portaloos with Nadine Shah reminding a slightly flummoxed Felix Maccabees how they are for ever bonded by Fierce Panda.

Indie stalwarts BOB came to play at the John Peel Centre, so I reconnected gently with Richard and Simon, bringing a little bit of the old-school Latymer School vibe to Stowmarket. And the year ended in traditional slumped fashion, with an ex-desperate journalist drinking it up at the annual Panda Christmas drink at the Stag's Head with a gang of indie roustabouts, a mini-feast of friendly faces from bands, from labels, from management. Am I aware at this point of proceedings, around 17 December 2019, that I may never, ever see that mini-feast of friendly faces ever again? Yes, yes I am.

Because all of this was enjoyed – if that is in any way, shape or form the right phrase – with a weary sense of sorrow, suffused as I was with a perpetual sonic gloom. Loneliness really is the cloak you wear. One afternoon in the Lord Clyde I did an interview with a man called Will Simpson from a magazine called *Long Live Vinyl.* He said I was fun and that I fizzed with scampish enthusiasm. I didn't feel very fizzy, or very much like scampi. But the 'fun' bit I found interesting. Most of the time I saw myself – with a few layers of irony – as fun boy one, the original golden Lonely Boy. But sometimes I would have a meeting in the pub, and another meeting in the pub, and another meeting in the pub, and I felt like I was fun boy two, three and four. Given enough refreshment I could be the fun boy five as well.

But away from being fun boy free you feel trapped. You send out thirty-one emails to A&R, at least five of whom you've known for twenty-one years, and you get one response, which is an out-of-office message. You arrange a meeting with a man at a recording studio in Old Street, except he's totally forgotten about it and while you're kicking around the cobbled alleyways out east he's at a parents' meeting at a school in north-north-west London. Glancing at Jess Panda's *London In Stereo* gig guide magazine, it's not that it's full of names I had never heard of – it's full of names I couldn't even pronounce. You want to check out live sets by KF Shkupi, Nõmme Kalju and TSC Backa Topola? Good luck with that – they're actually all Europa League soccerball teams from north Macedonia, Estonia and Serbia, but fiction is always way stranger than the truth.

Ironically enough, for such a big Talk Talk fan, it was a hapless lack of actual talk talking that so very nearly did for me. God knows I tried, or at least I thought I did. I tried to engage with people, tried to get them to the pub, to sit them down, to listen, to help. Some friends were brilliant – as the cash flow became ever more sluggish Fierce Panda was bailed out more times than a cracked canoe in a monsoon – but these were just plasters slapped on the unseen wound. Friends had their own problems, their own fun families, their own internal battles, their own joyful outburstings. I didn't feel as though I could dig any deeper or push it any further. I didn't want to be a bother. The ultimate curse of the happy depressive, perhaps.

Nor was there much point in engaging with the youth of today to try to make sense of it all any more. As if my ghoulish visage isn't enough to unsettle anyone under the age of thirty-seven, I was now encountering young people who didn't know what Fierce Panda was – in fact, I was meeting people who could barely grasp the basic concept of what a record company was. This was the streaming generation, the kids brought up on a waterfalling deluge of cheap, perhaps entirely free, music and bands and songs. The kids who pop out a pop song before breakfast and expect to retire on their Spotify riches by the weekend.

How apt then that I should find myself confronted by an audience full of bored-looking young faces towards the end of 2019. It is midday on an autumnal Friday. I am on a panel at the Wild Paths festival in Norwich. It's at the Epic Studios venue. The bar is open. Last time I was here was for Dingus Khan at a John Peel night with the Fall and the Undertones. I'm still gently fizzing from seeing Bag of Cans at Voodoo Daddy's last night, who sounded like a regally manic mix of Blur and Dingus Khan and all of whom seemed to be called George. I spent the night at the Premier Inn Nelson Hotel. Now I am onstage on a lunchtime panel that asks, very simply, not to say a little bit sniffily, 'Do you even need a label any more?'

We chew the fat. In fact, we have a proper debate. The panel is composed of a variety of music industry tykes – an artist, a distributor and other properly knowledgeable showbiz types. I put forward the case for the defence of the record label, but, then again, knowing me, I quite probably manage to question the validity of my entire existence at the same time. Still, come the end of the session I instigate a public vote. Me! The bashful blushing bumbling middle-aged indie boy! On a stage! Under the lights! Asking an audience to make up their minds! The public wants what the public gets, after all.

So do you even need a label any more? Everyone puts their hand up. It's an overwhelming yes. Apart from one outraged outlier who probably dreams about being on AWAL. He disagrees. He is in the minority. But he might be my future.

So I boo him.

WINTER 2021–22

On 30 December, i.e. New Year's Eve eve, Nigel Ugly Child comes up from Colchester and takes me to the Pickerel pub. We finally celebrate the uncelebratable anniversary of the Grand Malarkey in style, or at least in as much style as can be mustered by two ageing indie gents with a few pints of Stella and some sterlingly elegant bants about bands. Nigel says this is now our new tradition – we're going to be celebrating the uncelebratable every New Year's Eve eve from hereon in. I like it. Being a creature of very peculiar habit, I return to the same venue the following night, on New Year's Eve itself. This time I go with Scout to see Five Mile High play live. This being the Pickerel, Five Mile High play a set of covers. They seem to really like Biffy Clyro. They also seem to play a lot of famous alt-rock bands' fifth most famous songs, which is curious but I guess at least connects in some way with their off-kilter name.

Speaking of names, somewhere along the line I change mine. It isn't a radical switch. I'm not swapping Simon Williams for Lord Stanley Marmaduke Marmalade of Handsomeshire, no matter how much my friends want me to. In fact, I gently tweak my name in a very spontaneous manner, just casually signing off an email with 'Si'. It feels great. I test it out on a few more emails to a few close friends. Some recipients are politely baffled, but it makes me happy, supercharged, revitalised. It's a new dynamic me. I've streamlined myself, added a metaphorical go-faster stripe to my pasty bodywork to go with the Carlos Fandango superwide wheels of yore. Simon the Pieman is now Si Pie. I fire off messages from my SiPhone and my SiPad and I walk along the streets of IP14 listening to my – yes – SiTunes. You could even say I am Si as a kite. But that would be terribly, terribly rubbish.

33

FROM THIS DAY ON

People love the name Fierce Panda. I know this because whenever I have to give my contact details to people on the telephone or face to face to face, and once we've clambered over the old Fiat Panda hurdle, those people always say, 'Fierce Panda? That's a lovely email address!' So they love the Fierce Panda name, just not necessarily as a record-company name because, as previously suggested, it's a sensationally dumb record-company name. A few people even love the sensationally dumbly named record company. This we can tell because we do Independent Label Markets like a properly marketed independent label and now and again people shuffle over to stare down at our piles of Panda paraphernalia and tell us so.

The Independent Label Market is where a veritable glut of independent record companies quite literally set out their stalls and warily tout their wares in the midst of their friends, their peers and their deadly rivals. At one such event in King's Cross

Coalyard a happy-faced soul strode past our stall and said, 'Fierce Panda?? I had no idea you were still going!'

During the indie market in the thoroughly unpredictable summer of 2021 at one point in the afternoon three ghosts of indie past were collecting by the Panda super-stall. These ghosts did not have their own market stalls because their labels have stalled: one person has stopped his label due to a total lack of good local new bands; one has stopped signing new acts because they are simply a drain on back catalogue income; one of them despaired so much he is now very much being dazzled by the Hollywood screenwriting lights instead.

It's not just them – even at their most proactive, promoting barmy release schedules chock-full of thrilling new signings, some other indie label bosses don't take a penny in wages from record sales; they have other jobs to subsidise the entire starry-eyed enterprise. And, as most new bands are horribly aware, while it's clearly easier than ever to get your music out there in the marketplace, it's even harder to get heard and, even if you do get heard, it's tougher than tough to make any money in that marketing place.

But still, no matter. As an indie-label tiger, you fight, you flirt, you frighten the children. After the mighty success of Five Mile High at the Pickerel pub, I made a bold New Year's resolution: in 2022 I will attempt to go and see 365 live performances – not 365 gigs, not 365 different bands, but 365 specific *performances*. So yes, when the Korgis are supported by the Korgis at the 100 Club and when Ian McNabb is supported by himself at the John Peel Centre they do count double. My rules, my tools. We are helped in our ambition to get out of the house by the New Year Pandamonium event rattling the Victoria rafters in Dalston, which means we've clocked up eighteen or so sets before most people have polished off the last of the turkey sandwiches.

Also, rest assured that this is going to be the most sedate gig count known to middle-aged kind. Crisis? What crisis? No more mundane midweek solo excursions in the pouring rain. I make sure that I am always in good gigging company, whether that is with Chrisorder at Echo & the Bunnymen at the Roundhouse, or with Scout at Shame and Anorak Patch at the John Peel Centre, or any number of friends and allies at the Shacklewell Arms and the Victoria and the Lexington, or with Nigel Ugly Child at James Blunt at Wembley Arena – in fact, *especially* James Blunt at Wembley Arena.

Because, for me, it's a highly personalised musical world of Midsomer Murder Ballads, with all due respect to the idea of Lord Nicholas of Caveshire rocking up to Badger's Drift with a certain glint in his eye. From Brian and the C86 Village People marching along to *Sgt Pepper* to Jayne Houghton removing the Inspirals and the living-room carpet for a real-life rave to Green Day soccerballing with the straightedgy nurses in the nursing home to the blushing doctor in the Royal Free keeping me alive with tales of *Transatlanticism* . . . much to its own rage and embarrassment the music industry does not have a monopoly over music – it *thinks* it does, it *thinks* it controls the charts, it *thinks* it goes to the very heart of everything you love, but as we've said before, a little thinking can be a very dangerous thing.

For all its self-proclaimed worthiness, the music industry has an incredible capacity for making people feel utterly worthless. It has been suggested on more than three occasions that I take everything waaaaaaaaay too personally. Of course I do. I have to. I am the Panda, the Panda is me. And it drives me crazy, takes me to the edge, to the end of the earth and beyond. The label spins further and further away, away from the mainstream, out of the orbit, drifting off into oblivion. One day you're gently irreverent, the next you're totally irrelevant. And of course, no matter how far away you spin you still can't escape the spectre of death. Since I started this book, admirable people mentioned in passing have passed away: the live agent Steve Strange, DJ Janice Long, editor Alan Lewis, 485C manager and Food Records supremo Andy Ross, *NME* associate Gavin Martin. Old music hacks can now be found gathering together at the wakes of other old music hacks. Ashes to ashes, funk to funky. 'Til Death Cab do us part.

So then. Are you also the kind of person who takes everything furiously personally? Are you the kind of person who flicks through your mental Rolodex searching for things to fret about, forever looking on the blighted side of life? Are you the kind of person who lies crushed beneath the weight of their own intense stupidity? Are you the kind of person who rages against perceived injustices, no matter how slightly toasted or lightly buttered? Are you the kind of person who constantly gnaws on the utterly unknowable like a stray hound, searching for the zero inside yourself? Are you the kind of person who cringes at compliments, who flinches from praise like it's a prize punch hurled your way, who simply can't bear to see what everyone else sees? Cherish this book. Hold it close to your palpitating bosom. You're not on your own.

And so we end as we started: gently confused, young at heart, wide of eye and even wider of ear; the sugar-spun brothers and sisters, forever candy-flossed in music.

Please look after this bear.

Thank you.

PATHETIQUE
A Q&A Afterword

So what is Fierce Panda? Who is Fierce Panda? And, in the name of all that is holy, why is Fierce Panda? Are we namby-pamby enthusiasts of bedwetting anthemic-ness or exponents of lo-fi, low-flying indiepop dweebiness, or both of those and more? To answer this question, to dig to the core of the who and the how and the why of Fierce Panda, I thought I'd make a bold attempt to answer the most frequently asked Fierce Panda questions, aka FAFPQs, and those answers mostly look very much like these:

What is your favourite Fierce Panda single?

'Cerebra' by Hundred Reasons, which starts a little bit like 'I Will Follow' by U2 and only gets madder and more manic after then. As it was Ning 99, we suggested we do brown-coloured vinyl, like a chocolate Flake. The Pantone shadings just made it look, frankly, like poop. Transparent vinyl it was, then! Sarah Neve took us to see them at the Garage supporting Kittie and they were concise, brilliantly heavy math rock. Subsequent gigs were more ragged, raucous, screamo affairs, but for fifteen minutes they lived right up to their tag as the UK's answer to At the Drive In, and not just because of singer Colin's excitable hair.

Plus *Kerrang!* loved them, and we loved *Kerrang!* all the way through the time we released very loud albums and EPs and mini-albums by Capdown and the Blackout and thisGIRL and very especially Winnebago Deal, who consisted of two blokes called Ben and who we initially saw supporting Fugazi at the Town & Country Club – as first dates go, an especially fruity one. Hundred Reasons won Best New Band at the *Kerrang!* Awards and we sat at their table and watched them go onstage to collect their award and thank everyone and give us no credit whatsoever. It was the greatest awards ceremony I've ever been to.

What is your favourite Fierce Panda album?

Transatlanticism by Death Cab for Cutie is generally perceived to be the finest Fierce Panda album for indie kids and specialist doctors alike, so who am I to disagree? But the earlier album, *We Have the Facts and We're Voting Yes*, has some stunning moments: the implausibly patient 'Little Fury Bugs' opens with a gut-punch of a line and doesn't cheer up much after that; the double whammy of 'Company Calls Epilogue' and 'No Joy in Mudville' is kind of fearfully nostalgic flowery lyrical emo with flashes of post-rock and therefore utterly compelling.

We did three albums by Death Cab, pretty much by total accident. The first time I saw them was when Chris Myhill, by now their live agent, booked them at Club Fandango at the Dublin

Castle (on 7 August 2001) as they were in London anyway, a hop-off on their way home from gigging for their Spanish label. The gig was sold out, full of incredibly sussed emo kids. After the show we asked them if they wanted to do a single, the manager asked if we wanted to release 'The Photo Album'. Magic. We did that, and then we went back to license the previous album *We Have the Facts* . . . and we stuck together for the *Transatlanticism* album, although 'stuck together' might be putting it a bit strong seeing as how Barsuk had touted the album around other labels. This much I know because Jeff Barrett told me they'd approached Heavenly, but he turned it down because he already had one Barsuk band signed in Nada Surf, and he didn't want to over-egg the Heavenly/Barsuk pudding, as it were.

I always got the impression that Death Cab thought Fierce Panda was too small fry for them – a bit amateur, a bit shabby. There was one small fried influence we had on their career though: after the Dublin Castle, Chris booked them into the Garage in Highbury. It sold out on the day of the show and I remember watching the queue from the mini-bar window next door. Next time around, Chris wanted them to play safe and booked them into the Garage again. Problem was I'd worked out that we were going to be lucky to get Death Cab over for live shows more than once for each album cycle: they worked so hard on the road in the States it was always really tough to nail them down as they were either touring, so they didn't want to talk about the UK, or they were about to start touring, so they didn't want to talk, or they were just off tour, so they were too tired to think about it.

So Chris booked them into the larger ULU instead. It ended up being Fierce Panda's tenth birthday show, 12 Feburary 2004. It sold out on the day. The Cribs supported, alongside Medium 21. Steve Lamacq made it up from the *NME* Awards in Brixton, and noted that the entire crowd seemed to be comprised of cuddlesome couples who knew all the words. Next time round Death Cab sold out two nights at the Astoria, by which point they were signed to Atlantic. Could I complain? Not really. Their album pre-sales in the US had reached 250,000, so a major label had to step in. Sometimes there is logic in the system.

How many people actually work for Fierce Panda?

We run a tighter-than-tight ship. Chrisorder is label manager as I type, which means a) there are two of us, and b) he is the sixth label manager since 1994 if we include Ian Damaged Goods. Then came Philip Ingles, then Ellie Coden, then Jess Partridge, then Oli Knowles, then Chrisorder. That's quite tidy, I think. In fact, it's so tidy that Ellie told me she was leaving, after seven years' service, in the Canonbury Arms, and, by the time I'd got back to the office fifteen minutes later, Jess had already emailed offering her services. Damn, that's one speedy network. Along the way we've also had Tor Ferrell, Alice Platt, Gill Barker, Antonio Papaleo, Gareth Dobson, Guy Lowman, Emily Mules and Martyn Boyle all make significant contributions to the Panda pot. Whether or not they enjoyed their time with us as much as I enjoyed my time with them is open to conjecture, however. Rest assured several of them have gone on to have much more successful careers than I, which in several ways is how it should be.

What is your favourite Fierce Panda gig?

The second Coldplay Club Panda show at the Bull & Gate gets massive credit elsewhere. The Walkmen played a lovely wintery ULU yuletide (aka ULUtide) show just as we started working with them, when snow was settling on the hushed streets of Bloomsbury. And we have hosted some smashing events at the Scala in King's Cross, for Panda birthdays or otherwise, for the Walkmen, Desperate Journalist, Goldheart Assembly, the Crookes and the Pains of Being Pure at Heart, plus associated groovy supporting cast. But for pure musical excellence I'll plump for Pile, the post-post-hardcore hammer-timers. Oli and Jess reeled them into the Panda's clutches from the vibrant Boston scene (see also: Speedy Ortiz) but Pile were the originators, the influencers, the Bostonian band's band's band. They had a drummer called Kris Kuss who looked like Hagrid and they had a sound that was colossal, bendy and compelling. They played the hottest show ever at the Lexington on 11 June 2015 and it was my gig of the year.

Then they played a steaming sold-out 100 Club show on 2 November 2016 and it was my gig of that year as well. They could have played and played and played all night long and nobody would have ever left. Nobody would have bought the record either, they just ripped it – Pile fans knew the words to a stack of unreleased Pile songs better than Pile did, let alone their bewildered record company. We released two Pile records – 'You're Better Than This' on CD in 2015 and 'First Other Tape' on cassette (and no digital release – punk rock ahoy) a year later. I was very fond of telling perplexed folks that Pile sounded like Afghan Whigs being played backwards in a thunderstorm, and that is still as close as I can get all these years later. A million miles away, but close enough.

What is your favourite Club Fandango gig?

I'd have to be some kind of ghastly dehumanised moron not to plump for Arctic Monkeys at the Dublin Castle on 5 April 2005.

Andy Pointy reeled this one in, keeping constant tabs on the manager for months as the band's reputation in Sheffield grew and grew on Myspace. By the time the gig happened the timing was perfect. The soundcheck was virtually a gig in itself, such was the A&R fervour surrounding the band. The show itself was sold out well in advance with a perfectly divided crowd – kids at the front, industry at the back, leaving a clear diagonal corridor slashed, like the blood red sash on the Peruvian national football shirt, from the door to the bar, for me to wander along unimpeded. And the band were absolutely excellent – speedy, tight, nervous, nerveless. They reminded me of seeing Supergrass for the first time. Knew what they were doing, where they were going. Really great gig. Within months the Monkeys were headlining the Astoria. Way to go.

What is your biggest regret?

My main regret, which is a pretty profound one, is that I have never been able to set up a transfer system whereby independent labels like us would have been recompensed by bigger labels for our sterling work in building bands, much like Crewe Alexandra or some such small soccerballing team getting a wee transfer fee for developing a soccerball player when they are signed to a bigger club. But perhaps that is missing the whole point. Perhaps other indie people would have been more corrupt and exploited the system. Perhaps that corrupt indie person would have been me, wholeheartedly damaging whatever integrity we never had to begin with.

Do you really not like cheese?

I really do not like cheese.

Why is that?

If I asked my psychiatrist, I'm sure he would take it right back to a troubling tangle with a triangle of Dairylea in 1974.

Let's face it, if any label releases hundreds of singles then some of them are bound to be by bands who go on to do bigger and better things on biggerer and betterer labels. But what about the bands who managed one or two singles before they split up? Do you mark them down as failures?

Absolutely not. Some bands are destined to release just those one or two singles because it's the best they've got, it's all they have in the tank, and sometimes that's as good as it gets. We also worked with some bands whose best moment was our single purely because when they stepped up to one of those biggerer and betterer labels they struggled in the new system, worked with the wrong producer, got lost in the major label maze, never had the chance to make the most of their obvious talent and release anything better.

In essence, however, this tactic usually meant I ended up with a tremendous number of terrific records by bands few people have ever heard of, would-be headline acts who never made it past the opening slot of life: the morosely pop-tastic 'Ten Thousand Years From Now' by Tim Allon; the shimmeringly epic 'Never Seen' by the Immediate; the billowingly graceful 'Stars' by Phonotype; 'Careering' by Bellringers, a splendidly enticing Disco Inferno-lite nugget; 'A Day in the Life of a Production Operative' by Twig, a clanking industrial boulder that unsurprisingly caused the odd ripple in Peelie's pond.

Because for the most part I considered these records to be little miracles lurking on the margins. And these are songs I still play these to this day as, rather conveniently, I have the original versions in my office at home.

What about pizza? Do you eat that? It's not even got real cheese on it.

I take my meat feast pizza with no cheese. All cheese, no matter how 'non-cheesy', is real cheese to people who don't like cheese. Even halloumi. In fact, *especially* fucking halloumi.

Is it true your indie A&R kryptonite is girl-fronted bands?

This has been mentioned to me on more than one occasion, not always unkindly. In the early years, Kenickie, Tiger and Pullover moved on to larger labels, and these were just the tip of the girl-fronted niceberg. But here's something I only realised very recently: brassy Mancs Pullover were the first band to release more than one single with us; Leeds indie darlings Chest's *Mystery Superette* was our first ever mini-album release; berserk Anglo-Nordic trio Tiny Too delivered our first ever full album release with *Things That I Discover*; Kidnapper were the first band to release singles on the Panda under two different names, reappearing as Spy '51; Twist were the first ever all-female grunge pop outfit from Birmingham to hammer out a Panda mini-album called *Magenta* . . . I could go on, and in the admirable cases of Mercedes, the Hot Puppies and KaitO I quite probably should. Because in essence, without the girl bands Fierce Panda could well have stagnated, just continued flipping out one-off singles. But with many of these girl-fronted groups sticking around for a pair of singles, for a big-hearted album, mini-sized or otherwise, we had a chance to evolve, to make a brave attempt to better understand the greasy mechanics of the music industry. Plus they were without exception bloody lovely people to deal with.

What is your favourite Fierce Panda banda?

Politeness and diplomacy prevent me from picking out one specific band. But somewhere between the shabby charm of Seafood around 'Messenger in the Camp', the chirpy punkoid chutzpah of Idlewild circa 'Chandelier' and the intellectual, emotional heft of Death Cab for Cutie through our three album releases, there lurks the core of the greatest Fierce Panda banda ever. The sound of a flight of stairs falling down a flight of stairs falling down a . . . oh, you know.

Overcoming the politeness and diplomacy for a moment I will also enthuse delicately about Desperate Journalist, whose four-album stint means they are Fierce Panda's longest-serving artistes. I went to see them by wild accident – asking the kids in the Leroy House office what hot new combo of combos I should be checking out that night, they turned the tables by suggesting I go to the Lexington to see an old combo, Six by Seven, 'because you like them'. This was very true, but what really piqued my interest was the support: any sane booker would pick carefully with a view to appealing to the gigsmart Six by Seven audience, and the Lexington are generally very splendid with booking their bills in a sane manner.

And so, on 24 July 2013, the one-time desperate journalist ended up checking out a show by a band called Desperate Journalist. Very good they were too – angsty and angry and powerful and snappy and snippy with a fierce pop sensibility and a

growly gothic undercurrent. Turned out their manager James
was the singer in the Rocks, who appeared on our *On the Buzzes*
EP and entertained the Club Fandango masses a decade or so
earlier – a good sign. Since that night they have evolved through
a litany of increasingly terrific live shows, from the Tipsy Bar
in Dalston and the Buffalo Bar in Highbury to the Scala, the
Garage and Lafayette. They were simultaneously ahead of the
post-punk crowd and behind some of my absolutely favourite
Panda tracks, and given a windswept work ethic that has produced four albums and two EP releases in the space of seven
or so years, there are a lot of absolutely favourite tracks to
choose from.

Every six months, I ask them to let us release a *Hatful of
Hollow*-style collection of lost singles and EP tracks and cover
versions and we could call it *Batful of Bollow*, craftily based on
their collective love for the Smiths. And every six months they
look awkward and say they don't really like looking backwards
at their catalogue. Our role in their A&R process meanwhile
is incredibly intense: the band writes the album, records the
album and masters the album while sorting artwork, lyrical
concept and pretty much everything else any record company
could ever desire. Manager James then sends us the album,
saying, 'They've finished a new record – what do you think?'
Then we listen to the album and we pick out at least four
tracks that could be singles, which, luckily, tend to fit with the
band's own thoughts. As you can imagine, it's an exhausting
process for us.

Over the course of those four albums and two EPs, I have
constructed several press releases pertaining to Desperate
Journalist's many sonic skills. In that time it would appear
that I have described them as: 'Shadowy indierock scowlers';

'Glowering indiegoth melody crunchers'; 'Gently bruised post-punk protagonists'; 'Much-loved indiegoth dreamboats'; 'Noirish alt.goth roustabouts'; 'Noirishly nourishing north London alt.gothic rocksters'; and, of course, 'Deliciously dark-edged indiegoth lovecats'. Sometimes I suspect that Desperate Journalist think I'm a total idiot. I kinda like it. It adds to the fun.

Where did it go so horribly wrong for Fierce Panda?

Do you know what? Maybe it didn't ever go wrong. Maybe we over-reached, overachieved, actually hit all our unknown targets without even realising what we were aiming for. Tiny little Fierce Panda battling it out with the majors. It was destiny. You can't change anything.

ACKNOWLEDGEMENTS

The world, it has to be said, has scarcely been waiting for another gently morose, wildly self-deprecating indie kid's opus about confronting the madness of the music industry. Yet here we go.

When I first touched base with Pete Selby at Nine Eight Books in the spring of 2021, the chat revolved around a story of bittersweet indie wibblage. But I had a secret up my sleeve. One day in the Ship, I handed him a sealed envelope that contained a print-out of the (failed) suicide diary in its raw, crooked form. He, like so many other people, had absolutely no idea about the grand malarkey.

It is to Pete's eternal credit that he didn't run away screaming along New Cavendish Street. Rather he embraced the chaos and has shown unwavering enthusiasm and kindness ever since, from removing the handful of painkillers on the original book cover and replacing them with a coy toy ambulance to publishing that suicide diary in its spaced-out entirety, exactly as I wished. Nor is Pete the only one: thanks to everyone nice I've already mentioned in dispatches, who supported the Armstrong-Williamses through the toughest of times and kept Fierce Panda going when all looked mightily doomed.

Thanks also to: Discogs and Wiki, for reminding me of various half-forgotten lunatic releases online; the ghostly afternoon pubs where I sat in Highbury and Dalston and Stowmarket, for allowing the happy lonely boy to recall the good times while smoothing the prickles of the bad, sad times; the staff of the Royal Free and indeed all the doctors and nurses who have tended to my every foolish fractured whim the world over, from Whipps Cross to Koh Samui.

Very special gratitude goes out to the Framily, not least to Mr Russell Thomas for the bleedin' obvious and the ever-fretful, fruitful family – Liann and Scout, Willow and Spirit, and Kiibo and (of course) Panda, the ferreting ferrets.

Am I happy I'm still here? For anyone who has winced at the more graphic elements of the initial diary entries or who has yawned at the more self-indulgent latter stages of the mentally ragged Panda party, rest assured, I make no apologies. If reading *Pandamonium!* makes one other sad old man out there stop and think and think again about the fucktwatting consequences of his actions, then my work here really is done.

No coquettish punchline required.

FIERCE PANDA DISCOGRAPHY

Singles / EPs

NING 01 VARIOUS ARTISTS *SHAGGING IN THE STREETS* double-vinyl EP
(S*M*A*S*H, These Animal Men, Mantaray, Done Lying Down, Blessed Ethel, Action Painting!)
NING 02 VARIOUS ARTISTS *CRAZED AND CONFUSED* double-vinyl EP
(Ash, Supergrass, Gorky's Zygotic Mynci, Credit to the Nation, Noiseaddict)
NING 03 VARIOUS ARTISTS *RETURN TO SPLENDOUR* double-vinyl EP
(The Bluetones, Create!, Thurman, the Weekenders, the Nubiles, Alvin Purple)
NING 04 VARIOUS ARTISTS *BUILT TO BLAST* double-vinyl EP
(Green Day, Understand, China Drum, the Flying Medallions, Fabric, Joeyfat)
NING 05 VARIOUS ARTSISTS *FROM GREER TO ETERNITY* double-vinyl EP
(Lush, Splendora, Jale, Fuzzy, Ivy, Solar Race)
NING 06 CHINA DRUM / FLYING MEDALLIONS 'Wuthering Heights' / 'Riot'
NING 07 CHINA DRUM / FLYING MEDALLIONS / TRIBUTE TO NOTHING TOUR T-SHIRT
NING 08 SCARFO 'Skinny'
NING 09 PULLOVER 'This Is the Life'
NING 10 VARIOUS ARTISTS *SUZI QUATRO LIVES IN CHELMSFORD* EP
(Joeyfat, Scarfo, Ligament)
NING 11 SUZI QUATRO LIVES IN CHELMSFORD TOUR T-SHIRT
NING 12 OAS*S 'Wibbling Rivalry'
NING 13 PLACEBO / SOUP 'Bruise Pristine' / 'Meltdown'
NING 14 PULLOVER 'White Horses'
NING 15 VARIOUS ARTISTS *MORTAL WOMBAT* double-vinyl EP
(Super Furry Animals, Panda, Baby Bird, Mexican Pets, Spare Snare, Harvey's Rabbits)
NING 16 KENICKIE *SKILLEX* EP
NING 17 THREE COLOURS RED 'This Is My Hollywood'
NING 18 VARIOUS ARTISTS *SONGS ABOUT PLUCKING* double-vinyl EP
(Bis, American TV Cops, Bennet, Chopper, Number One Cup, Magoo)
NING 19 KITCHENS O.D. 'Feel My Genie'
NING 20 PULLOVER 'Holiday'
NING 21 DWEEB 'Chart Raider' / 'Space Invader'
NING 22 TIGER 'Shining in The Wood'
NING 23 CHEST 'Feel the Same'
NING 24 VARIOUS ARTISTS *SCREECHER COMFORTS* EP
(Snug, Symposium, Midget, Dragdoll, Inter, Tampasm)

NING 25 FORMULA ONE 'Start the Ball Rolling'

NING 26 THE PECADILOES 'Right Away'

NING 27 CHEWY 'Prime Time'

NING 28 FURTHER (US) 'The Fakers and the Takers'

NING 29 EMBRACE 'All You Good Good People'

NING 30 TOASTER / GOD'S BOYFRIEND 'Huggy' / 'I Don't Wash'

NING 31 KIDNAPPER 'Super Real Fiction' / 'Cake'

NING 32 MAGICDRIVE 'Had to Be You'

NING 33 TINY TOO 'If I Was a Boy'

NING 34 CHEST 'Aniseed'

NING 35 ULTRASOUND 'Same Band'

NING 36 KIDNAPPER 'Is This a Girl'

NING 37 VARIOUS ARTISTS *LISTEN WITH SMOTHER* EP

(Tiny Too, Chest, Ultrasound, Lo-Fidelity Allstars, Kidnapper)

NING 38 TINY TOO 'My Planet Tim'

NING 39 VARIOUS ARTISTS *BLESS HIS LITTLE COTTON ROCKS* double-vinyl EP

(The Crocketts, the Interpreters, Cassius, Libido, Massey, Pohoda)

NING 40 VARIOUS ARTISTS *CRY ME A LIVER* double-vinyl EP

(Theaudience, the Unbelievable Truth, Peach Fuzz, Pure Grain, the Clientele, Velocette)

NING 41 REGULAR FRIES / CAMPAG VELOCET 'Dust It, Don't Bust It' / 'Drencrom (Velocet Synthemesc)'

NING 42 IDLEWILD 'Chandelier'

NING 43 SPY '51 'Slow'

NING 44 VARIOUS ARTISTS *THE DARK SIDE OF THE RACCOON* double-vinyl EP

(The High Fidelity, Roo, Jam Pandas, Spraydog, Firebunnies, Jetboy DC)

NING 45 SEAFOOD 'Scorch Comfort'

NING 46 SUPER J LOUNGE 'Sorry'

NING 47 MOGWAI / MAGOO 'Sweet Leaf' / 'Black Sabbath'

NING 48 CHEWY 'All Over the Place'

NING 49 LLAMA FARMERS 'Paper Eyes'

NING 50A FIERCE PANDA DISCOGRAPHY T-SHIRT

NING 50B *HOW LONG IS A PIECE OF NING?* FANZINE

NING 51 SPY '51 'Crushing'

NING 52 BEAKER 'Monster'

NING 53 BELLRINGERS 'Careering'

NING 54 SEAFOOD 'Porchlight'

NING 55 SUPER J LOUNGE 'Billboard'

NING 56 ASTRONAUT 'What You Gonna Do?'

NING 57 ROTHKO / BILLY MAHONIE 'For Danny' / 'Hoon'

NING 58 LLAMA FARMERS 'Always Echoes'

NING 59 INNER SLEEVE / DAWN OF THE REPLICANTS 'Come Alive' / 'Born in Baskets'

NING 60 SPY '51 'Theme from Spy '51'

NING 61 THE INTERPRETERS 'Should Have Known Better'

NING 62 LAPTOP / SOLEX 'Whole Wide World' / 'You're So Square'

NING 63 VARIOUS ARTISTS *JOY OF PLECS* double-vinyl EP

(Chicks, the Monsoon Bassoon, Max Tractor, Cay, Fantasmagroover, the Samurai Seven)

NING 64 INNER SLEEVE 'Let Me Down'

NING 65 VARIOUS ARTISTS *THE PANDA IN A VANDA TOUR* EP

(Seafood, Tiny Too, Billy Mahonie)

NING-NING 66 SING-SING / LINOLEUM 'I Can See You' / 'Your Back Again'

NING 67 TINY TOO 'World Between Us'

NING 68 COLDPLAY 'Brothers & Sisters'

NING 69 TWIST 'Star'

NING 70 VARIOUS ARTISTS *DOPE IS IMPORTANT* double-vinyl EP

(Bikini Atoll, Bellatrix, Senseless Prayer, Magic House, Second Star, Alchemicals)

NING 71 TV ONE 'Third Wave'

PANDAMONIUM!

NING 72 SEAFOOD 'Easy Path'
NING 73 THE GREAT OUTDOORS 'It Looks So Easy'
NING 74 MALLUKA 'Who Can See The Wind'
NING 75 TWIST 'Shari Says'
NING 76 JIM'S SUPER STEREOWORLD 'Bonkers in the Nut'
NING 77 ASTRONAUT 'Stone Cold Sober'
NING 78 VARIOUS ARTISTS *OTTER THAN JULY* double-vinyl EP
(Fraff, Pop Threat, Rosita, Hofman, Mo-Ho-Bish-O-Pi, Scribble)
NING 79 MERCEDES 'Nailed'
NING 80 FIERCE PANDA MUG, AKA NING A-TEA
NING 81 TWIST 'Lay Low'
NING 82 SHOULD HAVE BEEN SECOND FIERCE PANDA MUG, AKA NING A-TEA TOO
NING 83 SEAFOOD 'This Is Not an Exit'
NING 84 CANOLA 'Test Pilot'
NING 85 BELLATRIX 'Jediwannabe'
NING 86 JIM'S SUPER STEREOWORLD 'Could U B the 1 I Waited 4'
NING 87 THE GREAT OUTDOORS 'Head in the Clouds'
NING 88 ASTRONAUT 'Just Can't Take It'
NING 89 SEAFOOD 'Belt'
NING 90 BELLATRIX 'The Girl with the Sparkling Eyes'
NING 91 TIM ALLON 'Ten Thousand Years from Now'
NING 92 VARIOUS ARTISTS *CUTTING HEDGE* double-vinyl EP
(The Junket, Pachinos, the Starries, Jellicoe, Twentyseven, Caretaker)
NING 93 LINOLEUM 'Sirens' / 'I'm in Love with a German Film Star'
NING 94 AKIRA 'I Dizzy You'
NING 95 SEAFOOD 'Led By Bison'
NING 96 BELLATRIX 'Sweet Surrender'
NING 97 TENNER 'Where Do You Come From?'
NING 98 ELECTRELANE 'Le Song'
NING 99 HUNDRED REASONS 'Cerebra'
NING 100A FIERCE PANDA CENTENARY POLO SHIRT
NING 100B FIERCE PANDA CENTENARY T-SHIRT
NING 101 BELLATRIX 'Jediwannabe'
NING 102 VARIOUS ARTISTS *CLOONEY TUNES* double-vinyl EP
(Interpol, Bright Eyes, the Fire Show, Hopewell, Fiver, And You Will Know Us by the Trail of Dead)
NING 103 EASYWORLD 'Hundredweight'
NING 104 VARIOUS ARTISTS *CHEFFING AND BLINDING* double-vinyl EP
(Six by Seven, KaitO, Brazil, Jameson, Purple Munkie, Stumble)
NING 105 ASTRONAUT 'Three'
NING 106 FIVER 'Chalet Motel'
NING 107 THE MUSIC 'Take the Long Road and Walk It'
NING 108 VARIOUS ARTISTS *VET SOUNDS* double-vinyl EP
(Brave Captain, Go Commando, Jamie Owen, the General Store, Chris T-T, Tompaulin)
NING 109 KAITO 'Cat-Nap'
NING 110 MEDIUM 21 'Plans Aren't Enough' x2
NING 111 PHONOTYPE 'Stars' x2
NING 112 VARIOUS ARTISTS *MOSH* (double-vinyl 7-inch)
(Caffeine, the Parkinsons, Rueben, Tung, the Suffrajets, Elviss)
NING 113 VARIOUS ARTISTS *GO* (double-vinyl 7-inch)
(Jimmy Eat World, San Quentin, Jetplane Landing, Kidsnearwater, Stapleton, Econoline)
NING 114 SIMPLE KID 'I Am Rock'
NING 115 DEATH CAB FOR CUTIE 'A Movie Script Ending'
NING 116 DEATH CAB FOR CUTIE 'I Was a Kaleidoscope'
NING 117 THE FAINT 'Agenda Suicide'
NING 118 VARIOUS ARTISTS *PANDAMONIUM 3*
(Kaito, Simple Kid, Death Cab for Cutie, Medium 21, Caretaker, Astronaut)

NING 119 COIN OP 'Democracies'
NING 120 (X) IS GREATER THAN (Y) 'SGW'
NING 121 THE PARKINSONS 'Streets of London'
NING 122 SIMPLE KID 'Truck On'
NING 123 THE POLYPHONIC SPREE *SOLDIER GIRL* EP
NING 124 VARIOUS ARTISTS *PANDAMONIUM 4* EP
(Medium 21, (X) Is Greater Than (Y), Simple Kid, Easyworld, Coin-Op)
NING 125 COIN OP 'Southpaw'
NING 126 DEATH CAB FOR CUTIE 'We Laugh Indoors'
NING 127 (X) IS GREATER THAN (Y) 'Mirrors and Cameras'
NING 128 COIN-OP 'The Curve'
NING 129 THE RAIN BAND 'The World Is Ours'
NING 130 REPAIRMAN *THE ORANGE ROOM* EP
NING 131 VARIOUS ARTISTS *SQUIRREL* EP (double-vinyl 7-inch)
(thisGIRL, Funeral for a Friend, Million Dead, Jarcrew, the Copperpot Journals, Engerica)
NING 132 FURTHER (AUS) 'Romance!'
NING 133 KEANE 'Everybody's Changing'
NING 134 AGENT BLUE 'Snowhill'
NING 135 CHIKINKI 'Time'
NING 136 CAPDOWN 'Act Your Rage'
NING 137 VARIOUS ARTISTS *FIERCE PANDA SPRING TOUR* EP
(Further, Le Neon, Winnebago Deal, (X) Is Greater Than (Y))
NING 138 CABLECAR 'Wasting Time'
NING 139 WINNEBAGO DEAL
NING 140 FIERCE PANDA 1994–2004 T-SHIRT
NING 141 LE NEON 'S.P.A.C.E'
NING 142 SIX BY SEVEN 'Bochum (Light Up My Life)'
NING 143 THE VACATION 'They Were the Sons'
NING 144 SAMMY USA 'Doorway of a Dancehall'
NING 145 thisGIRL *DEMO'S FOR THE FAMILY* EP
NING 146 THE FEATURES *THE BEGINNING* EP
NING 147 KEANE 'This Is the Last Time'
NING 148 THE RAIN BAND *THE ART OF MASS DESTRUCTION* EP
NING 149 DEATH CAB FOR CUTIE 'The New Year'
NING 150 THE FEATURES 'The Way It's Meant to Be'
NING 151 THE MINT CHICKS 'Blue Team Go'
NING 152 ATLANTIC DASH 'Leave It All Behind'
NING 153 AGENT BLUE 'Sex, Drugs and Rocks Through Your Window'
NING 154 THE LEGENDARILY SEMINAL FIERCE PANDA JACKET
NING 155 VARIOUS ARTISTS *ON THE BUZZES* double-vinyl EP
(The Rocks, S Rock Levinson, Razorlight, Ludes, the Rakes, the Souls)
NING 156 VARIOUS ARTISTS *GLOWING UNDERGROUND* double-vinyl EP
(Dogs Die in Hot Cars, Amateur Anti-Guitar Heroes, Ex-Tigers, Multiples, Odeon Beat Club, This Familiar Smile)
NING 157 VARIOUS ARTISTS *SHOCK & OAR* double-vinyl EP
(The Walkmen, the Twilight Singers, Echo-Static, Low Flying Owls, Film School, Thee Heavenly Music Association)
NING 158 DEATH CAB FOR CUTIE 'The Sound of Settling'
NING 159 THE DRAMA 'Nothing Can Tear Us Apart'
NING 160 APARTMENT 'Everyone Says I'm Paranoid'
NING 161 THE IMMEDIATE 'Never Seen'
NING 162 ALTERKICKS 'Do Everything I Taught You'
NING 163 YOUTHMOVIE SOUNDTRACK STRATEGIES 'Ores'
NING 164 ART BRUT 'Modern Art' / 'My Little Brother'
NING 165 GLEDHILL 'Resurrect Me'
NING 166 KARI KLEIV 'When Can I See You'
NING 167 ART BRUT 'Emily Kane' / 'These Animal Menswe@r'
NING 167S ART BRUT 'Emily Kane' / 'Moving to LA'

PANDAMONIUM!

NING 168 BLACKBUD *THE LIVEWIRE EP*
NING 169 BATTLE 'Isabelle'
NING 170 BOY KILL BOY 'Suzie'
NING 171 APARTMENT 'Patience Is Proving'
NING 172 THE REVELATIONS 'You're the Loser'
NING 173 ART BRUT 'Good Weekend'
NING 174 ABSENT KID 'Shame on Us All'
NING 175 SHITDISCO 'Disco Blood'
NING 176 AGENT BLUE 'Out with the New'
NING 177 MY ARCHITECTS 'Airborne'
NING 178 THE PISTOLAS *LISTEN LISTEN* EP
NING 179 MAKE GOOD YOUR ESCAPE 'Beautiful Ruin'
NING 180 THE MACCABEES 'Latchmere'
NING 181 THE HOT PUPPIES 'The Girl Who Was Too Beautiful'
NING 182 MY ARCHITECTS 'Under the Pines'
NING 183 ILIKETRAINS 'Terra Nova'
NING 184 WRECKLESS ERIC 'Whole Wide World'
NING 185 THE HOT PUPPIES 'Green Eyeliner'
NING 186 WINNEBAGO DEAL 'Spider Bite'
NING 187 DIRTY LITTLE FACES 'Piccadilly'
NING 188 DEAD KIDS 'The Dead Wife Pills'
NING 189 THE BLACKOUT 'Hard Slammin''
NING 190 DEAD DISCO 'Automatic'
NING 191 SHITDISCO 'Reactor Party'
NING 192 THE HOT PUPPIES 'How Come You Don't Hold Me No More?'
NING 193 MAKE GOOD YOUR ESCAPE 'Cut the Ropes'
NING 194 WINNEBAGO DEAL 'Reeper'
NING 195 CAPDOWN 'Keeping Up Appearances'
NING 196 CAPDOWN 'Surviving the Death of a Genre'
NING 197 MAKE GOOD YOUR ESCAPE 'Real'
NING 199 SHITDISCO 'OK'
NING 200 VARIOUS ARTISTS *THE ROCK, STOCK AND BARREL EP*
(Capdown, Winnebago Deal, the Blackout, the Disappointments)
NING 201 THE DISAPPOINTMENTS 'No Charades'
NING 202 CAPDOWN 'No Matter What'
NING 203 YOU SAY PARTY! WE SAY DIE! 'Monster'
NING 204 THE BLACKOUT 'The Beijing Cocktail'
NING 205 YOU SAY PARTY! WE SAY DIE! 'Like We Give a Care'
NING 206 SHITDISCO 'I Know Kung Fu'
NING 207 THE RAVEONETES 'Dead Sound'
NING 208 THE BLACKOUT 'It's High Tide, Baby'
NING 209 THE RAVEONETTES 'You Want the Candy'
NING 210 THE WHITE RABBITS 'While We Go Dancing'
NING 211 THE SPINTO BAND 'Summer Grof'
NING 211B YOU CAN'T PUT YOUR ARMS AROUND A DOWNLOAD T-SHIRT
NING 212 THE WALKMEN 'The Blue Route'
NING 214 THE RAVEONETTES 'Blush'
NING 217 THE WALKMEN 'In the New Year'
NING 218 THE SPINTO BAND 'Vivian, Don't'
NING 219 HATCHAM SOCIAL 'Murder in the Dark'
NING 220 CAPITAL 'Ruin'
NING 221 THE VON BONDIES 'Pale Bride'
NING 222 HATCHAM SOCIAL 'Crocodile'
NING 223 THE MOLOTOVS 'Come to Grief'
NING 224 THE RAVEONETTES 'Bang'
NING 225 TAXI TAXI! 'Big Old Trees'

NING 226 GOLDHEART ASSEMBLY 'King of Rome'
NING 227 HATCHAM SOCIAL *SIDEWALK* EP
NING 228 GOLDHEART ASSEMBLY 'Under the Waterway'
NING 229 VARIOUS ARTISTS *ZIP IT UP* EP
(Brilliant Mind, the Crookes, the Heartbreaks, Hoodlums, Ideals, the Molotovs, Sketches)
NING 230 VARIOUS ARTISTS *LICENSED TO DRILL* EP
(White Belt Yellow Tag, the Megaphonic Thrift, Twin Tiger, Sir Yes Sir, Mabel Love, Burn Before Reading, Ladydoll, France and the Habsburgs)
NING 231 VARIOUS ARTISTS *GRUFF TRADE* EP
(Hatcham Social, Wild Palms, La Shark, Fiction, Not Cool, Sex Beet, Still Corners)
NING 232 GOLDHEART ASSEMBLY 'Last Decade'
NING 233 GOSPEL MUSIC *DUETTES* EP
NING 234 THE CROOKES 'Godless Girl'
NING 235 KITTEN *SUNDAY SCHOOL* EP
NING 236 THE CROOKES 'Chorus of Fools'
NING 237 SISSY & THE BLISTERS *LET HER GO* EP
NING 238 THE CROOKES 'I Remember Moonlight'
NING 239 THE CHEVIN *CHAMPION* EP
NING 240 THE KABEEDIES 'Eyes'
NING 241 HATCHAM SOCIAL 'Dance with Me'
NING 242 THE CROOKES 'Afterglow'
NING 243 THE KABEEDIES 'Bones'
NING 244 HEY SHOLAY 'Burning'
NING 245 THE CROOKES 'Maybe in the Dark'
NING 246 HATCHAM SOCIAL 'Lois Lane'
NING 247 ULTRASOUND 'Beautiful Sadness'
NING 248 HATCHAM SOCIAL 'All Summer Long' (Harry Love Remix)
NING 249 DINGUS KHAN 'Plank'
NING 250 VARIOUS ARTISTS *TAKE BAT AND PARTY* EP
(Acres of Lions, Dingus Khan, Electricity in Our Own Home, Hatcham Social, Hawk Eyes, Het Sholay, the Crookes, the Kabeedies, the TenFiveSixty, Ultrasound)
NING 251 ACRES OF LIONS 'Reaction' / 'Set Me On Fire'
NING 252 MILO GREENE 'What's the Matter'
NING 253 HEY SHOLAY 'Wishbone (Wish Wish Wish)'
NING 254 WOODPIGEON 'Red Rover, Red Rover'
NING 255 MILO GREENE '1957'
NING 256 MELANIE PAIN *JUST A GIRL* EP
NING 257 DINGUS KHAN 'Knifey Spoony'
NING 258 MILO GREENE *WHAT'S THE MATTER* EP
NING 259 THE CROOKES 'Bear's Blood' / 'We Dance in Colour'
NING 260 ULTRASOUND 'Between Two Rivers'
NING 261 HEY SHOLAY 'Cloud, Castle, _____'
NING 262 THE HOSTS 'September Song'
NING 263 TOM HICKOX 'Angel of the North'
NING 264 TOM HICKOX 'White Roses Red'
NING 265 THE CROOKES 'Play Dumb' / 'Before the Night Falls II'
NING 266 THE HOSTS 'Give Your Love to Her'
NING 268 LONGELLOW 'Kiss-Hug-Make-Up'
NING 269 THE CROOKES 'Don't Put Your Faith in Me'
NING 270 THE PAINS OF BEING PURE AT HEART 'Eurydice'
NING 272 THE PAINS OF BEING PURE AT HEART 'Kelly'
NING 273 FELT TIP *SIMPLE THINGS* EP
NING 274 TOM HICKOX 'The Lisbon Maru'
NING 275/6 [Gets a bit confusing around here as digital-only single releases start to enter the fray. Meta Panda behaviour, obviously . . .]
NING 277 THE CROOKES 'Howl'

PANDAMONIUM!

NING 278 LONGFELLOW 'Medic'
NING 279 LONGFELLOW *REMEDY* EP
NING 280 THE CROOKES 'You're Just Like Christmas'
NING 281 FAKE LAUGH 'Kinda Girl'
NING 282 HELSINKI 'Rising Heights'
NING 283 DOE 'Avalanche'
NING 285 JURASSIC POP 'Jurassic Pop 4 1/2: The Erotic Adventures of Jeff Goldblum'
NING 286 ALBERT GOLD 'Into the Wild'
NING 287 PILE 'The World Is Your Motel'
NING 289 DESPERATE JOURNALIST 'Hesitate'
NING 292 ALMA 'The Great Escape'
NING 294 KIERON LEONARD & THE HORSES 'Underwood Milk'
NING 295 MATES OF STATE *YOU'RE GOING TO MAKE IT* EP
NING 296 THE LUNCHTIME SARDINE CLUB 'Dollars for Donuts'
NING 297 JAJA OK 'Give Me Your Money'
NING 298 DESPERATE JOURNALIST *GOOD LUCK* EP
NING 299 VLMV 'To the Stars'
NING 300 LONGFELLOW 'Choose'
NING 301 SURFER BLOOD 'Feast-Famine'
NING 302 LONGFELLOW 'Elastic Heart'
NING 303 ETCHES 'Do Nothing'
NING 304 ALBERT GOLD 'Handcuffs'
NING 305 BRUNCH 'Yowie'
NING 306 WHISTLEJACKET 'Stay-N'
NING 307 PESKY! 'Christmas (Baby Come Home)'
NING 308 GHOST SUNS 'We Are Not Good People'
NING 309 THE HOSTS 'Baby Move On'
NING 310 WHISTLEJACKET *WHAT I ATE ON SUNDAY* EP
NING 311 FAKE LAUGH 'Mind Tricks'
NING 312 WHISTLEJACKET 'Duck Soup'
NING 313 ALPHADUKA 'I'll Follow You'
NING 314 CAVALRY 'Lucerne'
NING 315 HUSH! 'Teenage Weekends'
NING 316 SEAN GRANT AND THE WOLFGANG *7 DEADLY 7* EP
NING 317 HELSINKI 'Choices'
NING 318 COQUIN MIGALE 'Grindie'
NING 319 THE HOSTS 'Make My Heart Turn Blue'
NING 320 ALMA 'The Lighthouse' (maybeshewill Remix)
NING 321 CHALK 'You've Fallen into That Trap'
NING 322 485C 'She'll Lie'
NING 323 WHISTLEJACKET 'Oh Brother'
NING 324 GHOST SUNS 'Wait Out'
NING 325 PILE 'Cut from First Other Tape'
NING 326 WHISTLEJACKET *OH BROTHER* EP
NING 327 WHITE GIANT 'Keep the Lights On'
NING 328 COQUIN MIGALE 'Pt 2'
NING 329 AFFAIRS 'Life of Leisure'
NING 330 DESPERATE JOURNALIST 'Hollow'
NING 331 ALMA 'Lighthouse' (Tom Hodge Remix)
NING 332 RAGLANS *AGAIN & AGAIN* EP
NING 333 COQUIN MIGALE 'Soft'
NING 334 JOEY FOURR 'Uhmericka'
NING 335 A LILY 'Shadow and Me Makes Three'
NING 337 DESPERATE JOURNALIST 'Resolution'
NING 338 485C 'Strange Medicine'
NING 339 GHOST SUNS *WE ARE NOT GOOD PEOPLE* EP

NING 340 NATIONAL SERVICE 'A Little More Time'
NING 341 PARK HOTEL 'Gone as a Friend'
NING 342 GHOST SUNS 'Cheers to Poison'
NING 343 DESPERATE JOURNALIST 'Be Kind'
NING 344 LEAONE 'Goldtooth'
NING 345 WOODEN ARMS 'Lost in Your Own Home'
NING 346 485C 'Better the Man'
NING 347 THE VELVETEINS 'Midnight Surf'
NING 348 ALBERT GOLD *OXYGEN* EP
NING 349 LEAONE 'Fly, My Swallow'
NING 350 LEAONE 'Young Green Eyes'
NING 351 LERICHE 'Under Covers'
NING 352 WOODEN ARMS 'Burial'
NING 353 DESPERATE JOURNALIST 'Why Are You So Boring?'
NING 354 LEAONE *OH, MY SWEETEST SIN* EP
NING 355 FIGHTMILK 'Pity Party'
NING 356 FIGHTMILK *PITY PARTY* EP
NING 357 EASY KILL 'Phantom Pain'
NING 358 LEAONE 'End of the World'
NING 359 NATIONAL SERVICE 'Timid Kisses'
NING 360 THE CARESS 'You're Always Miles Away'
NING 361 EASY KILL 'Constant Hum'
NING 362 THE CARESS *YOU SAY I KISS LIKE A GIRL* EP
NING 363 LERICHE 'The River Runs'
NING 364 KRIEF 'Automanic'
NING 365 LEAONE 'Livewire'
NING 366 LEAONE *WILD HORSES RIDE ON* EP
NING 367 ALBERT GOLD 'All This Time'
NING 368 FIGHTMILK 'NYE'
NING 369 THE CARESS 'Man Up'
NING 370 KRIEF 'Ordinary Lies'
NING 371 CAVALRY 'Black'
NING 372 ALBERT GOLD *SECOND* EP
NING 373 LERICHE *X DREAMER* EP
NING 374 CAVALRY *SEE THE NIGHT PERFORM* EP
NING 375 VLMV 'All These Ghosts'
NING 376 DESPERATE JOURNALIST *YOU GET USED TO IT* EP
NING 377 THE CARESS 'Breakfast with Leather Apron'
NING 378 DESPERATE JOURNALIST 'It Gets Better'
NING 379 485C 'Kapow!'
NING 380 EASY KILL 'Guilt Trip to the Moon'
NING 381 CUESTA LOEB 'Dive'
NING 382 ALBERT GOLD 'Endless'
NING 383 VLMV 'If Only I'
NING 384 AUGUST CHILD *BURN FOR THE TIDE* EP
NING 385 GHOST SUNS 'Nothing More'
NING 386 THE CARESS 'Suffragette Look'
NING 387 NATIONAL SERVICE 'Islander'
NING 388 VARIOUS ARTISTS *THE FIERCE PANDA EP CLUB* EP
(Ghost Suns, Leaone, Fightmilk, the Caress, Cavalry, August Child)
NING 389 485C 'Hoppy'
NING 390 THE CARESS 'Breaking Up'
NING 391 KRIEF 'Deo Gratias'
NING 392 GHOST SUNS 'Why Criminal?'
NING 393 S.G. WOLFGANG 'Souls Out'
NING 394 JEKYLL *JEKYLL* EP

PANDAMONIUM!

NING 395 JEKYLL 'Plan A'
NING 396 THE CARESS *IN TECHNICOLOUR* EP
NING 397 GHOST SUNS 'Cards on a Bicycle'
NING 398 SAD BOYS CLUB 'Sleepyhead'
NING 399 TOM SHAWCROFT 'Darling'
NING 400 ALBERT GOLD 'Give In'
NING 401 VLMV 'Little Houses' (feat. Tom Hodge)
NING 402 PEEPING DREXELS 'Ray Purchase'
NING 403 NATIONAL SERVICE *FOREIGN LOVE* EP
NING 404 SAD BOYS CLUB *YEAH PEOPLE TALK BUT YOU'VE FORGOTTEN HOW TO LIVE* EP
NING 405 SAD BOYS CLUB 'Silverlined'
NING 406 SCROUNGE 'Etch'
NING 407 VC PINES 'Garden of the Year'
NING 408 DESPERATE JOURNALIST 'Cedars'
NING 409 OCTOBER DRIFT 'Come and Find Me'
NING 410 PEEPING DREXELS *PEEPING DREXELS* EP
NING 411 GHOST SUNS *TESTIFY* EP
NING 412 DESPERATE JOURNALIST 'Satellite'
NING 413 SCROUNGE 'Crimson'
NING 414 VC PINES 'Vixen'
NING 415 HOW'S HARRY 'I Dreamt About You Last Night'
NING 416 ALBERT GOLD *LONDON CALLING* EP
NING 417 SKINT & DEMORALISED 'Boro Kitchen 4am'
NING 418 JEKYLL 'Echoes'
NING 419 VC PINES *INDIGO* EP
NING 420 VC PINES 'Vixen' (Live from Miloco Studios)
NING 421 CHINA BEARS 'Stay for Good'
NING 422 CHINA BEARS *I'VE NEVER MET ANYONE LIKE YOU* EP
NING 423 VARIOUS ARTISTS *THE FIERCE PANDA EP CLUB II* EP
(Jekyll, National Service, Sad Boys Club, Peeping Drexels, VC Pines, China Bears)
NING 424P COLDPLAY 'Brothers & Sisters' / 'Easy to Please'
NING 424B COLDPLAY 'Brothers & Sisters' / 'Only Superstition'
NING 425 SKINT & DEMORALISED '#Refugees Welcome'
NING 426 CHINA BEARS 'Sunday'
NING 427 SCROUNGE 'Purpose'
NING 428 NATIONAL SERVICE 'Concrete'
NING 429 NATIONAL SERVICE 'Witch Trail'
NING 430 NATIONAL SERVICE *MELTWATER* EP
NING 431 SKINT & DEMORALISED 'Superheroes'
NING 432 FIERCE PANDA 25 T-SHIRT
NING 433 JEKYLL 'Marionette'
NING 434 CHINA BEARS 'Cold Shivers'
NING 435 ITALIA '90 *III* EP
NING 436 ITALIA '90 'An Episode'
NING 437 ITALIA '90 'Road to Hell'
NING 438 THE COMSTOCKS 'Six Months'
NING 439 ALBERT GOLD 'Ghost'
NING 441 VC PINES 'Bones'
NING 442 SCROUNGE 'Badoom'
NING 443 SCROUNGE *IDEAL* EP
NING 444 SCROUNGE *IDEAL* EP
NING 445 SKINT & DEMORALISED 'Slim Jim's Liquor Store'
NING 446 ALBERT GOLD 'Ghost' (Remix)
NING 447 THE COMSTOCKS *THE COMSTOCKS* EP
NING 448 GHOST SUNS 'Stuck on the Wall'
NING 449 MEMES 'J.O.B.S.'

NING 450 VC PINES 'Bones' (Piano Version)
NING 451 JEKYLL 'I Do What I Can'
NING 452 ALBERT GOLD 'House of Cards'
NING 453 MOON PANDA 'Rick F***in' Dalton'
NING 454 MOON PANDA *MAKE WELL* EP
NING 455 GHOST SUNS 'On Off'
NING 456 GHOST SUNS *HORIZON* EP
NING 457 JEKYLL 'The Escapist'
NING 458 JEKYLL *THE WHISPERING GALLERY* EP
NING 459 CHINA BEARS 'I'm Not Eating Like I Used To'
NING 460 CHINA BEARS 'Statue Still'
NING 461 CHINA BEARS *STATUE STILL* EP
NING 462 ALBERT GOLD 'Satellite'
NING 463 MEMES 'Cheer Up'
NING 464 MOON PANDA 'Slow Drive'
NING 465 MEMES 'Cheer Up' (Danny Inglis Remix)
NING 466 ALBERT GOLD *MOOD* EP
NING 467 CHILI PALMER *CHILI PALMER* EP
NING 468 CHILI PALMER 'S.I.T.'
NING 469 CHILI PALMER 'A.O.M.L.'
NING 470 SAD BOYS CLUB *YEAH PEOPLE TALK BUT YOU'VE FORGOTTEN HOW TO LIVE* EP
(Expanded Version)
NING 471 NATIONAL SERVICE 'Caving'
NING 472 MOON PANDA 'Call It Fate, Call It Karma'
NING 473 CHINA BEARS 'Jolene'
NING 474 MEMES *MEMES* EP
NING 475 MEMES 'So What'
NING 476 DESPERATE JOURNALIST 'The Fear'
NING 477 MEMES 'Oll Korrect'
NING 478 JEKYLL 'Nightporter'
NING 479 GHOST SUNS 'Hurt'
NING 480 CHINA BEARS 'Hackensack'
NING 481 OLI SWAN *ALL MY FRIENDS ARE LONELY* EP
NING 482 OLI SWAN 'All My Friends Are Lonely'
NING 483 OLI SWAN 'Make Me Cry'
NING 484 NATIONAL SERVICE 'Last January'
NING 485 VARIOUS ARTISTS *THE COVID VERSION SESSIONS* EP
NING 486 SCROUNGE 'Leaking Drains'
NING 488 CHILI PALMER 'East End Boys'
NING 489 MOON PANDA 'Visions'
NING 490 DESPERATE JOURNALIST 'Fault'
NING 491 DESPERATE JOURNALIST 'Personality Girlfriend'
NING 492 DESPERATE JOURNALIST 'Everything You Wanted'
NING 493 JEKYLL 'Tear Ourselves in Two'
NING 494 JEKYLL 'Catherine Wheel'
NING 495 CHILI PALMER 'Cocktail Nights' (feat. Gia Ford)
NING 496 ALBERT GOLD 'Want Me'
NING 497 ALBERT GOLD *PATTERNS* EP
NING 498 WYNONA BLEACH 'Aubergines'
NING 499 HATCHAM SOCIAL 'If You Go Down the Woods Today (Three Cheers for Our Side)'
NING 500 A TATTOO ON SIMON'S LEFT ARM
NING 501 MOON PANDA 'Vacationer'
NING 502 MOON PANDA 'Cloud Watching'
NING 503 MOON PANDA 'Sunrise'
NING 504 MOON PANDA 'Falling'
NING 505 WYNONA BLEACH 'Moonsoake'